FRIENDS
OF ACPL

Toward a History
of the New Left

ESSAYS FROM WITHIN
THE MOVEMENT

Edited with an Introduction
by R. David Myers

CARLSON
Publishing Inc

BROOKLYN, NEW YORK 1989

Library of Congress Cataloging-in-Publication Data

Toward a history of the New Left : essays from within the movement /
edited by an introduction by R. David Myers.
     p.   cm.
   Includes bibliographical references.
   1. College students—United States—Political activity–
–History—20th century. 2. Students for a Democratic Society
(U.S.)—History—20th century. 3. Radicalism—United States–
–History—20th century. I. Myers, R. David.
LA229. T65   1989   89-25472
378.1'981'0973—dc20
ISBN 0-926019-23-6

Typographic design: Julian Waters

Typeface: Bitstream ITC Galliard

Printed on acid-free, 250-year-life paper.

Manufactured in the United States of America

This book is dedicated to the people who wrote these essays and to those who struggled to build a movement based on true democracy and social justice.

Contents

Introduction

R. DAVID MYERS

The six articles included here provide an important contribution to our understanding of the 1960s and the New Left. They are some of the best essays dealing with the history of the New Left written by leaders and theoreticians of the Movement. In view of two recent developments, these essays take on an even greater importance. First, after a period of relative disinterest, scholars, journalists and former participants are studying the 1960s and its incumbent passions with a renewed interest. Numerous books and articles have been published in the last two years.[1] Central to these studies is the role of the New Left in shaping the decade. Second, as Richard Flacks has recently suggested, the signs of a new movement are becoming apparent. Sons and daughters of 1960s activists and other students are anxious to begin another movement and are very interested in learning the history of the New Left.[2] For analysts of the 1960s and for future leaders of leftist movements, these essays provide an incisive look at the internal, and to a smaller degree, the external problems which contributed to the New Left's inability to build an enduring movement.

Attempts to understand the failure of the New Left to build a lasting program, of course, should never underestimate its many and significant achievements. The revolutionary accomplishments of the civil rights movement, the successful building of a far reaching anti-war movement, the creation of an atmosphere where the beginnings of the modern women's movement and the start of environmental activism all resulted in large part because of the New Left. Failure, then, is probably too harsh and too misleading a word. The contributions of the New Left are still felt in our everyday lives. But by 1972 the passions of the Movement had slowed considerably, and by 1975 few overt trappings of its existence remained. The history of its accomplishments and its contributions sketched against a decade of intensive passions and exciting events continues to provide fuel for passionate discussions.

1

A key element in understanding the Movement's history is the view of its own leaders and intellectuals. One advantage in studying the New Left is that so many of those who participated wrote extensively. While compiling an extensive bibliography on the New Left, I became fascinated by a series of articles written by leaders and participants which analyzed the history of the Movement. The necessity of collecting and republishing these articles was confirmed when I read Maurice Isserman's excellent study, *If I Had a Hammer . . . The Death of the Old Left and the Birth of the New Left*. In an endnote, Isserman urged someone to pull together these relatively inaccessible articles into a "documentary history."[3]

The six articles here are important for a number of reasons. They provide a history of the Movement from the inside. In different fashions, the authors discuss what was important in terms of theory and ideas, what were the major successes, and what factors contributed to the breakup of the New Left. Other writers have broadly described the history of the New Left as a move from reform to resistance to revolution. Many of the reasons for this progression are discussed and analyzed in these essays.[4]

Before discussing the articles themselves, a few words about the history of the New Left are necessary. Several writers have comprehensively recounted the New Left's history as detailed in the endnotes to this essay and in the Recommended Reading list at the end of this volume, but a few words will provide a context for the essays. Primarily these articles deal with the New Left's principal organization, Students for a Democratic Society (SDS). As the central force within the New Left, SDS has attracted the most attention, and its leaders have been the most vocal, then and now. One could easily argue that a focus on SDS ignores such pivotal organizations as the Berkeley Free Speech Movement, such key anti-war organizations as Resistance and specific feminist groups, but SDS set the agenda and frequently ex-SDSers led these other organizations.[5]

A starting date for the New Left is not as easily distinguishable as once thought. As Isserman's book has recently demonstrated, the division between the Old Left of Communists, socialists, Trotskyists, and pacifists and the New Left is not as clearly demarcated as once believed. Generally, most observers understood that the New Left had its beginnings in the early 1960s, but Isserman has shown that the New Left drew much more heavily on the Old Left than previous writers believed.[6] But clearly, something different did start in the early 1960s. The lunch counter sit-ins which began in Greensboro, North Carolina and spread throughout the South had a dramatic effect on the growing number of leftists and students in the North. The launching of the Student Nonviolent Coordinating Committee (SNCC), the Freedom Riders, and the struggle for integration roused northern students and contributed significantly to the launching of SDS in 1962.[7]

SDS had its roots in the Old Left. Its parent organization, the League for Industrial Democracy (LID) was a social democratic group which counted among its members Michael Harrington, author of *The Other America*. To build a more effective student organization, several student leaders gathered in Port Huron, Michigan in June, 1962 to launch an organization that represented a new direction for leftist politics in the United States, the Students for a Democratic Society. In the course of launching a new organization, these students drafted "The Port Huron Statement," the manifesto which outlined the basic philosophy and central goals of the organization. Written primarily by Tom Hayden, "The Port Huron Statement" is indicative of many of the New Left's guiding principles. Drawing upon the concepts of such social philosophers as Albert Camus and C. Wright Mills, this manifesto set the tone for the movement that ensued.[8]

Central to the new movement were several concepts. At the heart of these was the belief that personal politics was important; the individual could make a significant difference. Direct action based upon a personal commitment by individuals was a way to effect change. Most important, the concept of participatory democracy was first enunciated in this document. SDS, like SNCC, believed that change should come from the bottom up. Individuals, ordinary people not political leaders, should guide the way to change. True democracy could only exist when individuals committed themselves to building a better world by creating a world in which individuals could control their everyday lives. The major problem facing America, and other countries as well, was a huge uncaring bureaucracy. Political parties, labor unions and other agencies for change were no longer effective because they had become undemocratic and bureaucratic. SDS hoped to build a coalition of radicals, civil rights activists, liberals and progressive labor unionists committed to establishing true social justice.[9]

The work of SDS in the post-Port Huron days fell into three broad areas, but focused primarily on two. A general split among founders took place as one group stressed research while the other emphasized action. The research group, led by Al Haber, believed that SDS's essential function should be to locate on campuses and conduct research on the major problems of the United States and publish the results with recommendations for action. Part of this work would include organizing and educating students.[10] The action group, led by Tom Hayden and Rennie Davis, understood that effective change would come by working with and organizing those segments of society that were unable to improve their own conditions. The Economic Research and Action Project (ERAP) placed SDS activists in low income neighborhoods in such cities as Chicago, Cleveland and Newark to work with residents of these areas. The emphasis of these projects was to organize people to help them take more control of their lives through landlord pressure and confrontations with city officials. The third, very small, group sought to build a political coalition with liberals, but this group never attracted a following.[11]

Eschewing politics, New Left groups worked in the early 1960s largely to reform American society and its institutions through direct action, but a series of events which took place from 1962 to 1965 pushed these groups in a more radical direction. An early factor in the political atmosphere which encouraged leftist activity was the tone set by the John F. Kennedy administration, but disenchantment came quickly. The Bay of Pigs, the Cuban Missile Crisis, the questionable commitment to civil rights and the quiet buildup of military advisors in South Vietnam gradually convinced New Leftists that liberals were not all that supportive of fundamental change and that other avenues of action would have to be developed.

This belief became more apparent in the summer of 1964. Hundreds of northern white students joined with SNCC workers to register black voters, primarily in Mississippi. The violent response, including the murders of James Chaney, Michael Schwerner, and Andrew Goodman, combined with the general neglect of the Lyndon Johnson administration inspired a new militancy. One result of this incipient militancy was the formation of the Mississippi Freedom Democratic Party (MFDP). The new party elected a slate of delegates to the Democratic Party National Convention in Atlantic City and petitioned the Democrats to unseat the regular Mississippi Democrats because they had been chosen in an unrepresentative manner which excluded blacks from any hope of participation. The MFDP delegates rejected a compromise proposal delivered by a number of party liberals that would have seated the regular party delegation and given the MFDP two at-large delegates.[12]

SNCC and SDS members felt betrayed by the desertion of liberals. This attitude was reinforced throughout 1964 and 1965 as the escalation in Vietnam continued. Now the growth of U.S. commitment was no longer so quiet, and President Johnson, who had run as the peace candidate in 1964, seemed intent on involving American soldiers in a major engagement. Congressional support for the buildup was provided by liberals in the House and the Senate and by widespread vocal support from labor leaders. The growing split over the war further undermined an already shaky coalition.[13]

Other events in 1964-65 further recast the New Left. A major student strike at the University of California-Berkeley in September, 1964 convinced many New Leftists that college campuses could be a key component in radical activity. Led by organizers of the Free Speech Movement (FSM), thousands of students protested the university's refusal to allow the distribution of political materials on campus. One particularly important element of this protest was its emphasis on higher education's involvement in defense work and complicity in repressive government and corporate activities. The protest also called attention to the dehumanizing and bureaucratic nature of the "multi-university."[14]

The strike at Berkeley was complemented by other campus activity that took place a few months later. In March, 1965 the first teach-in was held at the University of Michigan-Ann Arbor. Faculty, students, and interested observers met for a marathon session to discuss the disastrous nature of America's deepening involvement in Vietnam. As teach-ins spread to other campuses, discussions widened to consider the full range of social and economic problems in America. The growing awareness of college students and faculty encouraged New Left leaders to realize the demand for organizing activities to a much greater extent on campuses. The demand was not ignored. ERAP workers gradually returned from the ghetto and SNCC activists returned from the South. Membership, particularly in SDS, began to grow, but with this growth problems began to emerge.[15]

By this time the whole question of the Movement's direction became a subject of heated debate. A fundamental change in SDS and SNCC was taking place which accelerated the alienation and radicalization of both organizations that had begun during Freedom Summer. The most important change within SDS was the changing character of its rapidly growing membership. These new members differed significantly from their predecessors. Known under the collective term "Prairie Power," they did not come from urban centers and generally came from the Mid- and Southwest. They were much less grounded in intellectual theory and much less interested in the idealism put forth in the Port Huron Statement. Prairie Power advocates had little patience for building coalitions with mainstream groups and had an intense dislike of electoral politics and bureaucratic government. This group also tended to be much more attuned to the developing counter-culture on campuses. The new generation dressed and acted more casually than their predecessors, and the use of marijuana and other drugs became much more commonplace at chapter meetings.[16]

Changes were also taking place within the civil rights movement. The primary New Left organization, SNCC, underwent a fundamental change. Embittered by the MFDP experience, SNCC leaders gradually became more radical in tactics, goals and ideology; black separatism became a popular philosophy. The development of black power and the Black Panther party were clear indications that the much-hoped-for integrated radical movement was becoming a less realistic goal. The explosion in Watts in the summer of 1965 indicated the changing nature of race relations and the move toward more violent action. Less enamored with white support, black activists became attracted to the separatist movement in increasing numbers.[17]

The new militancy in the New Left also became apparent in the character of and the involvement in protest activities. The most apparent was SDS's sponsoring of a major anti-war march. In the first truly national effort by the New Left, many peace and activist organizations joined with SDS to co-sponsor a march on Washington in October, 1965. The success of the march surprised everyone. Twenty to twenty-five thousand protestors listened to speakers and petitioned Congressional leaders. The march was a great success in temporarily uniting leftist groups and in demonstrating the burgeoning opposition to the escalation of the war. The clearest evidence of the march's success was a much greater interest on the part of the media and the government. Suddenly, SDS and other groups moved from being a curiosity to a leftist movement that for the first time since the 1930s demanded the attention of the press, the government and the nation.[18]

The Movement's new-found success had immediate positive results, but simultaneously and irreversibly cut short a promising leftist coalition of pacifists, radicals and socialists. The fervor of the growing opposition to the war attracted thousands of students and members of existing organizations to join SDS because it was the only national organization providing leadership on a range of activities and was the only leftist organization that was attracting widespread media attention.[19] Curiously, however, SDS leadership fairly quickly abdicated its role as the focal point of the anti-war movement. Leaders did not want SDS to become a single issue organization: other issues such as racism, black power, poverty, and the radicalization of campuses deserved as much attention. The abdication of the anti-war leadership came at a critical time. Prairie Power advocates were concomitantly pushing through an organizational plan of decentralization. The upshot of decentralization was that the National Office had a decreasing role in determining the direction of SDS. Local chapters gradually became more free to determine their own initiatives. Ironically, the National Office, always the focus of media attention, moved in its own direction which was often at odds with the local chapters.[20] The result was that SDS, despite its growing membership, did not play a guiding role in the anti-war movement.

Despite SDS's ineffectiveness, activity throughout the country indicated a flourishing movement. A new character gradually developed in the New Left as it moved from peaceful protest and coalition building to resistance aimed at blocking the government's involvement in Vietnam. A series of events in the autumn of 1967 indicated the extent and nature of the protest movement. At the University of Wisconsin, Madison in mid-October, students blocked Dow Chemical recruiters (the makers of napalm) from conducting interviews on campus. What began as a peaceful protest quickly accelerated into a widespread strike. City and campus police used tear gas and force to disperse students. On October 20, 10,000 protestors gathered in Oakland to block troop trains and resisted the forced dispersal attempts of the Oakland police. These were but two examples of local activity that took place throughout the country.[21]

At the same time, national activities grew in size and intensity. Other groups began to fill the anti-war leadership void left by SDS. Resistance, a group formed by, among others, Staughton Lynd and David Harris, encouraged young men to resist the draft and induction. National rallies called for this type of action as hundreds of draft-age men participated in a week-long draft card turn-in (October 16-21). Resistance members combined with the National Mobilization Committee to End the War (MOBE) to organize a major march on the Pentagon. An estimated 100,000 marchers used a back road route to reach the Pentagon to protest the continued U.S. involvement in Vietnam and especially to condemn the bombing of North Vietnam.[22]

The size and militant character of the march caught the government by surprise. Clearly, disenchantment with the war and with the American government had reached dramatic proportions. One result was that government investigations and interference in the New Left accelerated.

Within the New Left, a transformation also took place. A new militancy began to develop. Frustrated by the inability to change the course of U.S. involvement in Vietnam and a similar experience on other social issues such as poverty and racism, New Leftists sought alternative methods for changing society. This changing character was particularly evident within SDS. A new group, the May 2 Movement (M2M) which was the anti-war wing of the Maoist Progressive Labor (PL) party joined SDS. M2M members contributed to a changing dialogue within SDS. Radicals began to talk in terms of understanding imperialism and its role in perpetuating the war in Vietnam. Marxism and Leninism along with Maoism became terms of discussion within the New Left. Radicals began to identify with the National Liberation Front (NLF) and its banner began to appear at anti-war rallies where chants in support of Ho Chi Minh became commonplace. Another sign of change within the Movement was evidenced by the growing assertiveness of women. At SDS meetings, women began to caucus separately and to define issues on their terms. The Movement was beginning to split. One group called for raising the line of confrontation and transforming the sources of power; revolution as a concept began to creep into the literature and into conversations. Another group rededicated itself to organizing and educating to build a wide base of support.[23]

As a result of this growing split, SDS played less and less of a leadership role with the Movement. The National Office became further removed from the chapter rank and file. Ironically, however, SDS membership continued to grow and support for the New Left virtually exploded. But other forces were at work that continued to unravel the possibilities for a strong radical mass movement. The counter-culture was in full bloom. Many of America's youth turned toward drugs, psychodelia and alternative lifestyles rather than to political or revolutionary activity. The counter-culture found some leadership in such gurus as Abbie Hoffman and Jerry Rubin, who founded the Youth for International Peace party (YIP). Yippies concentrated on the absurd. Guerrilla theater and acts intended to outrage were the Yippie staples.[24]

A more potent force on the left emerged from the Black Power movement. The Black Panther Party became the dominant force and commanded the attention of militant blacks and dominated media attention. The "Free Huey" Newton campaign served as a popular rallying cry for Black Power advocates and their radical white supporters. The growth of Black Power, devastating riots in Newark and Detroit in 1967, revolutionary

8

dialogues in the New Left, and the significant growth of the counter-culture all pointed toward a more factionalized and isolated Movement.[25]

The year 1968 marked the culmination of New Left activity and government reaction. It was a year of such widespread activity that several books have been written that concentrate on that year alone.[26] The year began with Viet Cong's Tet Offensive which surprised American military leadership and stunned American television audiences as they watched Viet Cong commandos enter the compound of the American Embassy in Saigon. In response to widespread disenchantment with the war, Senator Eugene McCarthy announced his candidacy against the incumbent President Lyndon Johnson, and on March 13 scored a huge symbolic victory in the New Hampshire primary. Faced with the McCarthy challenge and on the advice from strategists, Johnson surprised the nation late in March by announcing that he would not seek reelection. Five days after the Johnson announcement, James Earl Ray assassinated Martin Luther King, Jr., in Memphis, Tennessee. King's death resulted in a series of riots, the most serious of which took place in the nation's capital. Shortly thereafter, the SDS guided one of the year's most dramatic events when students took over Columbia University. SDS members, led by Mark Rudd, occupied administrative buildings and effectively closed the university in an attempt to force Columbia not to build a gymnasium that would displace poor blacks in Harlem and to force the divesture of defense-related research and investments. Another assassination took place about a month after King's when Sirhan Sirhan shocked the nation by killing Robert F. Kennedy, who had been campaigning for the Democratic nomination.[27]

The climactic event of the year, and probably the decade, took place in late August in Chicago at the Democratic National Convention. Radicals organized by MOBE led by Hayden and Rennie Davis, and Yippies led by Hoffman and Rubin joined supporters of Eugene McCarthy to protest the nomination of Hubert H. Humphrey as the Democratic candidate. Under the glare of the national media, Chicago police brutalized protestors. The effect of this "police riot" was to radicalize New Left activists further. Chicago served as the symbolic end of the resistance phase.[28]

The New Left's turn toward radicalism accelerated as the decade drew to a close. Armed confrontations between Black Panthers and the government increased. SDS was rent asunder by a cadre of leaders who became increasingly dedicated to violence and by the constant ideological battles of such factions as the Revolutionary Youth Movement (RYM), Progressive

Labor and other groups. At the local level, however, much activity continued along the lines of resistance. SDS rank and file continued to participate in anti-war activity, to support action to overcome racism, to help build the growing women's movement, and to contribute to the nascent environmental movement. But national leadership continued its march to revolutionary actions and ideological splits.[29]

The culmination of these trends took place at the June, 1969 SDS national convention in Chicago. At the end of five days of heated debate, SDS split into three factions: PL, RYM, and Weathermen. It was irreversibly split and essentially finished as a national entity. The most notorious of these factions, the Weatherpeople (as they later renamed themselves) became the most violent manifestation of the New Left. The media focused heavily on such Weatherpeople acts as "Days of Rage" in Chicago and other violent acts. These activities were juxtaposed against the trial of the Chicago Eight (Chicago Seven after Bobby Seale finally had his trial separated), and the New Left garnered the national spotlight as it never had before.[30]

Clearly, however, national influence on the part of the New Left was beginning to ebb. Federal and local government actions against the Movement became more repressive. Leaders in the new Richard M. Nixon administration were less concerned with the civil rights of individuals and took a much more repressive stance against protestors and activists. Both the FBI and the CIA became more heavily involved in infiltrating the Movement and in encouraging violence. The beginning of troop withdrawals and the draft lottery served to quiet some protestors. With the dissolution of SDS, no national center for the New Left remained. Peaceful protest and civil disobedience no longer attracted the national press when compared to the violent acts of the more radical groups.[31]

To be sure, some activity continued into the early 1970s. Leftist journals and newspapers continued to be published; major protests against the war took place. Student strikes in such universities as Harvard and San Francisco State, and the brutal reaction of Berkeley, California area law enforcement agencies against the building of People's Park illustrated the continued dedication of activists.[32] Similarly, the major campus revolt against Nixon's invasion of Cambodia in the spring of 1970, which led to the killing of student protestors at Kent State and Jackson State, demonstrated the vitality of the anti-war movement. But by 1972, following the overwhelming defeat of George McGovern in the presidential election, the New Left was no longer a strong force. Media attention slowed and former activists began to move into professional positions and assume responsibilities that limited activism.

The failure of the New Left to build a leftist coalition and a continuing movement that could survive government repression and changing priorities form the focus of these articles. Before turning to the articles, a few points need to be made. First, these articles represent the views primarily of the first generation of leadership or the old guard of SDS. To date most accounts by New Left leaders and theorists have been written by the old guard or by those who are sympathetic to the first generation. With few exceptions, the second and third generation of New Left leaders have not written and published memoirs or analyses.[33] Second, as alluded to earlier, Richard Flacks in a recent article develops the theme that the New Left never really ended. Instead, he argues, it continued in the environmental movement, the women's movement and in the way many New Leftists settled into professional careers yet maintained a set of ideas and values developed during their participation in the Movement. Flacks further argues that a new generation of students are starting to pay more attention to the 1960s and the Movement. He finds that they are attracted by the ideas and the activities of the New Left. These new activists are interested in learning from veterans of the Movement. As he asserts, [they] "want to learn its lessons, pick up the threads."[34]

If what Flacks argues is true (and having watched dozens of young students listen to Howard Zinn in Madison with rapt attention and and these same students help elect a former radical mayor it is easy to believe), these articles take on an even greater importance. Besides providing some important lessons for present and future activists, these essays have the added advantage of providing a fascinating inside view of the Movement from the perspective of some of its most important participants.

One of the most explicit essays in analyzing the ideological problems of the New Left is Carl Oglesby's "Notes on a Decade Ready for the Dustbin."[35] Asked by the editors of *Liberation* to write an essay on the future possibilities for the Movement, Oglesby provided instead an analysis of the problems. His views are especially important. He was president of SDS in 1965-66 and one of the few early and mid-term leaders to stay active in leadership circles for a long time. He wrote the article after the 1969 SDS convention. Written in a choppy, almost stream-of-consciousness style, this article nevertheless provides a penetrating critique of post-1965 trends in the Movement. Oglesby attacks the split of SDS and especially chastises the Revolutionary Youth Movement, Progressive Labor and the Weatherpeople

11

for their role in the breakup. He argues that the theories of the early New Left were the most promising for changing the nature of American society and government.

The difference in the post-1965 generation of SDS leaders was the introduction of revolutionary theory. Oglesby criticizes white and black leaders for abandoning radical reforms and moving toward a theory of revolution for the United States and the West based upon Marxist-Leninist ideology. This theory failed to understand American culture, but, more important, slavish devotion to such ideology precluded the development of a new philosophy more in step with reality. SDS and the New Left groups' failure to develop shrewd policies or a concrete social program ensured its inability to build a broad-based movement. In response to those who argued that such policies would have led to co-option (one of the New Left's greatest fears), Oglesby offers some excellent advice for future leaders. The left, he argues, should not be wary about being co-opted but should instead concentrate on what needs to be done. The only real question is whether reform will be a fundamental challenge to class and help reconfigure the power structure.

A more focused portrait of SDS internal workings is provided by Richard Rothstein in his "Representative Democracy in SDS." It was first published as a pamphlet in 1971 by the New University Conference and later reprinted in *Liberation*.[36] Rothstein seeks to correct misinterpretations about the structure of the early SDS. One of the New Left's most important struggles was to keep from becoming an elitist bureaucracy like the United States government or the Soviet Union. SDS constantly tried to preserve participatory democracy so that it could be exported to the outside world. Rothstein wrote this article in 1970-71 to counteract those who had argued that the tyranny of leadership within SDS in the late 1960s proved that representative structures are undemocratic. To correct this misconception, Rothstein, an SDS founder, provides a fascinating history of SDS governmental structure and intertwines his thesis, which is that SDS's ongoing need for a more democratic structure allowing almost total participation combined with a constant effort to decentralize operations actually resulted in tyranny rather than democracy.

The abandonment of representative democracy began with a reorganization in 1963 when the representative structure was dismantled. What happened over the next few years was that local chapters were increasingly excluded from influence at the national level. The constant rotation of officers insured a new generation of leaders who never had to face the long term consequences of their actions, and their successors were never around long enough to learn lessons from the past. Power gradually fell to the National Interim Committee (NIC) which was "appointed and organized by the staff itself" and had the responsibility for operating SDS between meetings. Having the staff appoint its ruling body could only preserve an anti-democratic structure. In another search for wider democracy, the central ruling body, the National Council (NC) began to allow anyone who showed up at meetings to vote. This effectively eliminated the voice of elected chapter delegates.[37] Rothstein provides both an incisive look at the internal workings of SDS and many arguments for the creation of a sustaining democratic organization. In essence he shows how the breakdown of true democracy contributed significantly to the demise of SDS.[38]

In a very different type of article, Elinor Langer, a later activist, provides a personal interpretation of the New Left in her "Notes for Next Time: A Memoir of the 1960s."[39] To explain the New Left and its successes and its failures, she recounts her personal intellectual development which led to her participation in the Movement, her later disillusionment and her eventual turn to the women's movement. Like Oglesby, she studies the transformation of the Movement from reform to revolution, but unlike Oglesby, she became caught up in the momentum of the revolution after 1965. In her autobiographical approach, Langer makes several important points. She argues that the growth of Marxism within the New Left was understandable because it had been so inaccessible for American youth. This fantasy of revolution was in some ways very convenient because it was apolitical and effectively impossible. In other words, it gave some activists the ability to criticize without offering an effective alternative. She also chides later activists, like herself, for becoming too immersed in the promise of youthful counter-culture. It was a great notion to believe that such developments could fundamentally reshape or revolutionize America, but activists made a critical mistake when they failed to realize that America can accept anything as long as money remains the medium of exchange.

The central problem for the Movement in Langer's view was its failure to develop a clear and incisive analysis of American culture in the 1960s. In fact the Movement was anti-cultural. The underdeveloped "half-baked" Marxism gave activists several ideas that impeded a productive left. In much the same vein as Oglesby, Langer believes that later New Leftists developed a false consciousness which was used to explain away the fact that most Americans

13

failed to understand the theoretical relationship between advanced capitalism and the war economy and its relation to inflation and the denial of public services. Most Americans were tightly bound to the culture of the system. A second problem was "false internationalism." The highs from the National Liberation Front and Cuba precluded a systematic analysis of foreign communism. Other problems included the fear of co-option and repressive tolerance. The former paralyzed political initiative and the latter insured the New Left's loss of the higher moral ground. Finally, half-baked Marxism could not cope with America's huge middle class and the fact that there was a sense of social mobility. After 1965 life in the Movement became a brutal and continual search to meet the revolutionary test.

Richard Flacks' "Making History vs. Making Life: Dilemmas of an American Left"[40] is a much less personal history of the New Left. This article, the thesis of which was expanded into the author's recent book, *Making History: The Radical Tradition in American Life*, argues that the left will become an important force only when it appeals to a popular majority. Flacks, also an SDS founder, believes that society should be organized so that power and everyday life can be intertwined. Attempting to get to the heart of one of the early New Left's most important tenets, Flacks asserts that the primary goal of the left should be to help ordinary individuals gain the ability to make history—that is to have real decision-making authority over their everyday lives. This concept is the radical left's distinct difference from liberals. Liberals want to make decisions for the people based on their expertise, radicals want to give people the power to make their own decisions. The early New Left approached this philosophy. It was anti-dogmatic, anti-authority and anti-bureaucratic. Furthermore, it was open to experience and desperately wanted to avoid factional and sectarian infighting. It was to be an alternative to the Old Left and to the Democratic Party.

Additionally, Flacks enumerates the reasons why the New Left failed to build a wide-ranging coalition. In his view, the lion's share of blame lies with other organizations. Organized labor and other reformist bureaucracies had little real interest in a social movement. Integrationist strategies among the groups collapsed as labor and liberal groups continued their commitment to Cold War interventionist policies. Vietnam, Black Power and ghetto rebellions led to divisions in the social groups that might have built a radical coalition. He finds reasons for this failure within SDS as well. One failure was the inability to establish a cohesive group. Former leaders were regularly excluded from the decision-making process, and the old guard failed to communicate their vision to those who replaced them. The result was that once the founders were gone, little agreement on basic philosophy or moral approaches remained.

Another major failure was that the New Left did not develop an organization for its graduates. Once activists entered professional life, there was no organization to help them continue radical activities. A final problem was that many of the early leaders like Mario Savio of FSM and Robert Moses of SNCC did not wish to develop followings and abdicated their leadership roles to those who were less troubled by doubt and more secure in their ideological commitment. In the end SDS and other New Left groups failed to develop coherent policies because they fell prey to the worst excesses of the Old Left. For the left to be successful, it must give ordinary people the ability to make history. It can do this by stressing local politics, personal development, intellectual work and coalition building.

Trained in sociology, like Flacks, Robert Ross also takes a sociological/historical approach to the New Left and combines it with his own experience. In his "Primary Groups in Social Movements: A Memoir and Interpretation,"[41] Ross studies the changes that took place during the pivotal years of 1965-66, casting a particular eye toward the change in character and direction of the SDS leadership. He argues that the vote to hold the April, 1965 March on Washington prefigured the later generational split. The founding generation opposed such activity because it took energy and resources from local community organizing. This friction caused the old guard to begin a quiet withdrawal. Simultaneously, media attention and the resulting growth in membership contributed to the negative effect of giving SDS broader, unannounced goals. As evidence of this phenomena, Ross argues that the mass media interpreted participatory democracy to mean consensus in group decision-making, but, Ross argues, in the Port Huron context, the term was meant to extend industrial democracy to all forms of public life.

The lack of continuous old guard influence on the second and third generation of the New Left had a similarly negative effect as the Movement expanded. One of the Movement's critical problems was that it failed to meet one of the central requirements of an organized democracy. It did not have an influential group with skills in facilitating decision-making. This allowed SDS to be overwhelmed when new members poured into the organization and insured that the direction of the Movement could not be controlled.

This development forced the New Left in directions that were not in the best interest of building a strong radical movement.

The final essay, Todd Gitlin's "The Achievement of the Anti-War Movement,"[42] relates the history and importance of the New Left's struggle to end the war. He is particularly interested in the Movement's effect on the course of the war and the war's effect on the Movement. One of Gitlin's major concerns is that the New Left never really understood the full extent of its powers. Activists needed to learn patience and to build a broad-based coalition by working with such leaders as Martin Luther King, Jr. Instead, the New Left looked only for radical answers and in doing so, squandered much of its moral authority in a romance with the NLF. The consequences of this mistake were twofold: first, it alienated many potential supporters; and second, it gave moral title to the conservatives. In the end, the anti-war movement painted itself into a corner by determining that ending the war was an all-or-nothing proposition.

This all-or-nothing mentality hindered the New Left in developing an objective assessment of its role in ending the war. While the consequences were not immediately apparent, the protest movement did in fact play a significant role in ending a shooting war. It would have been an even stronger movement if it had broadened its appeal to include anti-war veterans, working class draftees, and it should have built a strong interracial alliance. Gitlin further argues that we have yet to understand the government's role in pushing the Movement to violence. The use of agent provocateurs in inciting a more radical direction within the New Left needs to be studied. He also admonishes present and future activists to criticize authoritarian socialism. The left's greatest chance of success lies with its commitment to ensuring elementary human rights.

It is fitting that this collection ends with Gitlin's essay. His study clearly demonstrates just how much one segment of the Movement accomplished, and it is the most hopeful in suggesting a positive course for the future. As all the writers suggest, the history of the New Left in the United States is, in part, one of mistakes and missed opportunities. It is important for past, present and future activists to understand these mistakes. But at the same time, it is equally important to understand the wide and far-ranging contributions of the New Left in the areas of civil rights, anti-war activities, women's rights and environmental awareness. The left of this country has made significant contributions to the betterment of its citizens and should be ready to do so again.

NOTES

1. Among the recent books on the Movement and the 1960s are: James Miller, *Democracy is in the Streets: From Port Huron to the Siege of Chicago*, (New York, 1987); Todd Gitlin, *The Sixties: Years of Hope, Days of Rage*, (New York, 1988); Maurice Isserman, *If I Had a Hammer . . . The Death of the Old Left and the Birth of the New Left*, (New York, 1987); Tom Hayden, *Reunion*, (New York, 1988); W.J. Rorabaugh, *Berkeley at War, the 1960s*, (Berkeley, 1989); Annie Gottlieb, *Do You Believe in Magic? Bringing the Sixties Back Home*, (New York, 1988) focuses on the cultural revolution; Russel Jacoby, *The Last Intellectuals: American Culture in the Age of Academe*, (New York, 1987) though not exclusively on the New Left, this book does contain two substantive chapters on the New Left in academe; Richard Flacks, *Making History: The American Left and the American Mind* (New York, 1988) is more of a blueprint for the future but contains a great deal about the New Left's past.

   The turmoil of 1968 has elicited special attention. David Caute, *The Year of the Barricades: A Journey through 1968* (New York); Ronald Fraser, *1968: A Student Generation in Revolt*, (New York, 1988) this title is misleading because the book deals with the whole of the 1960s; George Katsiaficas, *The Imagination of the New Left: A Global Analysis of 1968* (Boston, 1987); Irwin Unger and Debi Unger, *Turning Point: 1968*, (New York, 1988); Hans Koning, *Nineteen Sixty-Eight: Its Mark on the Country, the Government and You and Me*, (New York, 1987); Charles Kaiser, *1968 in America: Music, Politics, Chaos, Counterculture and the Shaping of a Generation*, (New York, 1988); David Farber, *Chicago '68*, (Chicago, 1988). Journals have devoted large sections to 1968. *New Politics*, New Series: 2, (Winter, 1989) includes seven articles and *Socialist Revolution*, 18 (Oct.-Dec., 1988) has articles on several countries including a particularly perceptive one by Maurice Isserman entitled "1968 and the New Left."

   Some literature on the New Left from the conservative perspective has begun to develop. See Peter Collier and David Horowitz, *Destructive Generation: Second Thoughts about the 1960s*, (New York, 1989); John H. Bunzel, ed., *Political Passages: Journeys through two Decades of Change* (New York, 1988); Guenter Lewy, *The Moral Crisis of American Pacifism*, (Grand Rapids, Mich., 1988).

2. Dick Flacks, "What Happened to the New Left," *Socialist Review*, 19 (Jan.-Mar., 1989): 91-92.

3. Isserman, *If I Had a Hammer*, 244.

4. Kirkpatrick Sale, *SDS*, (New York, 1973) organizes his study around this theme. This book remains the most comprehensive study of SDS.

5. Maurice Isserman and Michael Kazin, "The Failure and Success of the New Radicalism," in Steve Fraser and Gary Gerstle, eds., *The Rise and the Fall of the New Deal Order, 1930-1980*, (Princeton, 1989): 222.

6. Isserman, *If I Had a Hammer*, 173-219.

7. Sale, *SDS*, 35-37; Gitlin, *The Sixties*, 146-49.
8. Miller, *Democracy is in the Streets*, 41, 51.
9. Richard Flacks, "Making History vs. Making Life: Dilemmas of an American Left," *Working Papers for a New Society*, 2 (Summer, 1974): 67.
10. Sale, *SDS*, 103-104. Eventually the campus group would evolve into Al Haber's Radical Education Project (REP) headquartered in Ann Arbor.
11. Sale, *SDS*, 103.
12. The best descriptions of the Mississippi Freedom Democratic Party can be found in Clayborne Carson's *In Struggle: SNCC and the Black Awakening of the 1960s*, (Cambridge, Mass., 1981).
13. Sale, *SDS*, 159, *passim*.
14. Rorabaugh, *Berkeley at War*, 19-47.
15. Miller, *Democracy is in the Streets*, 180.
16. The growth of Prairie Power is explained in a number of publications, see Sale, *SDS*, 279-99; Gitlin, *The Sixties*, 252-55.
17. Carson, *In Struggle*, 191-211.
18. Sale, *SDS*, 228-35.
19. *Ibid.*, 246-52.
20. *Ibid.*, 519-20.
21. *Ibid.*, 369-87; Rorabaugh, *Berkeley at War*, 116-18; see also Nancy Zaroulis and Gerald Sullivan, *Who Spoke Up? American Protest Against the War in Viet Nam, 1963-1975*, (Garden City, N.Y., 1985).
22. Zaroulis and Sullivan, *Who Spoke Up?*, 137-39.
23. Sale, *SDS*, 390-403.
24. Gitlin, *The Sixties*, 222-27.
25. Carson, *In Struggle*, 191-211.
26. See note number one.
27. Any of the books on 1968 deal with these events; the most complete is Irwin Unger and Debi Unger's *Turning Point: 1968*.
28. Farber, *Chicago '68*.
29. Sale, *SDS*, 510-56.
30. *Ibid.*
31. *Ibid.*, 607-22.
32. Rorabaugh, *Berkeley at War*, 155-66.
33. For perceptive treatments by those who value the ideas of the latter generations see Katsiaficas, *The Imagination of the New left* and Winifred Breines, "Whose New Left?" *Journal of American History*, 75, (Sept., 1988): 528-45. Breines' article is a review essay of Miller's *Democracy is in the Streets*, Isserman's *If I Had a Hammer*, Gitlin's *The Sixties*, Mary King's *Freedom Song: A Personal Story of the 1960s Civil Rights Movement* (New York, 1987) and Katsiaficas. In the essay, she criticizes the authors, excepting Katsiaficas, for ignoring post-1968 Movement accomplishments because the authors focus too heavily on SDS. Another article in this vein is Paul Piccone's "Reinterpreting 1968: Mythology on the Make," *Telos*, No. 77, (Fall, 1988): 7-44.
34. Flacks, "What Happened to the New Left?": 92.

35. Carl Ogelsby, "Notes on a Decade Ready for the Dustbin," *Liberation*, 14, (Aug.-Sept., 1969): 5-19. Oglesby wrote another article entitled "Will Success Spoil SDS?" *Motive*, (Nov., 1968): 12-20 in which he describes meeting with liberal business leaders who were interested in developing a dialogue with leftists.

36. Richard Rothstein, *Representative Democracy in SDS*, (Chicago, 1971); *Liberation*, 16, (Feb., 1972): 10-18.

37. This operating procedure gave a disproportionate voice to such groups as PL who were much more rigid in their ideology and always willing to stay later than everyone else to vote on issues.

38. A latter generation SDS activist did publish a rejoinder to this article. See Norman Fruchter, "SDS: In and Out of Context," *Liberation*, 16, (Feb., 1972): 19-32.

39. Elinor Langer, "Notes for Next Time: A Memoir of the 1960s," *Working Papers for a New Society*, 1, (Fall, 1973): 48-81.

40. Richard Flacks, "Making History vs. Making Life,": 56-73. The same article was reprinted in *Sociological Inquiry*, 46, (1976).

41. Robert Ross, "Primary Groups in Social Movements: A Memoir and Interpretation." *Journal of Voluntary Action Research*, 6, (July, 1977): 139-51. A slightly revised version of this article was published in Jo Freeman, *Social Movements of the Sixties and Seventies*, (New York, 1983) under the title "Generational Change and Primary Groups in a Social Movement,": 177-90.

42. This article was originally published under the title "Seizing History: What Was Won and Lost at Home," *Mother Jones*, 8, (Nov., 1983): 32-38, 48. Professor Gitlin has retitled it for publication here.

Notes on a Decade
Ready for the Dustbin

CARL OGLESBY

The idea of trying to visualize ourselves five or ten years from now seems to me hopeless but necessary, so I'm writing a letter instead of a paper just because it seems easier in the former to float, stammer, and skip.

Hopeless—to put it most abstractly—because I don't think we have anything like a predictive science of political economy. We *approach* having an explanatory art of history, I think, and sometimes we can build up a head of steam-bound analogies and go crashing an inch or so through the future barrier, but it always turns out we land sideways or even upside down. And more practically, hopeless because in a situation as sensitive as what the world's in now, mankind as a whole lives under the permanent Terror of the Accidental.

But necessary, too, this idea, because even if we're never going to surpass improvisatory politics, we could still improvise better if we were clearer about ourselves and the country, and the effort to think about the future always turns out to be an effort to think about the present. Which is all to the good. So I'll start with the past—to get a sense of trajectory, if any, or the rhythm of our experience, to see if there's a line of flight:

1960-64

As well the Freedom Rides as Greensboro? But then, as well the desegregation decision as the Freedom Rides . . . etc. Whenever it began, this was the Heroic Period, the movement's Bronze Age. In transition ever since, the movement has yet to prove it will have a Classical Period, but maybe we're on the verge. Essentially, a single-issue reform politics; integration the leading public demand, although underneath that demand, there's a sharply rising sense that a structural maldistribution of wealth won't be corrected by the abolition of Jim Crow. An implicitly radical democratic communitarianism, projected correctly as both a means *and an end* of the movement, can still co-exist with a formless and rather annoyed liberalism because (a) the Peace People are obfuscating the Cold War without yet having become suspicious characters, and (b) the reform tide seems to be running, picking up velocity and mass, and has still to hit the breakwater. But there's a richness in the decentralist idioms of this period that has only been neglected, certainly not exhausted, or even barely tapped, in the intervening half decade of transition.

1965

Very quick, sharp changes, engineered in part by Johnson, in part by self-conscious growth within the movement.

The war abruptly becomes the leading issue for most white radicals. But not for community organizers, some of whom in fact are bitter about the new preoccupation. This is neither the first nor the last time that this sort of friction develops. What is its general form? A nationalist vs. an internationalist consciousness? It appears that some activists will always tend to visualize the American people mainly as victims, and others will tend to see them as criminal accomplices (passive or not) of the ruling class. This maybe points to an abiding problem for an advanced-national socialist movement—a problem which will be neither understood nor solved simply by the Trotskyist slogan, "Bring the troops home."

The teach-ins and the SDS April March on Washington repeat in a compressed time scale the civil-rights movement's growth from Greensboro to Selma. It's in this very brief, very intense period that SDS projects an unabashedly reformist critique of the war, our naive attack on the domino theory being the best illustration of this: "But the other dominos *won't* fall," we insisted, happy to give such reassurance to the Empire.

SNCC formalizes its transformation from reform to revolution, first, by explicating the connection between racism and war; and second, by focusing the metaphor of Black Power, which clearly (at least to hindsight) applied the forthcoming ghetto-equals-colony analysis and the shift from an integrationist to a separatist-nationalist politics, which of course was to bring two problems for every one it solved. This shift seems to have been necessitated by the impasse which integrationism confronted at Atlantic City the previous year.

What was the Atlantic City of the white student movement that was to go from pro-peace to anti-war, anti-war to pro-NLF, pro-NLF to anti-imperialist to pro-Third World revolution to anti-capitalism to pro-socialism—and then, with much more confusion and uncertainty than the schedule implies, to anti-peace (i.e., no co-existence) and anti-democracy ("bourgeois jive"), and which finds itself at the present moment broken into two, three, many factions, each of which claims to have the *real* Lenin (or Mao or Che) in its pocket? Riddled with vanguarditis and galloping sectarianism, and possessed of a twisty hallucination called the "mass line" like an ancient virgin her incubus (or is it just a hot water bottle?) the Rudd-Jones-Ayers SDS is at least an SDS with a past. I'll say later what I think is wrong with the mass-line stance, but the point here is to understand that it didn't just come upon SDS out of nowhere, not even the nowhere of the PLP, and that in the end, whatever you think of it, it has to happen: (a) because there was no way to resist the truth of the war, no way, that is, to avoid imperialism; (b) because once the policy critique of the war had been supplanted by the structural critique of the empire, all political therapies short of socialist revolution appeared to become senseless; and (c) because the necessity of a revolutionary strategy was, in effect, the same thing as the necessity of Marxism-Leninism. *There was—and is—no other coherent, integrative, and explicit philosophy of revolution.*

I do not want to be misunderstood about this. The practical identity of Marxism-Leninism with revolutionary theory, in my estimate, does not mean that Marxism-Leninism is *also* identical with a genuinely revolutionary practice in the advanced countries. That identity, rather, constitutes nothing more than a tradition, a legacy, and a problem which I think the Left will have to overcome. But at the same time, I don't think the American Left's first stab at producing for itself a *fulfilled* revolutionary consciousness could have produced anything better, could have gone beyond this ancestor-worship politics. It was necessary to discover—or maybe the word is confess—that we had ancestors in the first place; and if for no brighter motive than gratitude at not being so alone and rootless, the discovery of the ancestors would naturally beget a religious mood. That of the revival tent, no doubt, but religious all the same.

Again: Why did the white student Left so quickly abandon its liberal or reformist criticism of the war as policy and substitute its radical criticism of the war as the result of an imperialist structure? The former seems to have had much to recommend it: simple, straightforward, full of pathos and even sentimentality, it has by this time been linked (by liberals) to a still more pathos-laden cry to bring the boys back, and these two thrusts—save *our* boys and (incidentally) *their* babies—now make up the substance of the popular complaints against the war. (Harriman is now saying what we said about the war four years ago.) What happened was that the student movement traded this *easy* argument against the war for a much harder one. Not that we rose as one man to denounce imperialism, of course. It was in October of that year that Paul Booth told the nation that SDS only wanted to "build, not burn." But he got into a lot of trouble for his pains; and when about a month later, at the SANE-organized March on Washington, I used (without knowing it) all the paraphernalia of an anti-imperialist critique without once using the word "imperialism," nobody objected, nobody said, "This line commits us to an attempt at revolution and therefore, true or not, should be rejected as being politically impracticable."

Why did our movement *want* to be "revolutionary?" Very generally: An extrinsic failure of production (i.e., production turned *against* social reproduction) had already been intuited by that sector of the workers whose function is to *pacify the relations of production*. The most general means of this pacification is the neutralizing of the moral environment. This is what poets, political scientists, lit. teachers, sociologists, preachers, etc. are supposed to do. Deflect, divert, apologize, change the subject, prove either that our gods are virtuous and our direction right or that *no* gods are virtuous and *no* direction right and that rebellion ought therefore to forego history and take on the Cosmos. I think it can be shown that the practice of this essential work has already been jeopardized by the overall character of production in the late '50s. Those whose role in production is to *explain* production, to provide it with its cover of rationality, had found it impossible to play their role *convincingly* simply because production had become extrinsically anti-social. Workers who cannot do their work rebel. They do so, furthermore, in the name of their work, in behalf of its possibility, and therefore in the name of that reordered system in which their work would again become possible.

The main point here is that 1965 was the year in which both the black and white sectors of the movement explicitly abandoned reformism and took up that long march whose destination, not even in sight yet, is a theory and practice of revolution for the United States. For the West.

1966-67

The rise of the resistance (in all its variety) and experiments with a "new-working-class" analysis, both motions strongly influenced by Greg Calvert and Carl Davidson. Superficially, these developments seemed to be congruent and intersupportive. But it looks to me now as if they were in fact opposite responses to the general problem of conceiving and realizing a revolutionary strategy, each one being a kind of political bet which the other one hedged. There was, I know, a lot of heavy theorizing about the politics of resistance, and I don't want to turn a complex experience into a simple memory. Still, I think it's fair to take the slogans as being indicative of its political atmosphere—"Not with my life, you don't!" for example, or "A call to resist illegitimate authority." Even if only in embryo, I think "resistance" was at bottom a youth-based anti-fascist front whose most central demand must have appeared to any outsider's eye to be for a return to the *status quo ante*. That's not to say that its organizers were not radicals or that its inner content was anti-socialist or non-socialist. But in basing itself on the individual's rights of self-determination (mythical, of course: we were all hip to the con), and in trying to depict Johnson's as an imposter ("illegitimate") regime, the Resistance was easily as unassuming in its politics as it was extravagant in its imagination.

At the same time, Carl ("I Blush to Remember") Davidson, among others, was trying to work out a new-working-class concept of the student rebellion, the main purpose being to discover in this rebellion that revolutionary power which one feared it may not have. Wanting revolution (with all that implies about the power to make one) but only having spasms of campus rebellion, the student syndicalists needed to show that at least the seed of the first found fertile ground in the latter.

Meanwhile: The method of political action which had been reintroduced in Harlem-'64 or Watts-'65 was on some terms perfected in Detroit-'67. All whites are convinced that something will have to be done, but nobody knows quite what to do. Except, of course, for the Right, which understood at once that what was needed was a metropolitan police force equipped both militarily *and politically* for urban counter-insurgency.

1968

Confidence reappeared with Columbia and France, and then took an important turn with Chicago.

Columbia: (1) Conclusively, students have severely limited but formidable power to intervene in certain processes of oppression and to compel certain institutional reforms. (2) A practical alliance between blacks and whites became a concrete fact for the first time since Selma. The campus continues to be the main current locus of this alliance. (I say this, obviously, in view of Columbia's subsequence: Columbia's innovations proved repeatable elsewhere.) (3) Production relations constitute the life of class economy; distribution relations constitute the life of class society; consumption relations constitute the life of class politics. The stormed or barricaded factory gate of classical revolutionary vision is not the definitive image of any "final" or "pure" proletarian consciousness. The struggle at the point of production, when it occurs, is merely one expression of a more general struggle which, much more often than not, is ignited and fed by consciousness of inequities of consumption.[1] The worker comprehends the factory, in fact, as his means of consumption. It's in distribution patterns that the lifestyles of the class hierarchy are imposed; in the consumption patterns thus produced that the hierarchy of classes is most immediately *lived*. Production relations, as they are actually lived, are usually politically neutral: *the difference between an 8-hour day under U.S. capitalism and a 16-hour day under Cuban socialism is hardly to the former's advantage.* In fact, it's much more often a failure in the distributive or consumptive functions that creates political trouble for capitalism. How to finance further expansion? How to empty these busting warehouses? And it could even be argued that as between the ghetto rising and the militant strike in heavy industry, the former is closer to that famous "seizure of State power" that the latter is. But why try to choose at all? We are dealing here only with aspects of a unitary complex, not with elements of a compound, and the tendencies of a method of analysis to reproduce reality as a set of correlative abstractions should never be permitted to reduce aspects of a continuous social process to the elements of its model. What happened at Columbia/Harlem in the spring of '68 is just as important, just as pregnant and portentous, as what happened in Haymarket Square—but at the same time, *no more important either*. We have littered contemporary American history with a hundred aspiring preludes whose aggregate *current* meaning is precisely the fight for the last word about their meaning, but whose future denouement is not yet revealed to us. To make the point still more explicit: There is no such thing as a model revolution (or even if you think you have found such a thing in *la Revolution francaise, note that it materialized considerably in advance of the theory* that hailed it as such), and there is no revolutionary theory by means of which right and wrong sites of organization and agitation can be discriminated. The function of analysis is to clarify reality, not to pass judgment on it.

A few other points about Columbia: (4) "Co-optation" is obviously a useful concept. It warns you against being hoodwinked by those who've learned to smile and smile and still be villains. Unfortunately, just beyond that point at which it remains useful, it flops over completely and becomes disastrous: it can become a no-win concept masquerading either as tactical cunning or strategic wisdom. It instructs people to reject what their fight has made possible on the grounds that it falls short of what they wanted. If the Left allows its provisional victories to be reaped by the Center-Left, trust that those victories will very promptly be turned into most unprovisional setbacks. Am I saying that we should sometimes have people "working within the system's institutions?" Precisely, emphatically, and without the slightest hesitation! You are co-opted when the adversary puts his goals on your power; you are *not* co-opted when your power allows you to exploit his means (or contradictions) in behalf of your goals.

(5) The SF State strike retrospectively clarified one difficulty, maybe a shortcoming, of the Columbia strike. Other BSU-SDS-type eruptions suffered from the same lapse. Namely: *We very badly need a clear, sharp formulation of the white interest in overcoming racism.* All of us feel that this "white-skin-privilege"—if it is even a privilege at all—costs us something, and that the cost exceeds the gain. Yet we've had difficulty making it clear why we feel this way, and for the most part in the hurry of the moment have simply had to abandon the attempt, opting either for a purely moralistic explanation (which has meant that the white base of the strike is not represented in the strike leadership committee) or for the adding on of "white demands" (which tended to obscure the specifically anti-racist character of the action). Neither approach is any good. It is wrong for the base of the movement, any action, not to have a voice in tactical and strategic policy—witness, for one thing, the general bewilderment of the white SF State students who, when the strike was over, had little to do but return to business-as-usual classrooms. It is also wrong, or at least not quite right, for whites to demand "open admissions for all working-class youth" at the same time that the same whites

27

are (a) trying to help make a point about the *racist* nature of colleges, and (b) attacking the *content* of the basic college education on the grounds that it's a brainwash. The German SDS idea of the critical university, somehow adapted to our particular political objectives, might break through the current dilemma at the level of program. But especially since the dilemma may shortly materialize in noncampus settings, it's first necessary to break it at a theoretical or general level. Why does racism hurt whites? Or *which* whites does it hurt, and why, and how?

France, the May Days: "The revolt of the students is the revolt of the forces of modern production as a whole," writes Andre Glucksmann, a leading theoretician of the March 22 Movement. This intriguing formulation, like all new-working-class theorizing, is at bottom nothing but an attempt to find a new face for the old Leninist mask: Only "workers" can make 20th Century revolutions, so those who are creating a big revolution-sized fuss, even if they come outfitted with a few electrifying Sartrean neologisms, must therefore be some new kind of workers. I think this souped-up "New Left" scholasticism is worse than the Old Orthodoxy. Any common-sensical reading of the Glucksmann map would lead the revolution-watcher straight to the faculties of administration, technology and applied sciences, since it's within the meanings of the New Technology that these "forces of modern production as a whole" are being visualized. Maybe at Nanterre, where the fuse was lit. But certainly not at the Sorbonne or anywhere else in Paris, where the student base of the revolt, just as in the United States, came out of the faculties of liberal arts and the social sciences. Quite contrary to Glucksmann, the revolt of the students is the revolt *against* the forces of modern production as a whole—a fact which would doubtless be apparent to everyone if it weren't for the intellectual tyranny of Marxism-Leninism.

The more tradition-minded Leftists scarcely did any better with this out-of-nowhere avalanche. Not for one moment having imagined it was about to happen, insisting on the contrary that nothing like it ever *could* happen, and having finally satisfied themselves that all their curses and spells couldn't make it go away, the Old Crowd FCP determined to see in this Almost-Revolution a conclusive vindication of their theories, practices and political rheumatism all combined. "Behold, Lenin lives!" cried the Stalinists of France, even as they bent their every effort to killing him again.

The main fact about the Almost-Revolution is that it was *almost* a revolution, not that it was almost a *revolution*. As parched for victories as the Western Left has been in the post-war period, it may be forgiven its ecstasy at scoring a few runs. But what are we left with? No questions, Pompidou is not the only or the main or even a very important result of the May Days; as a minimum, the feudalism of the French academy has been jolted, and maybe it's still a big deal in the 7th decade of the 20th century to give academic feudalism a jolt. But it seems to me that all the lessons people are claiming to have learned are not lessons at all, only so many brute-force misreadings of the event. To claim that the student *foco* was a worker "detonator" is to dodge the awful question of the vanguard, not to face it and overcome it, and besides that, it tortures a meaning into "student" that has nothing to do with the students' evident meanings. On the other hand, the claim that the old problem of the "worker-student alliance" has found here the possibility of its solution seems to me the very opposite of what the facts indicate: Under propitious, even ideal circumstances, with the State isolated and virtually dumb before the crisis, with DeGaulle offering nothing more spiritual than an old man's resentment or more concrete than a diluted form of the students' program, with the army out-flanked politically and the police widely disgraced, with production mired in fiscal doldrums, the industrial workforce caught with a deep unease and its bureaucratized leadership dozing, it still proved hard for students and young workers to make contact, and (so it now seems) all but impossible for them to forge a lasting and organic revolutionary union.

It seems to me that the following are more defensible "lessons."

1. No key West European nation (Britain, France, Germany, Italy) can slide hard to the Left unless a Warsaw Pact nation can also slide equally hard to the right. France and Czechoslovakia constitute the gigue and the saraband of an unfinished political suite.

2. We're in a period in which, for the first time in modern history, the social base of a truly post-industrial socialism is being produced, delta-like, outside capitalism's institutional reach. (That is, a socialism which rejects capitalism because of its successes instead of its failures, and which comes into existence in order to supercede and surpass industrial society, not to create it.) But for a long time within the capitalist state, and for much longer within the capitalist empires, this new base will co-exist with that which needs to come abreast. This constitutes the protractedly *transitional* nature of the current period, a source both of confusion and opportunity within the world Left community, and above all a problem which the advanced-nation Left will have to solve by means of a post-Leninist theory and a post-Leninist practice.

Chicago: (1) Liberalism has no power in this country. It is not politically organized. The few secondary institutions in which it lives its hand-to-mouth existence are, at best, nothing more than insecure and defenseless sanctuaries. In none of the estates—not the church, not the media, not the schools—does it exhibit the least aggressiveness, the least staying power, the least confidence. *This country, in the current situation, is absolutely impotent before the threat of what Fulbright has lately called "elective fascism."*

I'll admit that this discovery surprised me. I had thought that the liberals had a little crunch left. McCarthy had always obviously been an ice cube in an oven; but even deprived of Kennedy, I had supposed that the liberals would have been able to drive a few more bargains. They were helpless at Chicago, and their helplessness has only deepened since then. (Observe the sorry spectacle of Yankeedom's main gunslingers, Harriman, Vance, and Clifford vainly trying to ambush Nixon, who knows and imperturbably defeats their every confused move.)

For the very simple truth about Chicago is that Daley got away with it, and there was nothing anybody could do. What "Big Contributor" dropped a word to the wise against him? What "Key Party High-up" moved even to censure him behind the scenes or slow him down? The *institutional mass* of the society is either neutralized or passively or actively supportive of reaction, and reaction can go, quite simply, as far as it determines it needs to go. Screaming their heads off at both the infant Left and the entrenched Right, liberals have neither base nor privilege, neither an organized following nor access to the levers of power. This is important.

(2) If only because it sharpens the melodrama, we may as well pinpoint Chicago, August, as the place and time of the "mass line's" formal debut: an unforgettable lit-up nighttime scene, Mike Klonsky taking the bullhorn at Grant Park to harangue the assembly about its "reformist" politics.

I've already indicated that I see nothing promising in *any* version of Marxism-Leninism—not PL's, not that of the now-defunct "national collective" of the Klonsky-Coleman period or of its apparent successor, the Revolutionary Union, and not that of the more diffuse and momentarily hazier grouping, the Revolutionary Youth Movement. But of course I don't claim that a mere statement of this view constitutes either an explanation of it or an argument for it. The argument will have to be made, very carefully, in another place, and I have to confine myself here to the observation that any revolutionary movement will all but inevitably adapt itself to Marxism-Leninism—or the other way around—because there is just no other totalizing philosophy of revolution. This philosophy then enables a representation of reality in something like the following general terms: "A desire in pursuit of its means, a means in flight from its destiny—these conditions constitute The Problem. Solution: tomorrow, when history's preplanted timebomb at last goes off, blasting false consciousness away, the words of the prophets will be fulfilled."

Chicago, in any case, occasioned these two terminal moments: the humiliation of liberalism, and the "official" reversion of SDS to a Marxist-Leninist worldview.

1969

The leading events so far: The SF State strike and the structurally similar conflicts that erupted across the country, the People's Park showdown in June, the SDS convention, and the Black Panther call for the Oakland conference.

San Francisco State: I want to make just two observations on this much-studied event.

First, the movement's characteristic attitude toward partial victories—more particularly, toward what is disparaged as "student power"—is mechanistic. It appears that every change which is not yet The Revolution is either to be airily written off as no change at all, or further than that, to be denounced as co-optation into the counter-revolution. People should only try to remember that the SF State strike did not materialize out of thin air, that it had a background, that it was that particular moment's culmination of a long conflictual process, and that just as with Columbia, where political work had been sustained at a generally intense level at least since May 1965, the explosive strike at State was made possible, maybe even necessary, by a long series of small moves forward, any one of which could have been attacked as "bourgeois liberal reform." More precisely, it was in large part those incremental "reforms" of curriculum and student-teacher and teacher-administration relationships carried out under the unseeing eyes of President Summerkill that created the general conditions in which the strike could take place. As with Columbia, the atmosphere had long been thoroughly politicized—that is to say, charged with consciousness of national issues. And a long reign of liberalism had, in effect, already *legitimated* the demands around which the strike was fought through, just as a long reign of reformism had created the institutional means of the strike. In the same way, the fact that the Third World Liberation Front leadership did after all negotiate the "nonnegotiable" demands, the further fact that this leadership then moved *to consolidate these bargaining-table victories within the changing structure of the institution itself*—this meant not that the fight was over, not at all that "capitalism" had suffered a tactical defeat only to secure a strategic victory, but rather that the stage was—and is—being set for another round of conflict at a still higher level of consciousness within a still wider circle of social involvement. For the net result of the strike's victories is still further to break down the psychological, social, and political walls that had formerly sealed off the academy from the community. This is a big part of what we are about—the levelling of all these towers, the redistribution of all this ivory, the extroversion of these sublimely introverted corporate monstrosities; and not just because we have willed it, whether out of malice or chagrin or a blazing sense of justice, but rather because capital itself, in all its imperial majesty, has invested these schools with its own trembling contradictions. Necessarily demanding a mass consciousness of and for its technological and political ambitions, it necessarily produces a mass consciousness of the servility of the first and the brutality of the second. Necessarily demanding an army of social managers, pacifiers of the labor force, it necessarily produces an army of social problem solvers, agitators of that same labor force. Necessarily demanding an increasingly sophisticated corps of servicemen to the empire, it necessarily produces a cosmopolitanism to which this empire's shame is its most conspicuous feature. Necessarily demanding a priesthood to bless its work in the stolen name of humanity, it necessarily produces the moral and social weaponry of its own political condemnation.

We play upon these stops. Not able to arrest this process, as Reagan wants, nor to let it go forward, as the liberals want, doomed to be blind in either this eye or the other, not able to teach us to serve without somehow teaching us also its inner secrets, not able to teach us those secrets without teaching us to despise it, capitalism in our time is forced upon—*forces upon itself*—a choice of mortalities. Either to continue that process whose most general form is simply total urbanization, with its attendant destruction of all the disciplinary taboos, of the family, of political religion, of nationalism, of property and the ethics of property, of individualism and the entrepreneurial style; or to try to reverse that process, in which case it destroys its fragile equilibrium, destroys the social base and dynamic of production and growth, puts on the airbrakes and turns off its engines in midflight. If it makes the first choice, it bursts like an egg: *social control over the means of education is necessarily only the proper prologue to social control of the means of production, distribution, and consumption.* If it makes the second choice, if it tries to freeze everything, then the living thing, the life inside the egg, dies out; a moment more, the shell collapses: *Already a fascism in its colonies,* the empire is obliged nevertheless to hold its facism at a distance; and when protracted "wars of liberation," wherever they happen (ghettoes, campuses), whatever unpredicted form they take (e.g., Peru!), succeed in driving this frontier fascism back upon its metropolitan front, then the whole political and social basis of the empire begins to fragment and dissolve. For a stable empire can be military only in its means, not in its ends—its end necessarily being a mode of production, distribution, and consumption; and the servicing of these ends ultimately requires exactly that metropolitan class *hegemony* (the classes passively accepting or even affirming the rule of the dominant class, the class hierarchy having therefore the firm structure of vertical consent) which fascism supplants with class *coercion.*[2]

One brief aside on a related matter: When I first met white New Leftists about five years ago, their most common fear was that they were not a serious threat. Along with this went the equally common belief that their seriousness would be proved only if they were vigorously attacked. (The current expression of this is the general view that the "vanguard" is whoever is being most vigorously attacked: it is not the people who pick their leaders, but the State). No one suggested that the Other Side might be holding less than a fistful of aces, that the adversary was not super smart, that he might be stymied by his own contradictions. Maybe it was my background that made me skeptical—grandson of the south's Last Peasant Patriarch, son of a first-generation migrant from a defeated rural economy to the industrial revolution (Akron: smoke, tires, factories, timeclocks, the permanently present memory of the "home" which you had abandoned in spite of all wishes and had thereby, despite yourself, helped destroy, and which you could never go back to again no matter how many rides you took those seven hundred miles on hot jampacked Greyhound buses that, once before Marietta, stopped every other mile to pick up or let off still another coming or going hillbilly, suitcase in one hand, baby in the other, eyes shot from whiskey and incomprehension . . . Another time I must deal with this.) I had thought that there was precious little need to go out of your way to provoke those distant people who worked on Mahogany Row, lived in the mansions of

Fairlawn, and owned all the cops and politicians. If the vague people of the vague middle were ignorant of how power worked and who had it and who did not, we who lived just at the edge of the black ghetto and whose lives were ordered by the vicissitudes of production—cutbacks, layoffs, speedup, doubles, strikes—were under no illusions. We knew their viciousness because man, woman and child we had it for constant companion. My mind was blown, its gears stripped, to hear someone say that the gift of authenticity was the Man's to give, that it came in the form of clubbings and jailings, and that, left unprovoked, he might withhold it. Not so: pursue your aims with stark simplicity and in all peacableness, put money in thy purse with the politest and gentlest of smiles—trust him, he'll get around to making you pay, and anybody who does not know this just hasn't been paying attention.

So. That's the first "observation"—the winning of a "reform" isn't always a bad business, and Leftists should stop being scared of being reformed out of things to do. The only real strategic necessity is to make sure the reform in question reforms the power configuration so that it becomes the basis for further and still more fundamental challenges to class rule.

The second observation is connected. It has to do with the question of what's called (disparagingly) "student power." The formula attack on the making of demands for such things as curriculum reform and greater student participation in campus government goes like this: "The young bourgeois, privileged already, exhibits here only his desire to extend his privileges still further. This desire must be fought by radicals. If not exactly in the *name* of the working class, we must see ourselves as fighting at least in its *behalf*, and since its interests are hardly served by the abolition of grades or the reduction of required credits, we must oppose such demands."

First, the outlines of a speculation. What if the multiversity is in some substantial part the creation of the advanced-world proletariat—not merely the plaything and mistress of the imperialists? What if it is partly in the multiversity that the proletariat has banked and stored up its enormous achievements in technology? What if the multiversity—the highest realization yet of the idea of mass education and the rationalization of productive labor—is in one of its leading aspects the institutional form through which the proletariat continues its struggle for emancipation? Behind how many of these so-called "bourgeois" children, one or two generations back, stands a father in a blue collar, a mother in an apron? The proletariat, says Marx, will have to prepare itself for self-government through protracted struggle. What if this struggle is so protracted that it actually must be seen as taking place, in one of its aspects at least, across *generations*? The revolutionary aspiration of whites in the 1930s manifested itself most sharply in factory struggles. In the 1960s, that aspiration has materialized most sharply on the campuses. What have we made of this fact? The function of a method of social analysis is not to reprimand reality for diverging from its model, but on the contrary to discover in reality the links and conjectures that make history intelligible and life accessible to effective action. An abstraction is not something to stand behind like a pulpit but a lens to see through more discerningly. Obvious? Then it is high time to confess: At the same time that it has been trying so desperately to live forwards, the New Left everywhere, in West Europe as well as here, has been just as desperately trying to think backwards. If Marxism is any good, and if we can prove it worthy of the moment, then we ought to be able to say what it is about contemporary relations of production that makes the campuses a primary site of contemporary revolutionary motion. Only when that question is answered will we have any right to pontificate about "correct" and "incorrect" lines, and it has not yet been answered. Meanwhile, even if it is good and sufficient, as I am almost sure it is not, to characterize "student power" as a fight for "bourgeois privilege," we would still have to ask: What *kind* of privilege? Assuming that there is nothing here at all but an intra-class struggle against the contemptuous indifference of institutions, against the mindless blather of the dons, the deans, the sycophants and the liars, against authority in particular and authoritarianism on principle, we would still have to say that the political balance of this struggle is *progressive and portentous*. To those who tell me that this fight neither equals, approximates, initiates, nor reveals the form of The Revolution Itself, I answer first, Neither did Nanterre, neither did Watts, neither did anything else in man's social history but a bare handful of uniquely definitive and epochal convulsions, each one of which moreover appeared only at the end of a painfully long train of indeterminate events which escaped their ambiguity only thanks to the denouement; and I answer second, If you are trying to tell me you know already what The Revolution Itself will look like, you are either a charlatan or a fool. *We have no scenario.*

Second, for what it's worth to a movement suddenly infatuated with the words of the prophets, Lenin faced a somewhat similar question in 1908 when certain radicals refused to support an all-Russia student strike on the grounds that "the platform of the strike is an academic one" which "cannot unite the students for an active struggle on a broad front." Lenin objected:

"Such an argument is radically wrong. The revolutionary slogan—to work towards coordinated political action of the students and the proletariat—here ceases to be a live guidance for many-sided militant agitation on a broadening base and becomes a lifeless dogma, mechanically applied to different stages of different forms of the movement." Further: "For this youth, a strike on a large scale . . . is the beginning of a political conflict, whether those engaged in the fight realize it or not. Our job is to explain to the mass of 'academic' protesters the objective meaning of the conflict, to try and make it *consciously* political."

The People's Park: Those few SDSers, unfortunately conspicuous this past year, who think Stalinism is more or less right on, ought at least to have admitted that "socialism in one country" is not exactly the logical antithesis of "socialism in one park." But it was the Stalinists, both pure and off-breed, who among all the Bay Area radicals found it hardest to relate to the park before the attacks, were most puzzled by the attack itself, and produced the most opportunistic "support" in the aftermath. Mainly because these curious rumbles of the hip are so hard to focus politically in terms of a mass-and-vanguard model, it's hard for people with old minds to figure out how to relate to them. That fact may be the basis of a touching epitaph; but a living politics for our period will have to understand that "decadence" is as "decadence" does, that the "cultural revolution" is not merely a craven and self-serving substitute for the "political" one, and that if the West has, indeed, a leftwards destiny, then neither its particular ends nor its modes of organization and action will be discovered through archeology. My guess: People's Park was one among many episodes of a religious revival movement—exactly the kind of movement that has heralded every major social convulsion in the United States—and as with all such movements, its ulterior target, its enemy, is the forces of the industrialization of culture. The difference now is that the virtual consummation of the Industrial Revolution, *within the West*, lends a credibility and relevance to such a program that it formerly has not had. That is: The anti-industrialism of early radicals like Blake and Cobbett, though it was fully anti-capitalist, could confront rampant capitalist industrial progress with nothing more powerful than a retiring, improbable, defenseless nostalgia; could argue against the system of "masters and slaves" only in behalf of the older and no doubt mythical system, allegedly medieval, of "masters and men." Every time it became a *practical* movement—whether revolutionary or reformist—socialism had to put forward simply a more rational version of the program of industrialization itself. This is not an irony or tragedy of history, it's just the dialectics of historical process. That it has so far been unsurpassable is in fact the essence of revolutionary socialism's general isolation to the backwards countries, or put differently, this limit merely expresses the wedding of revolutionary socialism to anti-colonialism, and on the other hand, its omnipotence in countries in which the industrialization process has been carried forward effectively (however ruthlessly) by the bourgeoisie. The thesis of People's Park, rough as it may be to deal with both in terms of our tradition and our current practical needs, is that the essentially *post-industrial* revolution, embodied most fully but still (we must suppose) very incompletely in the hip communities, portends the historically most advanced development for socialist consciousness.

"Most fully" because it goes beyond industrialization and in doing so implies (much more than it has so far realized) a genuinely New Man—just as new compared to Industrial Man as Industrial Man was new in comparison to the artisans and small farmers who foreran him.

But it would be useless just to approve of this cultural revolution without being very clear about its terrible limits. I see two limits. First: The "new values" (they are, of course, very old) can claim to be subversive only of the standing values of work, but not really of consumption, there being nothing in the structure and precious little in the texture of "hip leisure" that keeps it from being commercially copied (deflated) and packaged. Thus, in effect, the target of the attack detaches itself, refuses to defend itself, and in offering itself as the apparent *medium* of the attack is able (persuasively to all but the sharpest consciousness) to pose as the "revolution's" friend. There are a thousand examples of this process, whose minimum result is vastly to complicate the cultural critique, and which at the other limit succeeds wholly in disarming it. The quietism of which the hip community is often accused may thus be much less the result of a principled retreat to cosmology than of its flat inability to confront commercialism with a deeply nonnegotiable demand.

Second, even though the new anarchism is morally cosmopolitan—affirming in a rudimentary political way the essential oneness of the human community—its values are *practical* only within the Western (imperialist) cities, and are far from being universally practical even there. So the second and bigger problem the cultural revolution needs to overcome is its lack of a concrete means of realizing its sympathy with those globally rural revolutionary movements whose social program necessarily centers around the need for industrialization, not the surpassing of it. A resolution of this problem would no doubt also solve the first. This is why it's so important to subject the cultural revolution to a much more profound and critical analysis than what has been produced so far. For the point at the moment is not to be for or against the current reappearance of anarchism. It will be necessary rather to replicate its tradition (too many hippies think they are trying brand new things) and then to try to see if the balance of forces has changed sufficiently that this old movement for a cultural revolution against industrial society has begun to acquire a power which it formerly has not had.

The SDS Convention: I wasn't there, never mind why. At the last SDS thing I was at, the Austin NC, the handwriting was already on the wall. Having determined that SDS must become explicitly and organizationally committed to its version of Marxism-Leninism, PL would continue in its Trotskyist way of identifying organizations with movements and would try to win more power in SDS—that much was already clear in the spring. I didn't think, though, that PL people would force a split. As fiercely indifferent to this country's general culture as they seem to be, I still thought they would understand a split as contrary to their purposes and would therefore seek to avoid it, even if that meant a momentary tactical retreat. Either I was wrong, or PL misunderstood—and misplayed—the situation.

I want to make just one point about the current situation. What is wrong with PL is not its rigidity, its "style," its arrogance or anything like that. Its *ideology* is wrong. And not just in the particulars of emphasis or interpretation or application, but in its most fundamental assumptions about the historical process. Someone else may argue that PL's Marxism-Leninism is a bad Marxism-Leninism, and that is a view which can doubtless be defended. But I see no prosperity in the approach that merely wants to save Leninism from Milt Rosen here and Jared Israel there. The problem is deeper and the task much more demanding. It can be posed this way: Backwards as it is, our practice is more advanced than our theory, and our theory therefore becomes an obstacle to our practice—which is childish and schematic, not free and real enough. The general adoption of some kind of Marxism-Leninism by all vocal factions in SDS means, certainly, that a long moment of intellectual suspense has been resolved—but much less in response to experience than to the pressure of the *tradition*. We have not produced even a general geosocial map of the United States as a society—only as an empire. We have not sought in the concrete historical experience of classes a rigorous explanation of their acceptance of "cross-class" (Cold War) unity but rather have employed a grossly simplified base-and-superstructure model to explain away the fact that labor does not appear to think what we think it ought to think. We have taken a class to be a thing, not a process (or as E.P. Thompson called it five years ago, "a happening"), and have imagined it to be bound, more or less, to behave according to the "scientific laws" which govern the category. Most generally, we have imported a very loose and sometimes garbled theory of pre-industrial revolution, have tightened it without really clarifying it, and are now in the process of trying to superimpose that theory, thus reduced, on our own very different situation. The RYM group does not differ in this respect from PL, the Revolutionary Union, or even YSA or ISC. All these groups, opportunistic in widely varying degrees, claim to have the same ace in the hole, and Lenin's phrases (or what's worse, the Chairman's truistic maxims) are gnawed upon by every tooth.

For a long time I was baffled. Last fall the word began to reach me: It was being said that I had "bad politics." How could *that* be, I wondered, since I thought I had no politics at all. But by winter I conceded the point: no politics is the same as bad politics. So there followed a time in which I experimented with only the "mass line." Could Klonsky and Coleman be right? It didn't come to much. My mind and my instincts only became adversaries. By spring I had to deactivate, couldn't function, had to float. What I know now is that this did not happen to me alone. On every quarter of the white Left, high and low, the attempt to reduce the New Left's inchoate vision to the Old Left's perfected remembrance has produced a layer of bewilderment and demoralization which no cop with his club or senator with his committee could ever have induced. And my view of the split at the convention is that it merely caps a series of changes which began at the East Lansing convention in 1968, with the decision to counter PL's move on SDS by means of a political form—the "SDS caucus," i.e., a countervailing faction—which accepted implicitly PL's equation of the social movement with the organizations that arise within it. What walked out of the Coliseum was simply a larger version of 1968's SDS caucus. Certainly it had grown in awareness and self-definition over the year; and knowing that bare opposition to PL is no very impressive gift to The Revolution, it had spurred itself to produce an independent Marxist-Leninist analysis and at least the semblance of a program. My unhappy wager is that even in its RYM incarnation it remains a faction, that it will continue last year's practice of "struggling sharply" against internal heresies, that it will remain in the vice of the old illusions, that it will pay as little attention to what is happening in the country and the world as its predecessor regime did, and that whatever growth the movement achieves will be in spite of its rally cries and with indifference to its strictures. Nor is there a lot that can be done about this. The Western Left is perhaps in the midphase of a long, deep transition, and there is no way for SDS to protect itself from the consequences. They will have to be lived out. Which does not mean there is nothing to do. It means, rather, that any new initiatives will confront a situation very heavily laden with obstacles and limits. It isn't 1963 anymore.

The Panther Convention: It hasn't happened yet as I write, and I have no idea what its outcome will be. But certain doubts still need to be aired.

What's good about the Panthers has been amply hailed in the white Left: The Panthers have, in effect, done for the black lumpen of the northern urban ghetto what SNCC, years ago, did for the black serfs of the rural south—individual despair, given a historical interpretation, is turned into collective political anger. To the alternatives of tomism, crime, and psychosis, SNCC in the country and the Panthers in the town have added the idea of revolution—anti-racist, internationalist, and socialist.

But taken all in all—and for forcing historical reasons this is truer of the Panthers than of SNCC of 1960-64—this consciousness is a Word without Flesh, and that's what's got the Panthers trapped in a blind alley from which the only exits are either martyrdom or the "anti-fascist" popular front which it is the apparent purpose of the July convention to organize. To put it another way: The Panthers did not *organize* the ghetto, they only apostrophized it. So far as I know, the breakfast-for-children program represents the only serious attempt to relate concretely, practically, broadly, and *institutionally* to the black urban community as a whole. And it is very much to the point that the Panthers have recently promoted the breakfast program as their most characteristic political act—at approximately the same moment that the super-militants are purged, the public making of fierce faces greatly cooled, and the gun no longer presented as the leading symbol of Panther intentions.

This is all to the good, but it should have happened long ago. There ought to be dozens of programs like the breakfasts. Nothing else, in fact, gives stature, credibility, and social meaning to the gun; for the ghetto, as such, neither can be nor should be defended. Only when that ghetto is being transformed, de-ghettoized, by the self-organized activity of the people does its militant self-defense become a real *political* possibility. I'm not saying that social organization must always precede combat organization. If ghetto blacks were like the sugar proletariat of pre-revolutionary rural Cuba, and if the police were like Cuba's rural guard, then the opposite would likely be true. Even so, even if there is a proper analogy to the July 26 Movement, what would follow if not the obligation not merely to challenge the police, not merely to engage militarily and escape alive, but in fact to *defeat* the police, to prove to the people that the tyranny cannot impose its will on the countryside by force? The essence of J-26 politics lies in its valid presupposition of a popular will for social revolution and in its insight that it was mainly their common-sensical skepticism about overcoming the state military machine that held the people back.

With all respect for Cuba and the ardor of black American militants, I fail to see in the caste ghetto of an industrial city anything like a political replica of the countryside of a one-crop colony. The presence in the ghetto of the political gun meant a great many worthwhile, even invaluable things. But crucial as it is, "Free Huey!" is not by itself a social program or a revolutionary slogan. The irony is that nothing but a real social program, and the expanding base of involved, active, and conscious persons such a program alone could produce, would ever make Huey Newton's liberation even thinkable, never mind the means.

"But of course this has all been seen by now." Has it? The current Panther move to establish a white base of support does not persuade me that it has been *understood. The Panthers are in trouble not because they have no white support, but because they have too little black support; not because they have no white allies, but because, in the virtual absence of a wide array of real activities, real social programs in the black communities, there is nearly nothing that white allies can do besides pass resolutions, send lawyers, and raise bail.*

SDS will have to take its share of the blame for this. Much more interested in shining with the borrowed light of Panther charisma than in asking all the hard practical questions, much more interested in laying out the mere physical maxims that identify the "vanguard" than assuming real political responsibility, this SDS, which often chews its own tongue for being "petty bourgeoisie" most shamefully confesses its origins precisely when it tries so vainly to transcend them in worship of "solidarity" which really amounts to so much hero-worship. Bourgeois is as bourgeois does. Marx, Engels, Lenin, Trotsky, Mao, Chou, Ho, Giap, Fidel, Che, Fanon: which one plowed a furrow, ran a punchpress, grew up hungry? That, in the first place, ought to be that. Further, in the second place, it is not lost causes, however heroic, or martyrs, however fine, that our movement needs. It needs shrewd political and concrete social programs. Not theoretical (really theological) proofs that The People Will Win in the End, but tangible social achievements now. Not the defiance of the small, isolated band of supercharged cadre who, knowing they stand shoulder to shoulder with mankind itself, who face repression with the inner peace of early Christians, but a mounting fugue of attacks on political crime of all sorts on all fronts, at all levels of aspiration, from all sectors and classes of the population, so that repression can never return; never find a fixed or predictable target. Humble example: Yesterday's *New York Times* carries a full-page political ad—the American Institute of Architects, it seems, has come out against the war. What will the Panther or the SDS national office do? Send a wire? Make a phone call? Investigate the possibility of a combined action? Try to make two or three new friends in order to make a hundred or a thousand later. I guess not. For the AIA is as *bourgeois* as they come, awfully *liberal*, too. When even the Oakland 7 and the Chicago 8 are suspect, what chance do a lot of architects have? So the architects will never hear what we have to say about the empire, about the houses that are being built in Cuba, about what we take to be the extent and causes of the present world crisis.

But this loss is presumably compensated by our clarity about the "vanguard." Clarity! Any close reading of the RYM's Weatherman statement will drive you blind. Sometimes the vanguard is the black ghetto community, sometimes only the Panthers, sometimes the Third World as a whole, sometimes only the Vietnamese, and sometimes apparently only the Lao Dong Party. Sometimes it is a seriously Hegelian concept, referring vaguely to all earthly manifestations of the spirit of revolution. At still other times, it seems to be the fateful organ of that radicalized industrial proletariat (USA) which has yet to make its Cold War-era debut. Mostly, though, it's the poor Panthers, whose want of politics was never challenged by the few SDSers who had access to their leaders; this appointment—Vanguard to the People's Revolution—being, presumably, SDS's to make—and one which is defended, moreover, in terms of a so-called revolutionary strategy (see the Weatherman statement) in which the United States is to experience a military defeat at the hands of twenty, thirty, many Vietnams—plus a few Detroits.

But perhaps the ghetto=colony analysis means that the Detroits are already included in the category of Vietnams? In that case, for all real political purposes, (North) American=white; and the historic role of these whites, their "mission" in the many-sided fight for socialism, is most basically just to overcome. The authors of the Weatherman statement are of course perfectly right in trying to integrate what may appear to be *decisive* international actors into a model scenario of domestic change. From no viewpoint can an empire be treated as if it were a nation state. But although they face this problem, they do not overcome it. They might have said that the leading aspect of the US industrial proletariat remains, classically, its exploitation at the hands of US capital, and that it therefore still embodies a momentarily stifled revolutionary potential. Contrarily, they might have said that what we have here is a giganticized "labor aristocracy who are quite philistine in their mode of life, in the size of their earnings and in their outlook . . . [and who are] real channels of reformism and chauvinism" (Lenin, *Imperialism: The Highest Stage of Capitalism*). On its face, neither view is silly, but neither is one more satisfactory than the other. Weatherman's refusal to settle for one or the other seems to me to express a realistic *intuition*; but the problem is not solved simply by asserting one theory here and the other theory there. They cannot both be equally valid. I think the difficulty is embedded in the method of analysis: Weatherman takes class to be a thing rather than a process, and consequently tries to treat class as if it were, in and of itself, *a definite political category*. (That is, labor is fated to be Left.) But Weatherman also has a certain level of historical realism, and this realism always intervenes (happily) to obstruct the mostly theoretical impulse—a kind of social Freudianism—to idealize labor, to strip it of its historical "neurosis" by the simple and fraudulent expedient of viewing its neurosis as *merely* superstructural. In other words, Weatherman's confusions and ambiguities stem from a conflict between its model and its data, and it comes close to escaping this dilemma only when it forgets its static model of history and process. At such moments, it comes close to saying something really important, which I would paraphrase, over-optimistically no doubt, thus: "The labor force we are looking at today is not the one we'll see tomorrow, and the changes it will undergo have everything to do with the totality of its current and forthcoming experiences, which range all the way from the increasingly sensed contradiction between the rhetoric of affluence and the fact of hardship to the blood and money sacrifices it will be asked to offer in the empire's behalf." But this ought to be said up front, and it then ought to lead to the most exhaustive analysis of the real, living forces that impinge upon not just labor but the population as a whole. Every time something like this starts to happen, Weatherman breaks off and reverts to its concealed paradox: the vanguard of the US (Western would be better) revolution will be those forces which most aggressively array themselves *against* the US, those forces, in other words, which are most *distant* from white culture. Thus, *cause becomes agency*: the living proof of a *need* for change—the Panthers, the NLF, etc.—is defined as the political *means* of change; an almost absent-minded abstraction converts white America's sickness into the remedy itself.

The most succinct case of this kind of bad reasoning I've heard came at the end of a speech Bob Avakian made at the Austin NC. The racism of white workers would have to be broken, he said, because, when the revolution comes, it will be led by blacks, whose leadership whites must therefore be prepared to accept. If this were only an unconsidered trifle, it would be pointless to snap it up, but it appears to represent a serious, persistent, and growing school of thought in the New Left. The problem with it is just that it implies that there could be a revolution in the absence of a profound radicalization of the white working class, in the absence of profound changes in the political character of that class. What would make it possible for white workers to revolt would also make it possible—and necessary—for white workers to help *lead* that revolt. The very idea of a white working class revolution against capitalism that is, necessarily *presupposes* either that racism will have been overcome or at least that the conditions for that triumph will have been firmly established. The problem with this dreamed-of revolution will not be anti-blackism within its ranks, but the anti-communism of its adversary. "In revolution, there are no whites or blacks, only reds."

But beyond this, Avakian (as with the Weathermen) wants it both ways: blacks are a colony, on the one hand, outside the colonizing political economy and set over against it; and on the other hand, they are in and of the empire's proletariat. In the first mode, they press against the empire from a position which is outside it in every sense but the geographical. In the second mode, they press upwards against the bourgeoisie from within capital's system of social classes. It is of course not impossible that these modes really do coexist and interpenetrate one another. In fact, it is likely that they do. But both modes cannot be represented as simultaneously co-leading aspects of the black situation *vis-a-vis* white society. A white revolutionary strategy requires a decision as to which aspect is dominant and which secondary, *as well as an understanding that what is dominant now may become secondary later, may even disappear.*

So—an attempt at a clarification (which, as with certain other points I've tried to make in this letter, I'll have to elaborate and defend in some other, more ample space):

1. The persistence of integrationism, in a dozen disguises, and nationalism's struggle against it, make a strong circumstantial case for the view that blacks are above all blacks. They are not just another part of the workforce, not even just the main body of the lumpenproletariat; nor do they make up a *caste.* Industrial societies do not have, and cannot afford, castes; castes belong to pre-capitalist formations (or, at latest, to agrarian capitalism) and are in fact destroyed by the imperatives of industrial organization.

Obviously, blacks are assigned an important role in the US production-consumption process. So were pre-revolutionary Cubans. So are contemporary Venezuelans. The low-skill aspect of black production and the importance of the credit and welfare systems in black consumption constitute, in themselves, the leading features of *colonial* relation to a colonizing political economy. It is therefore appropriate to see the black ghetto as a colony. Thus, *true* black nationalism (much "nationalist" rhetoric is merely a Halloween mask for integrationist or even *comprador* demands) is necessarily anti-imperialist, and could consummate whatever military or political victories it might achieve in the independence struggle only through a socialist development of the means of production.

2. No more than the struggle of the Vietnamese can be the struggle of blacks to play a "vanguard" role in the problematic revolution of white America. *Vietnam and Detroit, the NLF and the Panthers, do not constitute the means of white America's liberation from imperialist capital. They constitute, rather, the necessity of that liberation.* They exist for white America as the living embodiment of problems which white America must solve. There are, obviously, many other such problems: the draft, high taxes, inflation, the whole array of ecological and environmental maladies, Big Brotherism at all levels of government, the general and advanced hypertrophy of the State, the fractionalizing of the civil society. Most of these problems are relatively diffuse; they are not experienced so acutely as the war or the ghetto risings. But they are still real to people, and they all have the same general source in the hegemony of capitalism: What sets Vietnam aflame is the same force that brutalizes the black population and poisons everybody's air.

3. The function of the white Western socialist is therefore, at this moment, to confront white America (white France, etc.) with the truth about the problems that harass it, to explain that these problems cannot be solved merely by repressing those people in whose lives the problems are embodied, cannot be solved by prayer or petition, and above all that they cannot be solved so long as the means of production, the wealth of that production, and the monopoly of political power that goes with those means and that wealth are locked up in the hands of the big bourgeoisie. You would as wisely ask the bullet to sew up the wound it made as to ask the monopoly capitalist to solve these problems. The capitalist cannot do it. But the socialist can. That is the point we have to make.

4. The rebellion of white students is provoked most fundamentally by the great *extrinsic* failure of capitalist production—by the fact, that is, that production has become so conspicuously anti-social. This is what gives the student rebellion both its power and its very real limits. But this extrinsic collapse has not yet been followed by an *intrinsic* collapse: the system of capitalist production is at the moment *both insane and rational*. If a failure of its administration should produce also an *intrinsic* collapse—if suddenly no one could buy and no one could sell—then the people of the West would come again to the crossroads of the 1930s, and would have to decide again whether they would solve their problems by means of war or revolution. It is at that point that the fight for the loyalty of the proletariat will become truly historical instead of merely theoretical, necessary instead of merely right, possible instead of merely desirable. *But no will, no courage, no ingenuity can force this eventuality.* If it develops, and if the crisis is prolonged enough for white American workers to grasp the need for revolution, then with the same motion in which they change their rifles from one shoulder to the other, they will simultaneously *de-colonize* the blacks, the Vietnamese, the Cubans, *the French*—for at such a moment, all the old paralyzing definitions will die and new definitions, revolutionary ones, will take their place. The world proletariat will have achieved, at last, its dreamed-of world unity. This possibility, this towering historical power, is merely the other side of what it means to be a white American. But again: no matter how well it is organized or how combative and brilliant its performance is, no Western socialism has it in its power to force or even to hasten the intrinsic collapse of capitalist production. If you are an unreconstructed Marxist, you believe that it will come about sooner or later; if, like myself, you are not, then you don't know. It could happen: the market seems pale, inventories are large,

the need to fight inflation in behalf of the international position of the dollar may lead to harder money, more unemployment, and still further slippage in demand; and if Nixon does not get the ABM, the whole system of the US Cold War economy will have received an ominous if mainly symbolic jolt. My view is that if this process starts unfolding, labor will have scant need of student organizers, and in the second place, that it will actively seek the support of student radicals. The "worker-student alliance" will happen when workers want it to happen, they will want it when they need it, and they will need it when and if the system starts coming apart. At such a conjuncture, students will have a critical contribution to make no matter what happens between now and then; but their contribution will be all the greater if they will have employed this uncertain threshold period to secure some kind of power base in the universities and such other institutions as they can reach, and if they will have used the opportunities of their situation to take the case for socialism to the country as a whole, aware certainly that class *implies* a political signature, but just as aware that it does not *necessitate* one. It is mainly to the extent that the white movement has done just this, in fact, that it has been of some occasional concrete service to the black movement, and the same will be true of any forthcoming relationship with a self-radicalized labor force.

Let me put this more bluntly. We are not now free to fight The Revolution except in fantasy. This is not a limit we can presently transcend; it is set by the overall situation, and it will only be lifted by a real breakdown within the system of production. Nor will the lifting of the limit be the end of our fight; it will be just the possibility of its beginning. Meanwhile, there is no point in posing ourselves problems which we cannot solve, especially when the agony of doing so means, in effect, the abandoning of humbler projects—"humbler"! . . . as for example, the capture of real power in the university system—which might otherwise have been brought to a successful head. Just look: Very little, even insignificant effort was invested in the idea of "student power," and the SDS leadership even debunked the concept as, of all things, "counter-revolutionary." Yet we have just witnessed a moment in which a few key universities very nearly chose to collide head-on with the State over the question of repression of the Left. That would have been a momentous fight, especially coming on the heels of the black campus insurgencies. It's our fault that it didn't happen. The fault may be immense.

This was supposed to be about the future. Thousands of words later, I have still said very little about the future. I'm not really surprised at myself, and I won't apologize, but simply sum it up by saying that if SDS continues the past year's vanguarditis, then it, at least, will have precious little future at all. For what this movement needs is a swelling base, not a vanguard.

Or if a vanguard, then one which would rather *ride* a horse than look it in the mouth. One which wants students to get power and open up the campuses, blacks to win the franchise and elect some mayors, architects to be against the war and advertise that fact in the *Times*, clergy to be concerned and preach heretical sermons, inductees to dodge the draft and soldiers to organize a servicemen's union, workers to have more pay and shorter hours, hippies to make parks on private property, liberals to defeat the ABM, West Europe to escape NATO, East Europe the Warsaw Pact, and the global south the Western empires—and the American people as a whole (by any means necessary!) to be free enough to face their genocidal past for what it was, their bloody present for what it portends, and their future for that time of general human prosperity and gladness which they have the unique power to turn it into. And for being still more "revolutionary" than this implies, let us confess that time alone will tell us what that might mean.

NOTES

1. "In eighteenth-century England the manufacturing workers, miners, and others, were far more conscious of being exploited by the agrarian capitalists and middlemen, as consumers, than by their petty employers through wage-labour; and in this country [England] today consumer and cultural exploitation are quite as evident as is exploitation 'at the point of production' and perhaps are more likely to explode into political consciousness." E.P. Thompson, "The Peculiarities of the English," *The Socialist Register*, 1965 (London), Ralph Miliband and John Saville, eds., p. 355.

2. If the biography of German Nazism seems to contradict this thesis, recall that *Junker* coercion was finally translated into the hegemony of the State itself not mainly because of risings in the colonies, but because of pressure from rival imperialisms dating back at least to the First World War.

Representative Democracy in SDS

RICH ROTHSTEIN

In its early years, SDS was organized and joined by young people whose experiences with the American electoral process, the Communist Party, and the American trade unions led them to be deeply mistrustful of bureaucratic structures and of representative democratic forms. SDS was initially organized with a traditional representative structure. As members became aware of the broad range of individual participations which a representative structure allowed, they blamed the structure itself for this lack of pure (participatory) democracy. Beginning in 1963, under the banner of "democratic" reform, the representative structure of SDS was dismantled. As each representative institution in the organization was destroyed, the organization became, in fact, less democratic. This increasing lack of democracy was seen by SDS members as further evidence of the failure of representative structures, and fueled the flames of new "democratic" reform movements to destroy the remaining representative institutions within the organization. Thus, destruction of democratic forms led to less democracy, and less democracy led to the destruction of democratic forms. Today, the movement is still retarded by an erroneous interpretation of SDS' history. Attempts to form new national or local organizations with a representative democratic structure are frustrated in part by the charge that "tyranny in SDS proves that representative structures are undemocratic." Since few of those who today must deal with these charges were members of SDS in the relevant years, it is hoped that this historical essay will illustrate that the opposite of popular belief is true: that it was the destruction of representative democracy in SDS which helped make SDS tyrannical.

SDS was organized as the Student Department of the League for Industrial Democracy. Its initial leaders were young intellectuals—graduate students and scholarly undergrads—whose main formative experience was the "Silent 50s." They were faced with a student constituency whose problem was not so much wrong political ideas as no political ideas. The standard description of the student population from which we came (a description we shared) was APATHY.

SDS initially shared a number of the assumptions of this country's liberal elite, particularly assumptions regarding the failure of past movements. The Port Huron Statement, drafted by Tom Hayden, stated that "the Communist Party (S.U.) has equated falsely the triumph of true socialism with centralized bureaucracy." The failure of trade unions in this country to mount an adequate reform movement was primarily ascribed to the elitism of trade union bureaucrats who were unresponsive to membership.[1]

It was common among us to see the U.S. and the U.S.S.R. as basically equivalent evils and the common denominator factor was the centralized bureaucratization of both societies where politics took place without "publics," without responsibility. We laughed, of course, at the anti-communist peace movement's pressure on SDS to balance all criticisms of U.S. policy with criticism of the U.S.S.R. ("No Tests, East Or West"), but laughed not at the politics of the pressure but at the compulsive need to prove anti-communism by saying the "obvious" all the time. The similarity of the "end of ideology," no public politics, assumptions of the U.S. and U.S.S.R. elites was one of the chief themes of a very important influence on the pre-PHS SDS: C. Wright Mills' "Letter to the New Left."

Finally, the influence of Michels' *Political Parties* was strong in the thinking of early SDS. Michels, together with Mills, was most quoted in 1962, and his description of inevitable bureaucratization in traditional organizations provided the chief framework for analysis of both the domestic trade union movement and the old Left communist party, both here and in the U.S.S.R.

The Port Huron Statement articulated the notion of "participatory democracy" as a society where the individual "share[s] in those social decision determining the quality and direction of his life; [and] society [is] organized to encourage independence in men and provide the media for their common participation." The remainder of the founding SDS' articulation of participatory democracy was largely generalizations adding up to socialism without the word: "economic democracy," "bringing people out of isolation and into community," etc.

SDS was established after the Port Huron convention with a traditional bourgeois, political party structure: the convention elected an unpaid President, Vice President and National Executive Committee; the NEC was instructed to hire a full time staff; between conventions, interim policy decisions were to be made by a National Council composed of the NEC and chapter representatives.

This organizational table was formally democratic; it was also precisely the organizational form through which trade union elitism emerged and about which Michels warned. Today, it is fashionable in the movement to assert that this organizational form was largely responsible for much of the recent unpleasantness and ineffectiveness of SDS. The words "pyramidal," "hierarchical," "elitist" appear frequently as self-explanatory descriptions of this traditional representative form; and much organizing in the movement today is as heavily inspired by a negative sanction—to avoid this traditional form—as it is by any positive vision of an alternative. Thus, in the Autumn 1970 *Liberation* exchange about the Seattle Liberation Front, one of the defenders of the SLF states that the "SLF coordinating structure was loose to allow for broad participation, unlike the elitist and rigid old SDS form."

The reaction in the movement to the "elitist and rigid old SDS form" is, at first, a reaction to these problems: male chauvinism in the movement, and particularly the deep personal chauvinism of many well known movement (and former SDS) leaders; the existence of debates in national SDS which had little relation to the actual work and problems of local chapters; the creation of national programs for the movement by national movement leaders while it was impossible for ordinary movement activists to have any control or decision making about those programs—e.g., the Democratic Convention demonstrations, recent Weather programs, the 1965 SDS "Build not Burn" program; the alienation of movement life in a period when the movement seems to make no political progress—national meetings and impersonal organizations become even more alienating when what is perceived to be necessary is face-to-face comradeship and intensive study to attempt to figure out what to do, not "mindless activism," announced at the top.

It is my belief that these movement problems are not really a function of the "elitist and rigid old SDS form;" that many of these problems were created, or intensified, not by the old SDS form, *but rather by its abandonment*; but that while some of these problems could have been alleviated by an attempt to consciously perfect the old form rather than abandoning it, these problems are political problems which do not have formal solutions.

For these purposes I want only to illustrate how the abandonment of the "pyramidal," "hierarchical," and "elitist" structure of SDS actually intensified or created the problems of movement elitism and authoritarianism which it is now common to blame on that structure. The successive leaders and activists of SDS who dismantled that structure did so for the same motives that representative democratic structures are not being attacked in the movement—a belief that these structures caused the absence of full democratic participation in SDS—but in doing so, those SDS leaders and activists intensified the very problems they had set out to remedy. At the very minimum, I think it can be shown that the increase of elitism and unrepresentative manipulation by SDS leaders from 1963-1969 was proportional to the progressive dismantling of SDS' original formally democratic structure.

As was implied above, the original SDS leaders were very ambivalent about the original SDS structure, and were very conscious of the need to differ from the way those structures resulted in present union and CP bureaucratization. "Participatory democracy" became the watchword of early SDS: "Robert's Rules of Order" were castigated and "abandoned"—but the adapted Robert's Rules were initially not much different from the "bourgeois" version, since the early SDS leaders were very skilled in the use of large meeting procedures, having apprenticed for SDS in the National Student Association.

Rotation of Office

One of the first conclusions reached by the early leadership was that a regular rotation of high office was a necessary antidote to bureaucracy. It was widely assumed that re-election to any post in the organization was to be avoided unless absolutely necessary. Hayden served a term as SDS National President from June 1962 to June 1963 (he had been field secretary of the provisional organization in the period immediately prior to the Port Huron Convention) but in June 1963 it was widely assumed that he must "retire," despite the unavailability of other leaders who could have taken his place. This resulted in the election of Todd Gitlin as president, who, while politically talented and experienced, was young, relatively new to SDS, and without any history of SDS organization leadership before his election. The consequence was that Hayden continued to provide ideological and programmatic leadership (together with Rennie Davis and Paul Potter) while Gitlin was largely a figurehead. Rotation in office did not eliminate Hayden's ideological clarity, his programmatic vision or his organizational skills. Rotation did make this leadership less publicly accessible to the SDS membership, less responsible to the organization and required the establishment of the fiction of Gitlin's powers to disguise the hidden manipulation of the actual leadership which was being exercised.

The principle of rotation was unquestioned and extended to all levels of the organization. Members of the NEC ceased running for re-election. Staff organizers were discouraged from continuing leading roles. In late 1964 and 1965, a political debate was waged in SDS which polarized the organization into two factions: one arguing for building bridges to liberal and labor groups to combat Goldwater-type facism; the other arguing for the creation of grass roots and community organizations independent of the liberal establishment. Dick Flacks circulated an influential memo to protest the extremity of polarization on these issues which concluded with the following paragraph:

> Finally, I'm upset that a lot of polarization has occurred around the figures of Steve Max and Tom Hayden. These guys should be reminded that they at least implicitly promised to withdraw from top staff or leadership positions in the organization in an effort to encourage the development of a new generation of leaders. I think they are not keeping their promise, and everyone would find things a lot happier if they stepped away a little.

However, the inability of the SDS membership and leadership to deal adequately with the complexity of the political issues was not helped by having the most articulate spokesmen for the two opposing positions "step away." They did, however, step away. One of them, at least, has continued to exercise movement leadership without even the minimal checks which SDS National Committee meetings and program votes provided. In place of that original leadership, SDS saw a succession of rapid-rising leaders, none of whom stayed around long enough to allow the membership to either ratify or reject the long-run implications of their initiatives; nor did the successors stay around long enough to learn any lessons from their initial errors of leadership. As those errors became more serious as the political situation became more intense, a "clean sweep" came more and more frequently to be seen as the solution to unpopular political initiatives of the leadership. These sweeps were accompanied by an absolutist moralism about the personalities involved (replace the bad guys with good guys—and they always were guys, because guys are not only accustomed to being on top but are also most accustomed to scrambling to get up on top in situations where any regular accession to leadership is seen as "hierarchical"), and without any admission of the importance of developing skills and mechanisms for more democratically instructing the leaders we've got.

When Hayden was SDS president, political initiative in the organization rested with him, the elected part-time organizational official. He was elected because of his articulated ideology and program, an ideology and program to which the organization wanted its staff to be held responsible. And it was: how many remember Jim Monsonis, SDS National Secretary under Hayden in 1962-63? One consequence, however, of the rigid rotation of political leadership which began in 1963 and the lack of organizational continuity which that implied, was increasing *de facto* power resting with the national staff. Succeeding national secretaries became more and more politically powerful in the organization (Lee Webb, Clark Kissinger, Paul Booth, Greg Calvert) and succeeding presidents became more and more figureheads (Todd Gitlin, Paul Potter, Carl Oglesby—elected president within three months of organizational experience—and Nick Egleson).

After four years, the charade became too embarrassing to be defended, but this embarrassment did not stimulate thought in SDS about how to revive the office of president or the political powers of the Executive Committee or National Council which at one time provided a minimal democratic control over the function of the office and staff. The increasing failure of debate in the NEC or the NC to have relevance to the day to day program being implemented by the office was not seen as a problem which could be remedied by strengthening the NEC or NC or by accentuating the political seriousness and representativeness with which delegates to these bodies were chosen. Rather, "participatory democracy" was turned to for a justification of staff hegemony. That "people should control the decisions which affect their lives" was interpreted in the organization as a justification for the trend which was developing—for whose lives did staff decisions affect more than the lives of the staff themselves? At times, even "workers' control" arguments were used, not only to resist notions of formal responsibility of the national secretary to the organization as a whole, but to argue for the abolition of the national secretary and the creation of a national office workers' collective. In any event, the solution for the powerlessness of the presidency, for the increasing control of the organization by its secretariat, was seen in SDS as the ratification of that trend. In 1967 the Presidency and Vice Presidency of SDS were abolished and the National Secretariat became the *de jure* political leadership of the organization as well. At a very minimum, one of the results of this move was to restrict national political leadership in SDS to those who could move to Chicago and work full time in the national office.

Three National Secretaries

This participatory democracy energy carried itself further than merely substituting an elected national secretary for an elected president. The office itself was "democratized" in 1967 by having the National Committee elect three secretaries to work together in the national office. The National Secretary, the Inter-Organizational Secretary and the Internal Education Secretary were all to be elected by the NC. It occurred to very few of those who participated in this decision that a triple election could result in much less democracy for SDS than a single election. For in a single election the organization would have to make a choice between competing political perspectives and programs; and then hold the winner accountable to the platform on which he or she was elected. The triple election formula allowed a situation to develop in which the politics and program of the national secretary, the inter-organizational secretary and the internal education secretary were vastly different.[2]

In an organization with a traditional structure, such dissension within the national office of SDS could have been dealt with by an executive committee, rather small in number, meeting in emergency session if necessary, and meeting frequently enough to be in touch with the details of the internecine battles of the office. But by 1968-69 this alternative was no longer available to SDS. The executive committee had been functionally abandoned, in the spirit of anti-hierarchialism and anti-elitism, in 1963. As soon as the National Council, in late 1963, became a functioning body, NEC members saw their role as only that of at-large members of the NC. Ashamed by the anti-representative spirit of SDS to admit the leadership responsibilities for which it had been elected, the NEC was ignored and atrophied for so long that in 1967 a new group of at-large leaders was instituted, called the NIC (National Interim Committee) whose function and structure was identical to that of the NEC which had never been formally abolished.[3] The NIC functioned for a short time in a supervisory relation to the national office, but it too was soon seen as too hierarchical and "bourgeois." Within a few months it was functionally replaced by the notion that the national staff should be responsible only to a "national collective" appointed and organized by the staff itself. The deeply anti-democratic nature of this shift was disguised by the use of the word "collective," for this word carried the moral sanction of the anti-structural forces in the organization.

This is not to say that the continued functioning of an executive committee from 1963 to 1969 could have removed the later political battles in the office to the membership at large: if the NEC had been elected with as little political self-consciousness as the national staff, the NEC might have been as deadlocked as the office itself. However, an NEC elected nationally on a political basis would at least have had a chance to bring those office debates to a more democratic membership forum, suppressing their continued expression in office struggle. The result of the "anti-hierarchialism" of eliminating the NEC was to make the national office staff less subject to democratic control.

The National Council (chapter delegates plus the at-large members of the NEC) stood even less chance of holding the national office accountable in any way. Not only was its membership very unstable in a rapidly growing and transient student organization, but National Council members were in no regular touch with the national office. The NC had no mechanisms for exercising ongoing supervisory authority but could only take votes at its quarterly meetings.

Moreover, the "ultra-democratic" mystique extended to a refusal to define National Council membership in any way. In its early years (1963-65) SDS encouraged all members to attend NC meetings in order to observe and become familiar with the organization. After a while, though, it was seen as oppressive and in violation of "participatory democracy" to prevent from speaking anyone in the room who might have something to say. In due time this was carried further and it was felt to be embarrassingly "bourgeois" to ask for voting credentials—anyone who showed up at NC could vote. By 1967, random members who showed up outvoted chapter delegates at NCs. This made it possible for non-chapter members to relate to SDS only at the top—i.e., the NC; the chapter was destroyed as the essential constitutive unit of the organization; there was soon little pressure to have a national program which was relevant either to chapter needs or campus constituencies.

Regional Power

Parallel errors were repeated with respect to SDS' regional organization. In 1962 SDS had one campus organizer—Steve Max. Max was responsible to the national secretary, the NEC, the NC, and the Convention—in that order. As SDS grew, however, more campus organizers were required, and it seemed reasonable to restrict the travels of particular campus organizers to particular regions. This, in turn, raised the rather difficult problem of deciding to whom the regional staffs and offices were to be responsible. The anti-hierarchical, participatory democracy, and decentralist instincts seemed to suggest that regional staffs should be as close to "the people" as possible, i.e., responsible to chapters in their regions; rather than being responsible to the distant and hierarchical national office. Had the SDS regions been strong enough and well enough organized to actually hold local staffs responsible, it might have made sense to have the staffs report in part at least to regional chapter councils. (Only in part, because so long as the national SDS organization continued to exist, it should have been able to implement national programs even in minority regions.) However, the decentralist argument went on at a time (i.e., 1965) when there were few local chapters strong enough to decentralize power to. The result was a series of virtually self-appointed regional staffs in a number of SDS regions. As the politics of SDS became "heavier" some of these staffs set about to organize political power bases in "their" regions—local chapters became, in effect, responsible to their regional staff and not vice-versa. Thus, for example, the "Weatherman" faction was able to exercise extraordinary power in the national organization in the months preceding the 1969 Convention, operating out of the Michigan-Ohio region where the regional staff had created chapters with its political perspective. Power in SDS came to rest much less on success in fighting for political perspectives in the organization as a whole. Again, a seemingly "decentralist" reform—responsibility of staff to their own regions—had a deeply anti-democratic effect.

It is not the case that there was no opposition in SDS to the series of anti-representative and anti-centralist changes described. But opponents of these trends were easily intimidated by their own acceptance of the moral categories in which the debate was couched. What now, in retrospect, seems to have been truly democratic instincts were branded as "bourgeois," and bureaucratic. The last SDS leader who was fully unashamed to admit the exercise of responsible leadership was Clark Kissinger, National Secretary from the winter of 1964 to June 1965. Kissinger's chief accomplishment was the organization of the April 1965 March on Washington, an initiative which took tremendous courage and foresight (it was proposed before the intensive bombing of North Vietnam began in the winter of 1965). At every step of this process, he scrupulously submitted initiatives to the NC for debate; despite derision from the "participatory" democrats, he made a point of describing his activities at every step as the "carrying out of NC orders;" and he maintained a bureaucratic enough office to insure that there was constant information going out to the SDS membership.

But even Kissinger felt it necessary to retire as National Secretary after one full year; the NC then took nearly four months to choose a new national secretary. In the meantime, the national office staff developed much more energetic notions of "anti-hierarchy and workers' control;" never again did adherents to forms of representative democracy and bureaucratic accountability have much self-confidence. Regardless of what the actual tallies would have been had any of these issues come to a vote, it was clear that the anti-hierarchical and anti-leadership forces had overwhelming moral hegemony. In December 1965, a national SDS conference was held in which these issues of democratic structure were a chief subject of discussion. Significantly, the only paper circulated at the December Conference which was critical of the prevailing anti-structure sentiment originated in SNCC and was anonymous.

The fact that so much of the anti-structure sentiment came to SDS by way of SNCC accounts in part for the extreme moral prestige which this position held. Abhorrence of representative democratic forms, accountability, and bureaucratic efficiency was even more intense in SNCC than in SDS—and at this time (1964-65) there was considerable movement back and forth between SDS and SNCC. The anonymous paper mentioned above (titled "Mississippi's Metaphysical Mystics") described SNCC as a place where

> the most final and cutting statement of rejection is "that's the way the society does things;" the implication being that anything done by the society must be beneath us, and our responsibility as the radical innovators is to discover new and fresh ways to do anything . . . The real danger is to allow ourselves to do *anything* the way the society does. "The society keeps books and records, so SNCC should not." "The society uses flush toilets so we should not," and so on.

ERAP Autonomy

The most direct representative of this mystique in SDS was the community organizing projects (ERAP) which most closely shared with SNCC a romanticism about society's outcasts, leading to a rejection of anything (e.g., representative democracy) which could be tagged "middle class." In many respects, "ultra-democratic reforms" within ERAP preceded and stimulated such movements in SDS generally.

The chief incident in this pattern was the abolition of the national ERAP (economic research and action project) office in March, 1965. Directed by Rennie Davis, the ERAP office had raised tens of thousands of dollars, established from 10 to 15 community organizing projects in poor white and poor black urban ghettos, and recruited over 100 students to work as community organizers in these projects. The ERAP office was formally responsible to SDS—there was an "ERAP Committee" elected by the SDS NC which was to oversee the ERAP office and its implementation of a community organizing program consistent with the "American and the New Era" statement of the 1963 SDS convention. However, as the community organizing projects grew, the legitimacy of the ERAP committee decreased. First, project directors were added to the ERAP committee; since these project directors, however, were appointed by the ERAP director, a project director dominated ERAP committee was unlikely to exercise any real supervision of the ERAP office. Next, inspired by the idea of "participatory democracy," most of the project director positions were abolished in favor of leaving direction of projects to their staffs as a whole (from 5-15 organizers per project), ERAP Committee meetings became virtually synonymous with national meetings of all community project staff members. Finally, the "hierarchical" nature of having an ERAP director and ERAP staff making decisions which affected the lives of project staff was attacked. Having no answers to these democratic arguments, the ERAP national staff decided to disband and join local projects as organizers.

These decisions had a number of little understood consequences:

First, ERAP project directors were all males, and all were much more experienced and politically sophisticated than most of the community organizers on local project staffs. The ERAP project directors, too, had little sense of how to train staff members in the political skills necessary to participate in genuine decision making. The abolition of the job of project director in favor of the "participatory democracy" of the project staff as a whole, did not alleviate these problems but accentuated them. As the most experienced, articulate and forceful members of the project, these directors (myself included) continued to exercise disproportionate power within the project, but the democratic ethos of the projects required that this power be hidden and disguised. Thus, leadership was transformed into manipulation; in addition, it is always harder to hold informal leadership accountable for mistakes than it is to hold formal leadership accountable—especially if the prevailing ethos requires a denial that any leadership exists at all.

Secondly, the control of ERAP as a whole by those it "affects" (first project director and then all community staff members) rather than those who empowered it (SDS), created an autonomous organization over which SDS had no control. SDS benefitted from political lessons learned in ERAP projects only to the extent that ERAP staff members moved out of local projects and back onto campuses (this was considerable). ERAP's autonomy also tended to isolate its community organizers whose own political development was narrower as a result of their decreased participation in SDS. In any event, whatever democratic benefits may have accrued to ERAP from its own self determination, this democracy conflicted with SDS' democratic right to control its own project. A political principle deeper than "participatory democracy" was necessary to resolve this problem.

Third, the dismantling of the national ERAP office resulted, within a few months, in the disintegration of all but the strongest ERAP projects. The financial assistance, staff recruitment and morale building which the national ERAP office had provided was essential to the weaker projects, but not to the stronger. In effect, the ERAP office was acting as the indispensable organizer of the weaker community organizing projects. Eliminating the national ERAP office on grounds of opposition to "hierarchy" did not speak to the essential political functions that office was performing. And not only the weak projects suffered. Within a few months of the national office's closing, the three remaining projects (Newark, Cleveland and Chicago) had nearly ceased communicating, since the regular channels for such communication had been abolished.

Fourth, the same democratic rhetoric which led to the abolition of project directors and the national ERAP office was soon quite logically applied to the communities in which the organizing was being done. If the ERAP office's attempt to organize the organizers was hierarchical and elitist, wasn't also the organizers' attempts to organize the community? This is much too complicated an issue to be dealt with briefly here, but the same instincts which led to the denial of project directorship, led organizers to attempt to deny their role as well. This resulted in a similar substitution of manipulation for self-conscious organizing and the eventual destruction of even the strong projects was at least in part influenced by the inability of ERAP organizers to develop a sophisticated notion of the role of an organizer which went beyond simple democratic slogans. "Let the people decide" was a powerful mass slogan, a weapon against the War on Poverty, urban renewal and the like. Mass slogans, however, are not always adequate tools for understanding political practice; in this case it led organizers to pretend (at times even to themselves) that "the people" were deciding issues that only organizers knew about, let alone understood.

The foregoing does not argue that SDS' problems would have been entirely avoided had it maintained a formally representative structure, complete with president, v.p., NEC, NC, ERAP committee, single national secretary, appointed staff, etc. SDS had many serious problems of ideology and practice, let alone its problems with democracy. This is not even an argument that SDS would have been a democratic organization had its formally representative structure been maintained. Male chauvinism in the organization, as well as political inarticulateness would have interfered with democracy even within a representative structure—as was noted above, the election of three staff members need not result in office warfare if the membership is sophisticated enough to elect the three from the same slate. Democracy can never be more than empty formalism if the base of an organization is not highly conscious and active in its own behalf. Fully participatory democratic organizations were probably impossible in the politically naive days of the early New Left; but formally democratic organizations would have been a good place to start.

But this paper does argue that the opposite assertions are false. Lack of democracy in SDS was not caused, not even related to its hierarchical, pyramidal and representative form. The attack in SDS on representative institutions in the name of democracy intensified SDS' lack of democracy.

We are now entering a period where activists are again thinking of building organizations—national organizations, like NUC, local organizations, sectoral organizations, women's organizations. In a period of much higher consciousness than the middle sixties, these organizations probably have a decent chance of success. But the organizers of these new efforts should beware the pitfalls of the sixties; they could do worse than to imitate the "rigid old SDS form."

Notes

1. In the Port Huron Statement, charges of elitism and bureaucratization of the Old Left (Stalinism) and the American union movement were toned down below the actual intensity of feeling on the subject by SDS people: for opposite reasons this was necessary to pacify the L.I.D. sponsors. L.I.D. had an uncritical admiration for LABOR and an uncritical anti-communist hatred of the U.S.S.R. The Port Huron Statement's moderate criticisms of both bureaucracies were statements of limited political independence from the L.I.D.
2. This need not have been the case if national politics in SDS had been developed to the point of sophistication where the three officers would be elected as a slate; but that sophistication had not developed—neither in the membership electorate nor in the candidates themselves.

   The result was that no coherent mandate could be carried out and that the chief political battles of the organization were fought out within the national office. Fighting out political battles within a national office is far less democratic than having those battles fought in a general election campaign for control of the office. Yet the troika model was adopted under the "democratic" banner.
3. The creation of the NIC was not really an exception to the anti-leadership mystique I am describing. The creation of the NIC was part of a package adopted in 1967 which included the abolition of the SDS presidency and vice-presidency. The NIC was seen as the decentralization of the two previously elected SDS officers.

Notes for Next Time:
A Memoir of the 1960s

ELINOR LANGER

*I long with all my heart for the most radical possible transformation of the
present regime, in the direction of a greater equality in the relations of power.
I do not believe at all that what is called revolution nowadays can bring this
about. After a so-called working-class revolution, just as much as before it,
the workers at R. will go on obeying passively—so long as the system of
production is based on passive obedience. Whether the manager at R. takes
orders from a managing director who represents a few capitalists or from a
so-called Socialist "State Trust" makes no difference, except that in the first
case the factory is not in the same hands as the police, the army, the prisons,
etc., and in the second case it is. The inequality in the relations of power is
therefore not lessened but accentuated.*

*This consideration, however, does not put me against the parties described
as revolutionary. Because every significant political group nowadays tends
equally toward accentuating oppression and getting all the instruments of
power into the hands of the State; some of them call this process working-
class revolution, some call it fascism, and some call it the organization of
national defence. Whatever the slogan, two factors always predominate: one
of them is the subordination and dependence which are implied in modern
forms of technique and economic organization; the other is war. All those
who favour the increase of "rationalization," on the one hand, and preparation
for war, on the other, are the same in my eyes: and they include everybody.*
—Simone Weil, 1936. In *Seventy Letters*, translated and arranged by
Richard Rees

These days I take for granted that The Movement is dead. This is, of course,
no news, but I am measuring it personally. Some of my friends, among them
some of the most original and inventive activists of the 1960s, have become

cultists: as isolated as the sectarians who preceded us on the left, the too-despised elders who we once had the common sense to know were wrong. Some are still doing the "power structure research" we thought we invented, not noticing that the caricatures and projections and charts that arise from their studies are still too hollow and one-dimensional to convince the American men and women at whom they are presumably aimed. Some friends work in the cities, caught up in the daily toll-taking work of the dissolution of old projects and the creation of new, hoping to find a "constituency" that their efforts will either move or serve. Some are mauling over their psyches in strange intense "collectives" across the country, hoping against the logic of their personal biographies and their location in history to become good communist women and men. More, as time passes, go back to work, or take up training for the professional careers their political involvement delayed. Some are in the country, learning building, farming, crafts; some are scaling mountains. A few are underground, institutionalized, or dead.

The streets of Vermont around me, like the streets everywhere, are filled with long-haired young women and men who could not be called "revolutionary" by any standard that does not mock history. Their businesses and careers are flourishing here, and they use their proceeds to buy land that the rising tax rate makes the local farmers unable to maintain. The stockbroker who commutes on weekends is scarcely different from us political exiles and communards: city folks perched atop land we scarcely understand, less able to pretend with every day that passes that our being here represents anything more than that, for now, we like to be here. We peel away successive layers of revolutionary ideologies, trying to understand how capitalism works chiefly because we have a sudden personal need to understand mortgages, investment, insurance, taxes. Once last summer, driving home from Cape Cod on a rainy Sunday, I took the alternate route and stopped for a moment at Plymouth Rock. The guide was a red-haired hippy Pilgrim, as spiritless and mechanical in his programmed misinformation about the Mayflower as the crew-cut Pilgrim who preceded him in that post, as the artificial ship-captain's wife in the Nantucket gift shop near the steamer, as every beaten down and lying tour guide posted along all the Freedom Trails of America. I drove back to Boston through the rain, knowing for sure—as I had known before, and doubtless will have to learn again—that America had outlasted its rebels once again.

I am surprised that these things should be so. It did not seem at the time as if there would ever be a discreet thing called "the sixties," as there had been the "fifties," "thirties," and "twenties," decades beginning in the 1890s to which the historians we read in college arbitrarily assigned colors like "mauve" or "brown." It seemed, on the contrary, like time itself, like the only possible reality; it seemed, as a friend of mine said recently, like the peak of history. Now of course we can seek that it was neither autonomous nor eternal. It was brought into being by social forces that preceded it and will last beyond it, and it was marked on both sides by external events, as were all movements that came before: though it is perhaps not yet so clear precisely which forces and which events will stake its boundaries in history. Right now I think that the radicals of my generation will never grow as arrogant and unseeing as those of the last, who became $40,000-a-year anthropologists and sociologists for the AID program of the CIA, publishers of above-the-fray magazines, and our enemies on the campus. Already we are luckier than they: their decade ended in World War II; ours has ended in the Watergate. Greater dangers for us, I think, are self-hate and despair, for we failed ourselves far more than we failed others, who never expected any different results. Boredom threatens too, for in withdrawing we are denying ourselves use of the very faculties—mental, moral, and political—that once gave our lives some energy and coherence. But I think if we have learned anything, we will try to use it better. We are a rich generation, God help us, we cannot shake that, and we have little material to lose or gain. I think that whatever we become individually we will be radicals to our graves if for no other reason than that we will never want "in." We started out "in," and didn't like it. The wanderings and confusions of the movement, which have seemed to outsiders so futile and indulgent, reflect a painful, personal, and therefore inescapable sense of some of the things that are really wrong with our country—even though we have acted them out in our recalcitrant lives and did not become soldiers in a post-industrial liberation army.

And yet it is clear that "our generation" is dead. I do not think this means that radicalism is dead or that there will never be a social movement in America that will drive the corporate moneylenders from their temples. I don't know. But the bands of sisters and brothers who marched and bled together on all the St. Crispin Crispian's days of the 1960s have withered away. We "failed" as a revolutionary generation. Everything we thought was wrong is still wrong, and more besides, and we are without the institutions, influence, or understanding to help change it. But the fact that the roots we sank are frail does not mean we have left nothing. Our mistakes are as important as our achievements because they are mistakes of the first—or at least one of the first—radical political movements in a post-scarcity capitalist society. Many of our errors come from that curse by an undefeatable law whose meanings are concealed in a Rosetta Stone we cannot yet read. It may be that our experience is anomalous, that we are premature, a post-scarcity episode or spasm on a planet in which all schemes for distributing resources will be governed by the unstoppable power of cynical and competitive social systems, or by the limits of nature. The post-scarcity idea may be a utopian delusion. Or, the idea may pre-date the reality by so much that our experience will seem insignificant. But, accident or portent, we were "post-scarcity" in our bones.

I think we should try to understand our time now, as well as we can. Romance is already setting in. I have students who confess to idolizing me as a relic of some brave revolutionary struggle whose meaning they didn't quite catch—their La Passionaria perhaps—and their illusions trouble me. The opposite is also true: we seem, as we seem sometimes to ourselves, confused, guilt-ridden, "irrelevant," or merely old. American radicals have never been able to reach each other across the decades very well. Each radical movement has risen and fallen in an historical moment gone before it has begun to be understood. Its leaders, its troops, its perception of issues, its solutions appear either sentimentally valorous, or else archaic, to its successors. But any movement for a different social order in America will not be the work of one generation alone. We have to mend discontinuities in the radical impulse if we can, head off generational misunderstandings, stand before others neither as false heroes nor as fallen idols. For this reason, it seems useful to try to begin to tell our story.

Most of what I have written here is personal. When I began writing, I distrusted abstraction and felt unable to make sense of anyone's experience but my own. Only autobiography seemed "true." More recently, I have been able to see how autobiography may also mislead, and not just in the simple senses of omission and individuality. Political autobiography, especially, emphasizes aspects of personality formed by culture. It offers a picture of a life shaped relentlessly by external events, a slide or chute whose angle controls the speed and whose rigid sides control the direction of one's course through time. It is apt to attribute to "the times" things that come from the chronological age of the writer at the time being recalled, or at the time of writing. I do not know how to cure possible distortions in this essay except by stating them: sociology is not the whole truth of a person, and political autobiography is not all of life. I know too that the "we" of this essay is small. At its largest it is white middle-class radicals who were active during the 1960s. More likely it is my friends. Perhaps it is, after all, only myself. Sometimes when I say "I" it would probably be more accurate to say "we"; sometimes when I say "we" I should probably be saying "I." Many friends contributed to the writing of this essay in both conversation and explicit criticism, and their lives as well as mine are imbedded in it. The "I's" and the "we's" do not clearly separate themselves out. But it does seem as we grow older that there were always more "I's" that "we" thought at the time: more separate people, more separate perceptions, more separate histories. Besides, we entered our joint history at different times. I was born the month after Hitler invaded Poland. I think I remember blackouts in Pittsburgh, and my father, who was not in the army, in the costume of an air-raid warden, but I am not sure that these things really happened to me and not just in the films and Movietone newsreels I saw later. For the most part my memories begin at the war's end. When Roosevelt died my parents sat around the radio for days, or so it seemed, frightened, stunned and crying. Later I understood that FDR was "their" President in a way our generation has not known. He stood over their adult lives like a guardian for more than a dozen years. They seem to believe that he had taken care of them all that time: fed them, clothed them, sheltered them from the storms of winter, and provided that their dying years would not be as bleak and penniless, as saturated with fear, as the dying years of the immigrant generation which preceded them. Over the years these emotions became a politics I could not share. The speech I heard so often became a set-piece in my mind, like the speech of the blind egotistical judge in *Little Murders* who does not notice he is speaking to an empty chamber. It went something like this: Of course things are not perfect but, dear, no human institutions are perfect and they are much better than they were. Working people can organize: do you know they once put your aunt in jail for helping to organize the ILGWU? People have a bottom under them: welfare, unemployment, social security, things that didn't exist when we were young. . . . On it went. My parents continued their patient climb from the pale of New York to the suburbs of Boston. This portrait of progress was true for them, but it was not my world. I could not find myself on the canvas.

When the bomb was dropped I had a nightmare. A man in a Santa Claus suit was flying low over the houses in our town, carrying a bomb shaped like a football which he was about to drop in our chimney. My mother came in to say it was all right, but of course it wasn't. Many people I know my age remember having similar dreams that summer. I absorbed the bomb into my adult life in the intellectual way I customarily handled traumas, by becoming an "expert." Shortly after college I became obsessed with the Manhattan Project. I read all the memoirs and chronicles and histories and apologies then available, and talked with anyone in Washington whose life had been touched by the bomb and who was willing to talk. Anyone who had played a decent role in the debate preceding the bombings, the attempt to set up the AEC under civilian rule, or the effort to establish international control, anyone who seemed human—from David Lilienthal to the Rosenbergs—was a titan to me. Lewis Strauss and Edward Teller and the men who tormented Oppenheimer were monsters.

I do not remember any deprivation during the war—or at any time in my life—or even any inconvenience, except for a long anticipated car trip for which my parents had been saving gas coupons. The car had four retread tires and they all blew out. What I do remember clearly is the burst of consumption at the war's end. It seems to me that at the very moment we were banging pots and pans on the streets of Newton (whether for V-E or V-J day I don't know) there was an explosion of fresh cream and strawberries. I carried nylon stockings to my first-grade teacher as if they were diamonds, a gift from my father who worked in a retail store. Suddenly we had a new car, a tan 1946 Oldsmobile with a slanting roof and huge windows. My father's initials were monogrammed onto the side, protected at first by a small cardboard square which covered them as a Band-Aid covers a rising vaccination blister. It was the first postwar car in the neighborhood and we drove it around and around the block, imprinting it forever, I suppose, on the hearts and minds of the teenage boys who gathered to look. I do not know what the spasm of goodies I remember had to do with the enormous expansion of production that followed the war on a long-term basis, and under whose effects we are still reeling. Perhaps it reflected only the snapping of controls. But it was the first time I had had whipped cream, and it was delicious.

My childhood seems, in retrospect, a "fifties" childhood: neutral and sentimental, separated from my later life by a geologic fault. In the first years after the war my parents, my sister, and I lived in a graceful eighteenth century town in western Massachusetts. My parents loved the architecture, the trout streams, the very smell of New England, and they passed that love to me. Postwar fortunes had not yet been made. Television had barely begun. There were few Jewish families, and each had the special burden of being "the kind of Jew" to whom their Yankee neighbors would not object. My mother organized Girl Scouts; I stopped off to light candles at the Roman Catholic Church as I bicycled to school with friends. For my parents, I think, the ovens of Europe and the betrayal of neighbors were never far away. I wanted playmates. When friendships seemed more safely secured by establishing differences than by ecumenicism, I had a burst of cultural nationalism and persuaded my parents to join a fledgling Reform Temple. One year we smuggled a Christmas tree into the house after dark so the neighbors would not sense our ambivalence. The next year I won the Sunday School essay contest on the topic "What Hanukkah Means to Me."

The town celebrated America whenever it could in patriotic pageants on the village green: solemn and quiet on Memorial Day, extravagant on the Fourth of July. We studied local history—mainly the French and Indian wars—and I still have the impression that all the rivers of Massachusetts ran red with the blood of the freedom-seeking ancestors of the families in the mansions around the green. I went to a Girl Scout camp at the western edge of the state. It was a community institution and every year before it opened whole families—mine among them—would drive up for a day of work, opening cabins, patching boats, clearing the mice-droppings from the kitchen. The camp prided itself on being nonsectarian, though it was nonsectarian in an exceedingly Christian way, and most Jews went elsewhere. One year three black campers came from Tennessee, on "camperships." We sang all the time: "I know a place where the sun is like gold . . .," "I would be true," and many Christian hymns. We were always struggling for badges and awards, but it was not, as I remember it, a particularly bestial struggle, and when the final banquet came, the night we sent our wishing boats—small pieces of bark alight with candles—across the lake, there were always prizes for everybody.

As I write it now, it does not sound so wrong. The small semi-rural community had decent intentions and traditions it did not seem necessary to doubt. Yet something was wrong with it, I still don't know exactly what. I have the impression that almost my entire life between 8 and 13 was spent in uniform: a square-flecked Brownie dress with a beanie, a masculine green shirtlike costume with a yellow tie, green and white striped shorts. I marched a lot and gave quite a lot of inspirational addresses. I do not feel comfortable with the intention of that past; I am not glad to have had it. I think that the songs that our clear children's voices carried across the mountain lake were not our songs but the songs of some upright nineteenth-century Protestant (General William Booth?) trying to stop time and mold our characters to fit a world that was already lost. Though I still love those melodies, I have never been able to feel that they are genuinely or rightfully mine.

Early in the 1950s my father was transferred by his company to Boston, and we moved back to Newton, where we had spent two previous years. The social structure of the schools was more complicated and demanding than the one I had left. There were not only Jews and non-Jews, but Jews within Jews: "Americanized" Jews like myself and my friends, and Jews whose families had more recently come from the ghettos of Dorchester and Roxbury and who still spoke in its accents. "They" were sexually more precocious than "we" (which led them to be known as "cheap") but less intellectual. We necked in their basements at parties but concentrated the energy of our daylight hours on our studies and friendships with the somewhat primmer Christians. The Christians set the standard: scholarship *and* athletics, advanced standing *and* cheerleading, intelligence *and* beauty. Grecian goddesses and gods preparing for a just and balanced Rule. It was difficult. One friend of mine, a small, brilliant, Jewish woman with a misshapen body, killed herself our senior year. I watched a gifted intellectual Jewish man, by Wasp standards homely, turn himself into a Princetonian with striped tie and straw hat, and lose his dignity in the process. I was afraid that someone at a football game would ask me to explain a play and I would have to reveal that I didn't, really, understand.

Those of us who fell short served on decorations committees for the victory celebrations, formed singing groups with school-inspired names such as the "Newtonettes" (with colors and uniforms subtly approximating those of the cheerleaders), patrolled the cafeteria for the Orange Shield (more uniforms), put out the yearbook, organized the Latin Club, and performed in a hundred other "after-school activities" that we knew in our hearts bore an unsatisfactory relation to the centers of social power. We also knew that the size of the columns listing "activities" after our pictures in the yearbook was directly related to "getting into college." We joined everything we could. It thus came to pass that at a certain time we were reading existentialist literature of alienation and despair, decrying "organization men" and the dismaying prevalence of "other-directedness" in our culture; and we never suspected that we, with our All-American masks and our premature anxieties, were the coming evidence of the philosophers' nightmares.

The school immunized us from politics. Compared to the sophisticated teaching of English and mathematics, our social studies were poor: standard pluralism, the problems are all solved. An assignment-in-the-world I remember took me to a family-run underwear manufacturer with a company union, paternalistic benefits, and a low turnover of personnel. I wrote an enthusiastic report. We did not much discuss McCarthy, MacArthur, Korea, Montgomery, or *Brown* v. *the Board of Education*. But there was more to it than that. Newton High School, the shining-jewel-in-the-crown-of-the-American-educational-system, the school that we were told day after day was the best in the country: that school had a track system and I believe its greatest achievement is that not one of us in those days would have understood the term. A ninth-grade student in a Newton junior high school recently published some sophisticated work demonstrating the correlation between a student's curriculum and the income level of his or her neighborhood; we scarcely knew that the poorer black and Italian communities existed. And a classmate of mine has written elsewhere about her discovery a few years ago that a black student who sat next to her in homeroom is now collecting garbage at her parents' Newton home. We did not know that was going to happen. To us there were simply four God-given curriculums. The reasons given were of course ordinary. People "learned at different rates," had "different educational needs and objectives." The triumph of the school was that it could provide quality teaching at all levels under one democratic roof. We believed we were an example of equal educational opportunity, and we were proud of it.

It seems to me now that the teachers were scarcely more than a thin overlay on the real function of the school, and that their work was not inconsistent with it. They were good people, the best of their kind at transmitting knowledge of the established order and its culture and its myths. I think of them individually with pleasure and respect. And yet I am appalled to see that I got A's for writing of Robinson Jeffers' sonnet, "Promise of Peace": "Mr. Jeffers has condensed into a compelling 14 lines the enigmatic paradox of the bewildered human race." I described Leon, in *Madame Bovary*, as a "sensual coward" (another A) before, I think, I even knew what organs the word "sensual" might be connected to, or how. And I wrote of *Hamlet*: "The play is about suicide in terms of killing an enemy, about endless delay in terms of incessant action," when I can't imagine I was talking about anything I understood at all. I was copying, I suppose, the styles of prose and perception of the ancient literary dons across the ocean and I cannot understand now why this psychological if not literal plagiarism was rewarded instead of challenged. What was the social function of this detached precocity?

During the same period of time I was president of a Jewish girls' club whose principal raison d'etre was an annual dance in a downtown hotel to raise money for a charity like cerebral palsy or mental retardation. I find, in the dance program hidden away among old treasures, that at 16 I made a speech that went:

Dear Friends—

It is my pleasure to welcome you all here this evening to the Curri Club's Annual Benefit Dance. Thanks to your generous contributions to our ad book and to your presence here tonight the Curri Club will again be privileged to donate over $1000 to Cerebral Palsy.

I would like to take this opportunity to compliment each of the Club members on her untiring efforts to make this dance a success. It has been a wonderful experience for all of us to grow and work together to achieve a single goal.

Once again, thank you all for helping us. Have a great time and take pride in knowing that you have indeed "Helped the Curri Club Help Cerebral Palsy."

The speech made me wince. Where was I in it? Who was I? Who put that prosperous, corny, and sentimental suburban matron into my 16-year-old body, and why? The pretension of schoolwork and the artifice of social life seems linked. The person who wrote the papers and made the speech was trying to get through adolescence as fast as possible: to be grown up, to be absorbed into a society where those adult roles and postures (and perhaps others) would have some meaning. It did not happen that way. Perhaps we were "sociological adolescents" (lacking what Keniston would call the prime sociological characteristic of adulthood, integration into the institutional structures of society) in the movement in part because we were sociological adults when we were children.

It is difficult to believe that this process was not at least in some vague cultural sense intentional. We were meant to slip without noticing it from childhood to adulthood, from marching on the village green to reporting for work in the office or factory. Public school was to make us obedient, skilled, repressed. This discipline was necessary, perhaps, for the generations throughout history which have participated in industrializing their countries. It may be necessary for most of the world now. But it was not necessary for us. When we stood at the edge of the adult world, we did not have to join its two-step procession.

Yet societal explanations, somewhere, fail to nourish. That geologic fault was also human. There was a jolt in my family when I was an adolescent. I could not believe in the stability of homes or in commitments that endured or in security through the piling up of goods. I saw them fail. Beyond that, I do not want to tell. I am not Philip Roth. My parents' lives are their own. But the social wreckage I saw and felt, I saw in part because it corresponded with my own ruined fantasies. What was the crucial link, what was the mixture of fuels, what was the synergy that bred the sense of disjunction that bred radicalism, I am not sure I know.

Arthur Schlesinger, Jr., begins his account of John F. Kennedy's *Thousand Days* in his usual purple: "It all began in the cold." My recollection is different: it began as it ended, on TV. Watching the debates between Kennedy and Nixon in the basement of my college dormitory in 1960, I concluded that, contrary to Schlesinger's pamphlet of that year, it did not "make a difference." I threw away, as they say, my first vote on a Socialist Labor candidate on my absentee ballot.

It has been convenient to think of that act—a vote cast at the beginning of the decade and of my political adulthood—as representing a tentative, individual, political alienation that would later join with others in the movement, and I think it is a useful symbol. I learned subsequently that many people soon to be in the movement had independently done the same thing that year. But the more I think of it, the more I see that that vote was not really a political act at all, at least not if politics implies engagement. It was something else: the statement of an intellectual position and a cultural attitude which I believe were widespread at the time and turned up in many masks later.

I went to Swarthmore from 1957 to 1961. During those years there was almost no political activity. There was a folk festival, a tradition, a sort of bohemian remnant, organized in part by many of us who became radical

73

later. We had some idea, I think, that folk singers were "real": Reds or Blacks, prisoners or miners, or Elizabethan minstrels still uneasy in the New World. Inviting them to the campus seemed slightly dangerous. The friends from Harvard and Wellesley who flooded the campus for this annual event were jealous and dazed by its aura. Our only political organization was the Forum for Free Speech, another remnant. It invited "controversial speakers from the left and right" and drew more energy from its vague associations with political danger and a radical past than it did from the themes or passions of its speakers. Nonetheless we felt proud of the relative liberalism that the college's critics always called "radicalism," and we were vaguely conscious that there was some tradition we were helping to keep alive. A chapter of the National Student Association was begun at some point, and though we contributed to its collectives (clothes and money for South Africa, I think) some instinct led us to keep away, as we kept away from conventional student government.

Our other political encounters grew out of immediate circumstance. A Negro friend received a hate letter; we tried to devise some collective response. A Ghanaian friend was sometimes insulted in Philadelphia and refused admittance to local bars. We remonstrated with the bartender, whom we needed because he did not look too closely at our phony IDs. At a certain point we began to make cultural forays into nearby Chester, a black hell where the SDS students who followed us at Swarthmore later worked. Our adventures were limited to segregated bars (we patronized both black and white) and after-hours clubs, but these treks, together with our jobs in the dining room, brought us into contact with the black people who worked for the college and lived in Chester. At one point we had a battle with the administration after it ruled that "the help" could not enter campus buildings by the front door. I think we were hungry even then for associations with "the people," whom we already felt we were not. Two years in a row we escaped the cultural divide and organized softball games with the painters, truckers, plumbers, and their families, whom we had met drinking in our favorite white bar. They arrived on the campus both years with huge kegs of beer we smuggled into the fieldhouse, and it seems to me that we played, and drank, and talked, all night. Of course these relationships had limits. I remember an evening's crush on a housepainter named Jim ending in the explicit recognition between us that "it was impossible," as if armed guards monitored the frontier between our different lives. But I don't think either of us knew exactly who the guards were serving or how they happened to be there.

Toward the end of college we watched Operation Abolition, identifying with the anti-HUAC demonstrators, who looked like us. We entertained black visitors from Tennessee and North Carolina who were integrating lunch counters and trying to get northern student support. We did some token picketing of Woolworth's in Chester. We heard before we graduated that some freshmen had set up a Marxist study group, and were more or less amazed. Marxism was critical to the European past, we thought, but it did not explain contemporary politics. I know that in other colleges at that time students came away either ignorant of Marx or with conscious anti-Marxism. That was not true for us. We understood that he was a towering figure, that judgments or quibbles about the "correctness" of his formulations were a waste of time. But precise mastery of his works and ideas also seemed to be a waste of time. That corollary did not seem questionable until later. At the possibility of a political use of Marx we felt slightly embarrassed and fearful that Swarthmore's intellectual traditions were in jeopardy.

For our real life at Swarthmore was intellectual. Our academic work dwarfed our love affairs and made politics unimportant. Most of my friends and I were drawn to studying history, and for a lot of reasons we felt we understood a great deal about revolution and change, about how history happens. Our teachers made us feel capable of criticizing every historical theory and any particular piece of writing, regardless of the reputation of the author. Before scholarship we were arrogant, not humble. We were taught that people disagree, that "fields" and "theses" are too narrow to contain human experience, and it is not the fault of the college per se that the universities into which it dispatched us for graduate work had narrower and more disappointing interests and ideas, or that forces at work in the world had uses for knowledge other than its reproduction and extension. There were exceptions to the humaneness and common sense. I remember a seminar on the British Empire that still cloaked it in the mystique of the West and considered most problems from the point of view of the governors, who wrote all the books. We became familiar with the worst of the anti-Stalinist analyses of the Soviet Union produced in the 1950s, but we learned at the same time that the works were shallow. Our teachers had been to the Soviet Union and knew that the parts and the whole did not fit together exactly the way our textbooks said. I took away, and I think that many others did also, the idea that no decent people disapproved of revolutions. They might take wayward paths, always they would fall short, but they were exciting times in the life of mankind, they meant to open up new worlds for ordinary human beings, they burst with energy and life. We identified with every revolution we could discover, and every revolutionary, those in the papers (Cuba, and for a time, we thought, Egypt) as well as those in the past. Knowing what we "knew" about revolutions in history, it was difficult to understand how politicians could be so stupid as to oppose them in the present, or why they would not just sit back, like our teachers, observe, and wish the people well. From the breadth of our reading and the spirit of our discussions we somehow acquired a kind of non-technical, logical, Marxism-of-the-heart: maybe just a conviction that things happen for a reason. I think this understanding is part of the heritage of the left. It partly accounts for the fact, for example, that in 1965 more radicals than policy makers knew why the United States could not win in Vietnam. They had their tables, charts, reports, technology, power, spies; we had a sense of how things flow. This sense sometimes seems mere sloganeering about revolutionary invincibility, but it also measures something true that governments rarely see.

Now this college radicalism seems romantic and intellectual. It was not based on experience. Because we loved history we assumed we loved politics. We have never understood the essential distinction that history, in elegant books and passionate tracts, is art and idealization and that politics is not the history of its own times but something quite different: something that, as one of my friends said recently, always lets you down. This intellectual mistake, though it is fused with many other things, is one of the reasons that we later became so quickly disillusioned, bitter, and desperate. I am not sure now that I would have felt any more at home among the revolutionary exiles in Geneva and Zurich than I sometimes did at the political gathering spots in Washington and Berkeley. But I took for granted at the time that I was meant for the cafes and barricades, and I was sorry to live in a country where affairs were so peaceably settled.

What we were really prepared for with our unearned profundity was not engagement but detachment. If history is inevitable it is also morally neutral. The only time I remember being touched by the idea of *courage* came in the form in which I suppose such an event was bound to occur in my life: intellectual, and about history. Alan Bullock, the British biographer of Hitler whose work we had all read, was speaking one evening at a nearby college on the then surprising subject of German resistance to Hitler. Bullock was a rumply, donnish, gentle man who, if I remember rightly, had just gotten off the plane from Europe. He described what he knew of the organization, the bomb plots, the assassination attempts and then began to explain how perilous resistance was. "For my part," he said, in a taut English voice I remember perfectly, "I do not think I should have had the courage to resist." I loved him for saying that. It seemed to me he was very brave to make his confession before an audience of young idealists. It punctured the pretensions of the heroines and heroes of imaginary revolution—myself and my friends—who believed at that time there was nothing we would not do for the sake of justice. It gave me a new sense of "profound understanding"—this time of the Germans and their real situation—and consequently a new weapon to use against moralistic and undereducated adults who, not understanding the consequences of action for ordinary Germans, still had the easy certainty that they would have behaved differently. I "understood"; they didn't. It was a posture brave and abject simultaneously. I say I loved Alan Bullock, and I am still impressed by his saying that. But later in my life the question has come to me: what does it mean that for so many years my definition of courage was linked with this quiet English scholar who thought he would not have stirred when 6 million Jews were gassed alive and Europe was tearing itself apart? That soupy diffuse "understanding" without rights and wrongs seemed appropriate in our benign protected atmosphere. Nothing was terribly wrong that we knew of. Our problem was historical interpretations, not social reality. This distance did not help, and later came to seem sinister—the whole of my Swarthmore education with it—when people were murdered in Birmingham and Mississippi and the news began to slip in from Asia about the wreckage of Vietnam.

Other attitudes bred by college or coinciding with it wove in and out of our political lives. We came to maturity in an atmosphere of cultural disaffection not even breached until Dylan and rock. The critics of culture spoke a great deal then of "middlebrow" and "highbrow," of "masscult" and "midcult." We accepted these distinctions and added our own, snobs searching for a special niche within an already snobbish tradition. If our parents listened to Beethoven, we would listen to Bartok or Berg. If they read Plato, we read Camus. If they like Monet or Picasso, we stood admiringly before the huge blank canvasses in New York museums, and spoke knowingly of "texture." We also preferred esoteric folk to fifties rock.

It is obvious that we were an elite. We were limited not only by our social class in the largest sense but by being a fragment even of that class: the most privileged among the already privileged. Just as we discovered at Swarthmore that we had each been at the top of our class in high school, so we discovered in the movement, especially in its early days, that "everyone" had been among the best students at his or her university. We were never surprised to be sought out, to be in the public eye, to be known. Of course: if we were journalists we must be Orwell; if filmmakers, Godard; if scientists, Fleming; if novelists, Tolstoy; if revolutionaries, Che. If we were not these things we would simply shift our course and try something new. We expected distinction, respect, fame as surely and deliberately as the Kennedys, Rockefellers and Harrimans expected public office: not for us the obscurity and struggles of the garret or the rigidity of large tedious organizations. And others agreed with our self-assessment. Throughout the decade scholars and journalists would justify and explain the movement on the basis that the best and the brightest had turned to it. We felt we had no place else to go. Our talent, our elitism, and our lack of use for them, are connected with the astonishing sense of self-importance that led us to overrate every twist and turn in our later development (though that tendency has other sources): to spend years examining our lives and our strategies, scarcely looking outward, to see the world as an enlargement of a microscopic scraping from our cells. Not understanding our place in history, we linked ourselves with it nonetheless. I remember one of my friends, somewhere in her trajectory from SDS to the women's movement to the gay movement, stopping off in my backyard one day at a difficult moment in her personal life to cry in confusion: "I don't want to be an example of the breakdown of capitalism." It is as if we took our dignity not from our internal selves but from being a part of History's process. If our arguments became more and more stale, parched, withered transplants of the divisions among the Old Bolsheviks, that was explicable and justified by the same logic. History could legitimate us if society would not. Our self-importance was grafted onto its opposite, insecurity.

But these things came later. In 1960 there was no group identity, no "we," only a great many people separated from one another by the stone walls of their separate colleges and universities, experiencing privately the same vague dislocation that led me to vote for a third-party candidate. What could you do when you knew that Camelot was a myth from the beginning? We had criticized Schlesinger as a sentimental and false historian from reading *The Age of Jackson* before we turned 21. We knew, from his works on Russia and economic development, that the heart of Walt Whitman Rostow was definitely in the wrong place. We knew that the entire court was riddled with apologists, though at the time we did not know what they were apologists for. The Kennedys never fooled us. We despised alliteration and felt that hunting and horsemanship and interior decoration were forms of aristocratic pretension, decidedly inferior to our own. Jackie might flirt with Leonard Bernstein who himself slipped much too trickily into and out of the world of "seriousness": she could not "understand" the Philharmonic. It was hard for us to participate in the post-Camelot blues because we had never believed in Camelot.

What was our real relation to the New Frontier? We shared with it, I think, a resurrection from quietism, a refreshed fascination with images of what human societies can accomplish, political grandiosity, and even, deep in both of us, a schoolchild's idealism about America and its messages for the world. At the space of some dozen years I concede that in an historical sense the Kennedy regime made the movement possible. But we were not, I think, powered by the same engine. Kennedy meant to "get America moving" toward a modernized empire, fueled by and refueling the major internal powers of the corporate state. We were the flotsam the ship of that state tossed about in its wake: too educated for its jobs, too sensitive for its dullness, and finally too suspicious of its intentions. We floated this way and that, trying different things, until public events and the emergence of the movement itself tied together the threads of our separate histories and gave them, for a while, a kind of sense.

I left college for Washington: a job at the Washington Center for Foreign Policy Research and graduate work at its parent school, the Johns Hopkins School of Advanced International Studies. I had mistakenly thought that the study of "international relations" would be the study of the causes of war and that those involved in it would have the passionate discipline I associated with the Carnegie Endowment's many-volumed series on the consequences of World War I. At those places I learned instead about the cold war and the corruption of scholarship in the service of government, which seemed to me then its worst effect. The men who worked at the research center were not anti-Communist emigres, like the cluster around Strausz-Hupe at Pennsylvania, or nuclear rationalists like the men at Rand and later the Hudson Institute, though they published in these fields from time to time to keep their oars in the swamps. They were saved from obvious extremism,

I think, by their semi-aristocratic or in some cases western European or British origins. They seemed to be the last of a generation of European-oriented gentlemen-scholar-diplomats, with closer ties to the State Department than to the Pentagon or the CIA. Thus they were the strategists of NATO and of European integration, the exponents of "neutralism" in the "emerging nations." Many of them were "former" one-things hoping to be "future" something-elses, if administrations changed. Christian Herter was there periodically, for example, and Gerard C. Smith, a former secretary and assistant secretary of state (Smith subsequently became head of the arms control agency) and C.B. Marshall, a former policy advisor to Harry Truman: all contributing architects of executors of the cold war. There was also a double "former" (and a double archetype), a "former" CIA employee who had been a "former" professor of renaissance history before he got caught up in the OSS. Like the spy who came in from the cold, he was rumored to have been dismissed from the CIA for drinking.

The work of the Center's "scholar-practitioners"—that is what they called themselves—seemed to me more boring, badly written, and superficial than sordid, and I disliked them for nonintellectual reasons. The nicest person there, the youngest son of one of America's leading millionaire-ambassadorial families, put a shotgun to his head that year, presumably for reasons having nothing to do with politics. The other men seemed egotistical, anti-semitic, and what I would now call sexist. The last two, particularly, were a surprise. I know I was sheltered, but I had not run into these attitudes among "intellectuals" before. The men used the women for rehearsing their speeches, recording their observations at conferences, telephoning their wives, and balancing their bank accounts. They did not notice, respect, or encourage the competence of the subordinate—that is to say female—staff. I see now that this was not part of their job, as it had been the job of my teachers. But I thought at the time and still think it is simply something nice people do for one another when some have position and resources and some do not. I also thought it was a hell of a way to run an organization. Most of the women on the staff were, like myself, social mongrels. The men gave preferential treatment to a contemporary of mine working there that year, a Radcliffe graduate with no interest in politics. L. had gone to an eastern finishing school and was from a well-known family. Her love was fine arts; later she studied architecture. but she was part of a Georgetown culture and I was not. I learned from innumerable signs—her invitations to cocktails at my boss's house, her more delicate Christmas presents, the greater deference paid her around the Center—that there was in fact a social establishment somehow linked up with political control and that no matter what I might do I would never be a part of it.

More important to me was the professor with whom I studied Soviet foreign policy at the Hopkins school. He worked at the time in the Russian section of the State Department's Bureau of Intelligence and Research and next at the Nixon White House, where he turned up in the papers as one of the men Kissinger ordered bugged. He now holds a high position in another department. I liked this man and he liked me. He was not a snob, and I could see that his relations with others around the Center were somehow afflicted by a streak of mongrelism in his ancestry that paralleled mine, though I never figured out exactly what it was. But he was the first contact I ever had with a political intelligence wholly divorced from humane ends: or, more precisely, attached to a narrow chauvinistic base whose defense was more important than the truth. He was an "expert" on the Soviet Union as my college teachers, perhaps more so, at least in the Kremlinological sense then in vogue. But unlike my teachers he seemed scarcely to grant the Russians the right to exist. He was not moved, as we had been, by the monumental undertakings of the men and women who made the Revolution. Russia to him was a wily enemy; his work an interesting intellectual chase.

I suppose this is obvious now that the ties between government and scholarship have been described and discredited. It was harder to understand then. My job carried with it a certain amount of local prestige as well as the approval of the college professors who had helped me get it. I could not grasp what it was I didn't like, but I felt uneasy, bored, sullied. When a year was up, I quit. I worked briefly for the *Washington Post* then took a job as a political reporter for *Science*. I became friendly with a group of people—more or less the left wing of the Kennedy administration—who were about to found the Institute for Policy Studies as an antidote to government-funded research groups. I married one of its founders. We spent the missile crisis together, the women, come to think of it, making coffee and setting the table, the men trying to figure out by what chain of who-knows-who they could reach the higher authorities with their proposals and demands. I met I.F. Stone and James R. Newman who alone of all the adults I encountered seemed to know something worth learning and to stand for something worth becoming. I worked locally in the civil rights movement and helped raise money during Mississippi Summer. I was uncomfortable giving cocktail parties instead of working in the South. Stokely Carmichael called me "ma'am" in my own house when I was about 24, and I thought he saw my confusion and was being purposefully malevolent, like Genet's Blacks. He probably was. SNCC workers stayed with us often in their periods of cooling out from the South, but I was a hostess, not a comrade. I cooked a lot and felt guilty. Marriage and a new job had enlarged my income and affected my style of living, and it troubled me. I was fascinated with my new work as a journalist. But I felt restless and old and in some kind of emotional and moral jeopardy.

Movement I: Attitudes

I said people entered the movement at different times. The change in my life came with the Free Speech Movement. I spent six weeks in Berkeley in the spring of 1965, after the major incidents of the FSM but while its spirits and energies were relatively intact. Two things were especially powerful. In Berkeley, everyone was young. My Italian knit suits and grown-up pocketbooks and high-heeled shoes and leather briefcases, and the grey coats and black ties and professional styles of my Washington friends, suddenly seemed to me like the disguises of people trying to sneak into middle age unnoticed. In the streets and cafes of Berkeley, people walked with a bounce, dressed roughly, carried their babies in canvas sacks on their backs or breasts. Perhaps it was the ancient attraction of Bohemia. All I knew was that I felt at home.

More important, I think, I discovered that the students were "right." I was there as a reporter, a role I liked till then. In my work in Washington I frequently felt partisan, but I had learned the trick of a journalistic even-hand, and most of the institutions and events I covered interested me chiefly intellectually. But the FSM's analysis was as convincing to me as its character was compelling. One of its pamphlets seared itself into my brain. The university was controlled by "business regents" representing "the Bank of America, three other big banks and a few smaller ones; two oil companies; three aircraft manufacturers, two shipping lines, two airlines; a trucking line and two railways; two giant utilities; several chain stores; two publishing empires; half the [California] food-packing industry; and hundreds of thousands of acres of irrigated farmland." I interviewed these gentlemen, who sat in large oak-paneled offices beneath their own portraits. I could not doubt that they were running the university in the interests of California's economic development, nor that they intended the graduates of the system to fill the slots in their own empires. Their opposition to political activity among the students (for, remember, that was the issue that created the FSM) had to be an attempt to maintain a status quo favorable to themselves. Furthermore, there was little difference of opinion between Clark Kerr and Mario Savio on this point. They agreed that the University of California was a vast business that had little to do with education. Scholarship was merely tolerated and scholars were dependent upon perpetuating the tolerance: hence their wailings about "the destruction of a great university," hence their wafflings, hence their refusal to support tactics aimed at securing ends in which they claimed to believe, hence hypocrisy. That whole package—business-cum-degrading-ideological-rationalization—was liberalism. For the first time, I think, I understood what the blacks in the Mississippi Freedom Democratic Party had seen at Atlantic City the previous summer. Liberalism was a mute, inglorious lie. From being an accolade, it became an epithet. More than that. Politics and morality had their first conjunction in my mind. There might be the opportunity—even the necessity—to take sides in my lifetime. It was a powerful conversion.

One night before I left Berkeley I interviewed a leader of the FSM. He was glad I saw what I saw, but warned me not to be misled by the relative innocence of the FSM's language. A lot of it was still liberal reformism, he said, a constitutional or Kerensky phase or front. What the FSM was really about was revolution. He told me about SDS, how all over the country young people were moving into ghetto communities to organize the people into community unions that would become a base from which to challenge established power. He said the war in Indochina was growing worse, and these people were opposed to it. He showed me a picture of one such group, I think in Texas, that had appeared in that day's *New York Times*. They were sitting in some basement, in shirtsleeves, their faces intelligent and intense. I wanted them to become my friends.

By the time I became involved in the movement it was already completing the phase which had produced the Port Huron statement and inspired early SDS: the period which is now usually seen as having been capable of producing a fresh understanding of America, and a new strategy for change. The movement's departure from that phase is referred to in many ways; and its labels, its causes, and the policies that belong to each of its sequences, are categorized somewhat differently.[1] In the broadest sense the spans are seen to be from liberalism to radicalism, or from reform to revolution. But regardless of how these transitions are named, most people seem to agree that there is a first stage of the movement that is fresh and "American" and vigorous and full of potential, and a second stage that proved to be sectarian, irrelevant, and self-destructive. Most people seem also to agree that this change is somehow, more or less, bound up with the movement's disintegration. I want to turn this theory around and around and look at it from many points of view, as well as I can understand it, because it is clearly the central question of the movement. Since the "it," the "change," the "transition," is not really a single thing but a process—a combination of some executive decisions, some intellectual analyses, certain experiences, a long period of time, and the diffusion of beliefs among great numbers of people—its causes and its effects are all tied up with each other. One trouble with many of the analyses is that they assume that errors of radical judgment followed each other like synapses along some intellectual spinal column. I think "it" happened for a more thickly tangled web of reasons. But I think it is important to understand first that the "sectarianism" usually attributed to the later sixties—to Progressive Labor and to the declining SDS and Weathermen—is less significant than the fact that the movement as a whole was sectarian in a broad sense as soon as it defined itself as revolutionary.

In 1965 there were several marches in Washington against the war. At the first Paul Potter said we had to "name the system" we were dwelling in; at another, Carl Oglesby gave it a name: "corporate liberalism." In his book, *A Name for Ourselves*, Potter says he wished at the time the christening had not come so readily:

> What I meant to say in 1965, and what I think Oglesby meant to say as well, was that we needed a name to describe what was wrong with America that had authentic political content for us. I did not fail to call the system capitalist because I was a coward or an opportunist. I refused to call it capitalism because capitalism was for me and my generation an inadequate description of the evils of America—a hollow dead word tied to the thirties and a movement that had used it freely but apparently without comprehending it.
>
> I talked about the system not because I was afraid of the term capitalism but because I wanted ambiguity, because I sensed that there was something new afoot in the world that we were part of that made the rejection of the old terminology part of the new hope for radical change. I was disappointed in Oglesby's speech not because I disagreed with it (I thought it was brilliant) but because it sacrificed the ambiguity which I felt was such an important part of our movement for a term—corporate liberalism—that didn't particularly stir me.

Oglesby, writing in *Liberation* in 1969 (August-September), was thinking similarly. He asks the question, "Why did the white student Left so quickly abandon its liberal or reformist criticism of the war as policy and substitute its radical criticism of the war as the result of an imperialist structure?—a process he furthered in the corporate liberalism speech which he describes as using, without knowing it, "all the paraphernalia of an anti-imperialist critique." He argues that the shift had to occur:

> (a) because there was no way to resist the truth of the war, no way, that is, to avoid imperialism; and (b) because once the policy critique of the war had been supplanted by the structural critique of empire, all political therapies short of socialist revolution appeared to become senseless; and (c) because the necessity of a revolutionary strategy was, in effect, the same thing as the necessity of Marxism-Leninism. There was—and is—no other coherent, integrative, and explicit philosophy of revolution.

I think Oglesby's analysis correctly and simply states the movement's course, and I wish Potter had said at the time what he said later. It would have been useful to know that others had their doubts. Marxism-Leninism, or rather the muddied versions of it from which we drew our slogans and tactics, did not make much space for political action in America despite the fact that in some ways it did correspond to what we saw. Marxism offered a theory of the system; Leninism a set of precepts for right behavior within a radical movement. The disease and the cure. Neither offered guidelines to useful political activity along the way to rehabilitation. Once we took up this "only available revolutionary ideology" we lost the impulse to develop another.

Nonetheless I think this description locates the source of the movement's political evolution too mechanically and too much within the leadership. As a group, as a generation, we were romantic, involved with images of revolution, dazzled by abstract ideas. By 1965 we also had evidence. We had counted toilets in Cambridge, Maryland; exposed the profiteering of drug manufacturers; harangued the welfare departments of a dozen cities on behalf of the neighbors we had joined in the ghettos. We had seen monks burn and Diem fall and the war go on unchanged. We were young and free and intelligent, and we had to try to understand the meaning beyond the apparent facts and numbers and chronicles. In grasping for theory we were only trying to understand what we in fact saw. The phrases of our spokesmen fell on ready ears. That Marxism had been so inaccessible to so many young people, that the United States had forcefully opposed every revolution that had occurred since the eighteenth century: all that only increased the alchemical magic of our discovery. Eureka: we have found the formula. And, damaging though it became, I think in some ways the formula suited us. It was, curiously, apolitical and elitist. Because revolution was effectively impossible one did not have to dirty one's hands in compromise, nor mingle much with the hoi polloi (meaning: the middle class; the un-Chosen) along the way. And it was also ahistorical and smug, since it mistook revolution, a rare historical event, for a moral choice. I do not think that we as a movement wanted to hook into the American political system and miscalculated, but that at some level we did not want to do so. John Brown is a good symbol for us. At one point he wanted to run a school for Negroes but he came to find the idea *too small*: he had to attack Harper's Ferry.

By "sectarian" then, I mean something broad: being "revolutionary." Using language most Americans did not understand, and tactics that they feared, on behalf of a goal they did not desire. I think this impulse had many roots. With objectivity it could have been overcome. But our inability to come up with fresh perceptions fed on itself. For one thing, by that time we hated intellectuals. This was neither irrational nor unjustified. The best advertised intellectuals and academicians of the decade were in fact shallow and discredited, and every month brought fresh evidence of the extent of their corruption. We hated their class position and their defense of it: exchanging truth for power, they also sullied truth. But if our hatred was not irrational it was unfortunate, for by hating thinkers we came to hate thinking. Once we saw the social abuses of "standards"—the connection, for example, between educational testing and lifelong tracking, or between class and race, on the one hand, and "approved" grammar on the other—we were left without any standards to apply. Logic, evidence, proofs—the tools of our training—came to seem attributes of social class alone, therefore immoral, therefore useless. This is the true source, I think, of our apparent anti-rationalism; the reason we filled our magazines and speeches and lives with half-developed ideas and poorly demonstrated theories and charges that alienated as many people as they drew and left the majority indifferent. It was almost as if illiteracy was the proof of our transcendence, our escape from the stigma of class. The poisoning of standards is also related, I think, to the complaints of nihilism and "programlessness" brought against us in the later sixties in connection, among other things, with the rebellions at universities. It was difficult to think constructively about "salvaging" the "good parts of the university" because we genuinely could not see what these might be; just as we could not see that schools, whatever stamping, molding, and tracking they might be doing, still offered the only point of entry into the system for blacks and many others. Thus at the same moment that we were exposing the cultural imperialism of the institutions and their curricula, black people were struggling for open admissions. Our Marxism, such as it was, was insufficiently dialectical, and we were not detached enough to see the roots of these anomalies and attempt to eradicate them.

We became anti-cultural for the same reason we became anti-university: because "culture" equaled the Lincoln or Kennedy centers, expensive midtown mausoleums catering to a selfish class. Symphony halls across America were filled with bigots who drove to concerts through blighted downtown areas in their air-conditioned sedans with their doors locked, and went home feeling sorry for *themselves*. It was as hard to see a human function for their art as it was to see anything worth saving in the schools: an East Side anarchist street gang piled Lincoln Center with trash. Some of us adopted the music and culture of the blacks, awkwardly; later we created our own, the "youth culture," or had the illusion of creating it, and it certainly widened our connections with other young people until it too became visibly corrupt. Youth culture was a great romance: music, energy, drugs, a cultural disguise. But it was part of our revolutionary fantasy: we were guerrillas among the people, "fish in the sea." Patton's nephew attended the premiere of *Patton* with long hair and we saw militarism crumbling. We forgot that America could support any lifestyle, as long as it used money as its medium of exchange.

Our revolutionary politics made it difficult for us to respect the role of civil liberties in America: again, as in the case of the universities, a justified and explicable perception that had a negative effect. By our logic, no major agency of a capitalist society could be other than the instrument of its ruling class. This made it difficult, in our literature and propaganda, to clarify the relationship between the judiciary and other powers of the state. It also made it difficult to interpret victories in the courts when they occurred, except by romanticizing "the people"—i.e., the juries. The ideology of the ACLU—used and vilified in about equal measure throughout the 1960s—seemed morally distasteful and politically impotent. What is the function of free speech in a country where neither words nor proofs have any effect on a policy of murder? "To defend to the death . . ." was Enlightenment bullshit. We wanted people to support us because we were

87

right. Because we could see the branches of liberty (in the big trials and the many smaller ones, the harassment of our newspapers and leaders, the violence of the police), because we could see, above all, the persecution of moral men and women for brave acts that only a criminal society would have made necessary, we dismissed the principles. We remained hostile to the idea that we should be judged by a constitutional system so plainly corrupt: though perhaps the reaction was as much to judgment as it was to corruption. In any case the conviction of being right and the tactics such as disruption of speeches that followed from it helped make the movement seem dangerous and incomprehensible to millions of men and women who did not understand the pseudo-Marcuseanism on which it was based, and who, whatever they will or will not accept in the name of national security, would not tolerate a suspension of the Bill of Rights by the left.

Thus the change in the movement from opposing particular policies to identifying and opposing "the system" was bound up with our political isolation. It also limited our tactics. "The system" is difficult to attack because, although it is everywhere, it is difficult to locate. It is easy to look both ridiculous and violent when you attack the symbols you think represent it—trustees, boards of directors, the Council on Foreign Relations, defense secretaries—because even though they stand for it, are part of it, administer it, they are not exactly "it." They appear as persons protected by normal rules of property and civility, and their opponents as vandals. They are personally immune to attacks because of the baggies they live in: their own ideologies, their estates, the endless company of like-minded people, their power. Even if they were not immune, their individual conversions would solve nothing. This problem, like the others, was real. It was not a result of the distortion of our intellects or perception, and it was self-reinforcing. We had a rough idea where power was, but we couldn't get to it. Representative government implied conventional—electoral—political tactics, but these did not work. The energies controlling the society appeared to be individual family wealth, giant corporations, new technology, the military establishment, and bureaucracy. A "representative" Congress would have its seats filled with file cabinets, Xerox copiers, fastback autos, missiles, anti-missiles, brigadier generals, oil rigs, and bananas, with a few small-time get-rich-quickers and admen on the sides. Or you could turn that idea upside down and say the government did represent those forces, precisely those forces, but it led to the same conclusion. Either way, reform by traditional means seemed impossible and human votes to have no effect. Watergate is the first restatement of identifiable responsibility for anything governmental in a long time, and that is responsibility only for the corrupt fringe of the system and not its corrupt heart. Since the problem was structurally connected with the unbalanced growth of Executive power, in theory it could be changed by a refreshed Congress attempting to make its policies and the tangible world connect. But Congress was stone dead during the life of the movement, and it is not clear, as this is written, whether its boldness around the edges of Watergate is anything more than playtime: Lilliputians teasing a fallen Gulliver who is bound to rise again. We correctly understood that in watching conventional politics we were watching a puppet show, but we could not name or capture the puppeteer. We could not invent tactics that corresponded in a convincing way to what it was that we did understand.

Outside of the factional leadership of the movement there was no serious attempt to apply the principles of Marxism-Leninism or to follow its precepts. But there was widespread among the rest of us a kind of half-baked lower-case marxism, or some kind of commonly held analysis that we thought was "Marxism." The analysis gave us several ideas that I think impeded the development of a productive left political movement.

The first was the idea of *false consciousness*. In the wrong hands, which were ours, or perhaps in the wrong times, this idea has terrible political consequences. There may be times in history when societies collapse, when such an abstraction helps enlighten people, meshes with their lives, and lifts them to a new plane of understanding. But ours was not such a time. We used "false consciousness" cheaply, to explain away the inconvenient phenomenon that Americans were in fact bound up with the culture and the system. Our failure to admit that was the source of the idea that they could be dislodged in single, dramatic acts of terror or, for instance, in the Weatherpeople's "jailbreaks." It is a useless idea for explaining why people do what they do; why people responded to George Wallace, why the hardhats marched on Wall Street, why more workers tolerate speed-ups than resist them, why most people still get up in the morning and go to work, why flags fly from every school and firehouse in every town across America, why in June 1973, 45 percent of the people said they would vote again for Richard Nixon. The people who do these things most likely do have "false consciousness" in the sense that they do not understand the theoretical relationship between advanced capitalism and the war economy, between the war economy and inflation, or between inflation and the decay of public services. They certainly have false consciousness in the sense that they do not understand the idea of false consciousness. But they may or may not have "false consciousness" in the sense that they feel dissatisfied, realize they are working for the Man and not for themselves, understand that few are rich and many are poor or struggling. Usually they do realize these things. But the point is they choose to live with them and except in an acute situation (layoffs, or inflation, or unemployment on a grand scale) they are likely to continue to do so. Thus in terms of what men and women can expect to accomplish or experience, how they want to spend their time on earth, they do not have false consciousness at all. If anyone has it it is radicals who mistake the abstraction for the reality. Furthermore, when used on a personal basis, the idea becomes both elitist and insulting. We tended to think that being "poor," being a "worker," being "black" was the whole identity of a human being. A person's human-ness is never defined solely by his or her economic position and to think that it is is to deny that they have any power of choice. Once last winter I was arguing about the war with a black friend who grew up in Bedford-Stuyvesant. I said: "Blacks are dying in Vietnam in disproportionate numbers." He said: "Right, but they are also killing in disproportionate numbers." I meant: poor blacks, I feel sorry for you, victims again. He meant: it is as wrong for blacks to kill in this war as it is for whites. My radicalism had become charity. We were always telling people, or at least implying, that if they didn't agree with us they were "victims of the system," or "brainwashed." We didn't respect most people, or the conclusions they drew from their own experience. On the whole we did not understand what their experience was, only about what our idea of their experience was. This was equally true of the radical women's movement as of the "male-dominated left." Women have "false consciousness" if they fail to perceive their enslavement and seize the time for their liberation. The problem with this idea is that it mistakes the connection between "consciousness" and life. Because ideas are powerful for us we assume they will move people out of conditions to which they are really tied, or in which they feel secure. But ideas do not go deeply enough. "Consciousness" not coincident with immediate material interests will not produce a revolutionary movement.

Another idea from which we suffered, I think, was a kind of *false internationalism*. Revolutionary imperialism is at least as old as the American revolution. At least since then, revolutionaries have had international identities, participated in an international revolutionary culture. Russia was not the first to make use of this phenomenon, only the most theoretically explicit and the best organized. Our internationalism took the form of third world rhetoric, Cuba-philism, later Maoism We assumed our identification with the third world countries was self-evidently justified because we had a common enemy: U.S. imperialism. They could not be free until we were, and vice versa. Our feelings had much in common with the Russia-inspired radicalism of the twenties and thirties, mainly, I think, in that the justification for the movement depended in both cases on the imminence and importance and validity of a worldwide revolutionary upheaval. It is easy to see now that Russian or Communist radicalism was not helpful to the long-run work of identifying problems in American society; easy to see that it was an escape that built little, helped create false enemies to focus people's uneasiness (e.g., the Rosenbergs), and fed internal convulsions (like McCarthy) that led to the obscuring of real social issues. A lot of the energy of several radical generations was spent trapped in that circle or undoing its effects, all for the sake of restoring an inadequate liberal consensus that made it possible to begin radical work again but did not suggest what to do. I don't know why that happened to people in the twenties and thirties. Perhaps Russia was genuinely too interesting to resist; or perhaps, like us, the Red intellectuals then were too impressed by fancy ideas and too estranged from American themselves to be able to say, fine, that's what the Russians have to do, now what is our work in America? and so slid easily into emulation. Perhaps it is the idea of internationalism itself that is so attractive. Maybe it is just fun to travel.

But there was a phenomenon in our lives that corresponded to "I have seen the future and it works." It was widespread long before it was spelled out in the official ideology of, for instance, the Weathermen. We called it an "NLF high." Here is an example of how it worked. I went to Budapest in the fall of 1968 with a group of radicals mainly from the antiwar movement to meet with a delegation of North Vietnamese and Viet Cong. This was the second such meeting. A similar one had taken place in Bratislava, Czechoslovakia, the previous fall. There were innumerable smaller meetings between American radicals and Vietnamese. Many people went to Vietnam and many more began to go to Cuba. By 1970-71 there were trips to North Korea. Now there are trips to China.

In Budapest the Vietnamese cast an incredible magic. It was like being caught up in some splendid fairy tale of revolution peopled with live heroes and heroines. Each of them was wonderful: physically beautiful, warm, sensitive, smart. They had made enormous efforts to attend the meeting, some of them walking from liberated areas of the South to Hanoi where they took a train across Asia to Moscow to fly to us in Budapest. They wanted to work hard: to hear our impressions of the movement, politics, and the war, and to tell us what was happening in their country. They showed us pictures of their villages torn apart, spoke of the husbands and wives they knew or thought were dead, their imprisonments and tortures, their escapes. They told us of the times their tactics succeeded and the times they had failed. They seemed so real, so many-sided. One night, after a long working session, they entertained us in their embassy in the city with Vietnamese food and a display of their culture, song and dance. We sang back, ad hoc rock and whatever freedom songs by then did not sting too bitterly on our lips. We felt scruffy, a band of wanderers whom these elegant and loving warriors from a splendid and integrated culture were somehow forced to take seriously. The very form of the meeting, the earphones and translations and documents and toasts by our hosts, the Hungarian Communists, made us feel, however unworthily, like a government in exile. I remember one of the Americans leaping down the graceful steps of the old embassy building afterwards, saying "My god, I'll eat peanut butter the rest of my life if that's what it'll take to help these people be free." If we loved the Vietnamese, they also loved us. They thought we were the best America had to offer, brave dissenters in a country that was destroying theirs. They felt we *had* to help them end the war, and we felt it too. And it was true.

For weeks or months after we got home (usually weeks), we would know what we had to do. We would talk to friends whose spirits might be flagging, try to make speeches, plan more demonstrations, write. For a while we would be full of energy and our course would be clear. The first thing to do is stop the war; the rest could come later. But always there would be a crash, energy flowing out of us, whether it was being thrust back into sectarian fighting from which distance had allowed us a brief certainty about "priorities," or the objectively real difficulties of mobilizing actions that included a lot of Americans and had any effect on the war. Soon we would stop opening the brown envelopes that came from Hanoi, stop reading the newspapers, turn to other things: new projects or a rediscovery of private depression. Within a few months we would not even recognize all the Americans with whom we shared the trip.

That's an NLF high. The rhythm of a Cuba high appeared to be similar, except there the priority was even more difficult than "end the war." It was "smash imperialism." Foreign revolutionaries increased the pressure on us out of a combination of self-interest, frustration, and comradely good intentions. The political work that seemed to follow from meeting with the Vietnamese was antiwar work; the work that followed visits to Cuba seemed to be organizing more visits to Cuba. It is difficult even now to think of how "false internationalism" could be replaced by real internationalism. These trips gave us at least an intermittent sense that we were responsible for the brothers and sisters overseas being murdered or pauperized by America. At times they cut through our chauvinism and self-absorption. But they also fed our romanticism and our easy identification with other countries' heroes. We had very little discussion that I can recall about the real nature of foreign communism. The near-revolution in France in 1968 had little impact. Our internationalism was chiefly worshipful. We made little progress in discovering what the real relationship between a U.S. radical movement and foreign countries ought to be.

Two related ideas that we also used badly are the idea of *co-optation* and the idea of *repressive tolerance*: again a kind of diffused Marcuseanism that didn't particularly depend on having read his works. They led us into simplistic thinking about culture and politics and social institutions. We believed that no dissent is possible because anything you are allowed to do (that is permitted to do without being repressed) the society "wants" you to do. Whatever you think, you are still its instrument. "Co-optation" derailed any explicit, critical, or analytical ideas we might have had about American culture because anything cultural was merely its evidence, and interest in cultural criticism was in turn evidence of middle-class taste. It also paralyzed most political initiatives short of terror or disruption. The idea had to lead to a stance as far outside all existing institutions as possible. And it made it impossible to claim victories when they had in fact occurred because victory meant the consolidation of reform within a standing institution. The movement was good, a friend said, at snatching defeat from the jaws of victory. Thus again these abstractions reinforced our revolutionary isolation and alienated people for no particular purpose, because our revolutionism had not much content beyond throw-the-rascals-out, and made no practical difference. Nonetheless we submitted our thoughts and actions to periodic checkups for symptoms of co-optation as if to a mobile x-ray unit. That blemish of the brain was one of the known danger signals of revolutionary demise.

But perhaps our most serious error was our conception of the uses of *class analysis*. Obviously this is not a bad idea in itself. Understanding the class structure of a country is critical to any intelligent political activity inside it. But in America at the moment it is an enormous muddle. The reality is confusing and the theories are at odds. Middle-class workers labor on intellectual assembly lines. Factory workers live in garden apartments and own motorboats. There is an expense-account proletariat. Marxist theory escapes these confusions. It says that these distinctions, based on income level or lifestyle, are epiphenomenal. They are the categories of "bourgeois sociology" (this is true) and ipso facto incorrect. Marxist theory continues not only to define class but to predict its political activity solely on the basis of its relation to the means of production. This has a wonderful effect. Sometimes when I am puzzled I consult a small pamphlet by Ernest Mandel. For about 15 minutes I am happy and relieved. I understand the classes, forces, categories, tendencies, pushes, pulls, inevitabilities, certainties, and questions. But when I go outside and talk to people again, it all seems useless. When I talk to workers they tell me about their hunting camps, not their shops. This does not surprise the Marxists. They know that in America the middle class and the working class alike have been bought off by CorningWare and skimobiles. That is true enough, again, but the conclusion is not simple. Marx named the "proletariat" and for 60 years or more people acted as-if-they-were proletariat and in certain measure consonant with his laws. But capitalism has drastically changed. No matter how they are labeled in America by leftists the "masses" do not respond. This may be because, despite everything, there is still a sense—and a reality—of social mobility here. It may be that people's self-images are so controlled and shaped by the media that only those categories proposed by the establishment have any possibility of taking root. It may be that the correct categories have not been named. I suspect that the first is closest to the truth. If that is right, finding the correct categories (as well as locating the base for a strong social movement) depends on whether or not social mobility has in fact ceased to be real for a large number of people for a long enough period of time. It depends, in other words, on whether our overall economic analysis of the potential of capitalism is correct; on whether things will stay fixed long enough to permit revolution-enabling categories to solidify.

The movement did have a class base and authentic reason for rebellion. It must have had. It rebelled. And, as Keniston has pointed out, no event is as interesting as one every theorist has failed to predict. But the movement did not understand its own rebellion. We are either "the new working class" or, more cynically, "the new non-working class": it is the same class in the sense that the foreman and the lineman are the same class or the office manager and the file clerk are the same class: representing mainly a fringe of privilege that doesn't affect the underlying structure. Mandel-inspired observers would say that our disaffection is a product of the decline in unskilled jobs as a result of automation. This produces rebellion not just among students pushed into the job marked through training in a knowledge-factory for factory-like intellectual work, but among blacks pushed out of the job market as the skill level of the economy advances. By the logic of revolution, these two forces would eventually join up. Anarchist theoretician Murray Bookchin has a different view. His argument implies, I think, that the middle class has achieved its historic function (industrialization and liberalism) and has no more work to do. The children of the middle class are therefore in a sense classless, or part of an emerging group for whom class is not the factor that determines political direction. Our "revolutionary" aspect derives not from our class but from our rejection of it: "the traditional class struggle ceases to have revolutionary implications; it reveals itself as the physiology of the prevailing society, not as the labor pains of birth" (*Post-Scarcity Anarchism*). Revolution and social class are no longer precisely tied.

It seems to me that whatever class truths a revolution of the future might reveal, and regardless of whether the neo-Marxist and the anarchist taxonomies ever merge, the Mandelian analysis represents a large-scale truth about the economy and the Bookchin analysis expresses something about our subjective experience of it. The jobs the multiversity opens up may be essential to the economy as presently arranged; or they may be automated. In either case they are not personally essential to us. Our philosophy did not emerge because we are better people with a keener morality than our parents, but because we don't need money and are surfeited with goods. Our parents have the money for us if we should need it badly enough, and we will inherit the goods if it should just-so-happen that in our old age we should seek possessions, or even if not. Of course there are individual variations. A large-scale economic crisis could undercut these calculations even now. And, by the time the movement drew to a close, it had in fact expanded into working-class schools and communities where the relation to the economy was different. But by and large if we didn't get our money from our parents, we got it from the state through welfare, unemployment, and so forth, thus paradoxically subverting the needs of the state (assuming it needed to integrate us into the work force) through mechanisms it established to prevent rebellion in another era.

This rejection of class, or rejection of the duties historically associated with class, created a sense of placelessness. It was like living in space, beyond the reach of gravity. Subjectively we felt lost, discredited by privilege, and not capable according to our own ideology of being the "agent of change" we believed we needed. We had no pride in ourselves or expectations of a decent future, for the future reeked of technology and large-scale enterprise, or work and the necessity of work, and that never felt right. We felled our Tsar when Lyndon Johnson withdrew from the 1968 presidential race and it didn't make any difference. Throughout the decade we all knew better what we did not want than what we did. This confusion was the deepest source of our inability to put content into a social program with meaning for anyone including ourselves, a design that would convince any other group of people we had something to offer. We were too puzzled to imagine freely or act effectively, least of all on our own behalf. We were insulted when people linked our values with our position and said we were rich kids protesting who didn't understand; but in a sense of course they were right.

Feeling inexplicable, if not worthless, we began our search for an "agent of change." The results of our groping for a "vanguard" were, if history is gentle with us, ridiculous. Paul Potter, Kirkpatrick Sale, and others report that the hunt for a seed-carrier of revolution began early in the movement's history. I don't know for myself about the early period. But I know that by the time I became involved the movement was embarked on a desperate and absurd search for a "vanguard" class (or sometimes vanguard party) to be the "agent" of our revolution. We tried on every one we could think of: workers, the new working class, radical professionals, students as proletariat and students as professionals, GIs, blacks in general, the Panthers in particular, third world forces, street people, prisoners, and finally fragments of ourselves: women, gay women, gay men. I remember one of my friends who had transferred her energies to the women's movement waving a copy of Shulamith Firestone's *The Dialectics of Sex* at me and crying out "We have an analysis. At last we have an analysis." It reminded me of Peter Pan and Wendy: "We have a mother. At last we have a mother." We needed an "analysis" to survive the hostile implications of our own Marxism.

Our arguments were not genteel arguments as occur among academicians, for example, though there came to be as little cross-fertilization among them as between academic departments: a monograph here, a monograph there, or even long-range arguments: the Constitution was framed in the interests of the ruling classes or it wasn't: dialogue at an exalted level over a long period of time. Our ideas came and were discarded in a frenzy of conferences, manifestos, treaties, new projects, and alliances. Each carried with it a bewildering imperative, officially "strategic" but actually also moral, because it was necessary for us to know at every moment that our individual and group relation to the "vanguard" was the correct one. If white workers were the vanguard it was OK to take a factory job or organize in a white working-class community; if they were objectively reactionary it was blind to do so, probably self-serving, possibly retarding the course of history. If something new was afoot among the middle classes in America it made sense to organize doctors, lawyers, journalists; if not it was helping to perpetuate elitist notions about the likely sources of change. If students were the vanguard, campuses were justified battlegrounds; if not we were turning our backs on real people and real struggles. If blacks were the vanguard we were all in trouble because we were limited to false threats to liberate Bobby Seale from his New Haven jailhouse.

We thus had no "theory," no common understanding of where or who we were, only a confusing array of "theories" more divisive than unifying. For me the worst symbol of our confusion is Chicago, 1968. There we were, thousands of us, being beaten back by the Chicago police, pushed against the tall glass windows of the Hilton till our bodies made them crack. Running and stumbling to get away, maybe to regroup, half the crowd looked up at the police and soldiers, shot out their arms, and shouted "Heil Hitler." The other half of us waved our arms to the soldiers and shouted "Join us." In the middle of Chicago, at the nominating convention of one of America's two major parties, half of us thought we were in Germany and half of us thought we were in Russia. We carried on our ideological debate at the top of our lungs until they were filled with tear gas and the American soldiers and the Chicago police had scattered us away.

Movement II: Encounters

Life in the movement was difficult. Women think it was difficult because of male chauvinism. Gay men think it was difficult because they had to conceal their gayness. Refugees to the counter-culture think it was difficult because it was competitive, bureaucratic, authoritarian. People call one another bad names like "liberal," "opportunist," "sectarian," "egotist," "escapist," "counter-revolutionary." Worse, people call themselves some of those names. These things did not begin with the decay of the movement: they were present within it. Those were brutalizing years. We suffered as much at the hands of "friends" as we did at the hands of enemies. In my case, considerably more, since I was never physically hurt, beaten, or jailed but was always shredding my soul, hoping to come up with a new version of it that would meet the revolutionary test.

This is an important subject. I think personal unhappiness is the real reason most people left the movement. Yet it is hard to talk about honestly, for three reasons. First, it is too easy to be glib. One can say: "The movement mirrored America in its social relationships, power hunger, chauvinism; this is inevitable; who could expect such a society to breed decent revolutionaries?" and leave it at that. It is easy to say that the outside world was worse. Second, it is the aspect of the movement that will be most vulnerable to reinterpretation in time, as the pain and the ache of it recede. It is already the most vulnerable to autobiographical confusion: to a false distribution of "causes" between the mere act of growing up and the vocabulary in which growing up took place because of the moment it was, or is, in the life of our society. There's a lot of dirty laundry in those trunks full of city clothes I packed away in New York. Let the moths get them. Who wants to see those old things again? Arguing with myself, I have made all the qualifications I can make: no two people are alike; how do I know whether my history contains a profile? But I can see no way to avoid it or to escape into theory. We are the only source of historical and political evidence about this it will be possible to have.

Let me stop for a moment in the middle. I was having dinner over a year ago with a New York editor who had read a draft of this manuscript up to about this point. He said: "I don't understand exactly what you mean by 'entering the movement.' How did you enter it? Were you ever really in it? You were a 'committed journalist' (a deadly phrase, I thought, perhaps meaningless) but were you really 'in the movement'?" This is an interesting question because it reflects the strong sense of inauthenticity that being around the movement provoked. The only inviolate movement job description, I think, was "organizer," and the only secure institutional affiliation was SDS. Draft resistance was a doubtful category since it was thought to be moralistic rather than revolutionary. Antiwar work, including work with GIs, was OK or not depending on whether it rested on a "revolutionary"—that is, anti-imperialist—critique and was not corrupted by liberal alliances or pacifism. It was acceptable to work on underground papers or news services or for specialized research or service organizations such as Health-PAC or the North American Congress on Latin America. And it was always all right to be on trial or in jail, whatever the reason. But it was best to be an "organizer" of something. Nonetheless, despite the fact that unlike most others I usually had a professional job, I "knew" I was "in the movement." After 1965 my friends changed. They were "organizers" even if I was not; "worked full time" in movement organizations; had a history of radical activity and leadership going back to the early 1960s. I no longer saw my old friends, lost touch with the intellectuals I had been close to in Washington, and gradually with professional colleagues. If I did see these people, or "straight" friends still working in the universities, the gulfs between us were very great. I was divorced and my new lovers were all movement men. I don't know what the movement's directory would say even now to the editor's question. But psychologically and socially, and measured by the content of what I believed, for better or worse I was "in" it.

A lot of my time in the few years after I returned from Berkeley was spent dissolving the relationships with the conventional institutions to which I had been attached. My marriage went first. I suppose now that it would have gone anyway, in time, because I had not wanted in wholeheartedly enough and I knew it, but there was no women's movement then to help me understand the reasons I did not like being married. I felt guilty that I was not "satisfied" with my "good husband" and that I hated my "perfect house." I was failing myself in all my own images of womanhood, and I was in despair over the pain I was bringing to my husband, who did not deserve it. The conventional Washington psychiatrist to whom I took my bank account and my neuroses was no help. The substance of that analysis, if indeed there was any, has left no trace on my life. The shrink lived (I knew) in a big house in Chevy Chase. He received enormous fees. He had to have—clearly had to have—accepted very much about the culture I distrusted in order to be functioning at all. I charged my husband, as I charged the shrink, with all the sins of the bourgeoisie. He was "liberal" and I was not, anymore; he was clean shaven and academic and I wanted a lover who was a man of the people and the streets; he did not share my guilt at our large income or my way of expatiating the guilt, which was to turn our house into a hostel for the radicals who were more and more frequently passing through Washington. But that description is slightly false. I wanted "movement people" to stay at our house in part because one of them—and we all knew which one—was going to be my lover after we separated. My husband was no less open-handed than I; just reacting to the fantasies he could feel were all mixed up with the new ideas I was using against him. The truth is, of course, we were not divorced for "political reasons" in a narrow sense at all, but because marriage was intolerable to me for a thousand reasons I can only now begin to understand. I used having-left-him, having-given-up-a-bourgeois-household and so forth in fashioning my new image (just as I used psychoanalysis: he was repressed and I was not, of which the second part at least was certainly not true) and I suppose a lot of people believed me because it fit with what they wanted to think about these things. But it was not deeply true, and I suppose the people who knew me best always knew it.

At the same time my job at *Science* began to confuse me. *Science* is a prestigious scientific weekly, read widely in the science and technology-related academic and business communities, and throughout the government. Early in the 1960s, when federal support for science was rising, the magazine created a political news section to provide information for these communities. The section was developed chiefly by a talented journalist, Dan Greenberg, who stayed with it for many years. He established a wide scope for the news department, and an independence from the editorial board and from the publisher, the American Association for the Advancement of Science, that is unusual in the relations between reporters and magazines, or reporters and newspapers, in this country. By the time I began work, in 1963, it was well established that the editor would not usually know in advance what the news department was writing about, and would rarely even read our material before publication. It simply went from our typewriters to the printer, stopping off down the hall for copy editing only. Occasionally on very controversial issues (reports on scandals internal to the scientific world, which Dan usually wrote; those that I did were politically controversial outside the scientific community) the editor, a geophysicist named Philip Abelson, would check the material, become alarmed, and urge us to alter or suppress it. But for as long as I was there, and I believe until Dan left, when these issues arose they were invariably decided in our favor. In tense moments Dan would threaten (sincerely) to resign, and always got his way. The news department itself was growing while I was there. At first I was an apprentice; later a member of a community of equals.

Gradually I became the house radical. I went to Berkeley every other year after my first visit, and reported on other student rebellions. I spent two weeks at Howard Levy's court martial. I went to New York when new documents were uncovered that the defense hoped would lead to the freeing of Morton Sobell. I met Ralph Nader and reviewed his book in the long-ago days before he became a corporation. I spent a long time in Denver to describe the development of one of the first neighborhood health centers under the poverty program. I followed the spastic resurrection of HUAC in its attempted entrapment of Chicago physician Jeremiah Stamler, and kept a growly watch over possible lapses into McCarthyism of other governmental and nongovernmental committees and agencies. I wrote about secret research, the CIA, the imperial uses of anthropology. I covered the AMA. Before I left I spent four months in research and writing on the extensive U.S. development of chemical and biological weapons. In all these things the support from the magazine was unquestioned: money for travel, expenses, phones, no questions asked, all the time necessary to do a decent job, and the space needed to report the results freely. Of course the AAAS was rich, and these reports were popular, but it also seems to me now—and seemed then—to have been a miracle of tact and restraint on the part of Abelson, who did not agree at all with what I wrote and had to defend its publication to outsiders. There is also no doubt that whatever I and others wrote gained incalculably in publicity and credibility from the prestige of the AAAS.

But something was coming to seem artificial to me about the role. Each morning I would come in and read my mail, or leaf through articles with my name on them, and I would know for a little while who I was. Recently I saw a friend, who was feeling low, check out his contributions to humanity in the *Encyclopedia Britannica*, and I could see that he was looking in a mirror for his mind in the same way. But having a public identity made me uncomfortable as well. I knew I needed it, and knew that I needed not to need it at the same time. It was hard to acknowledge to myself or my movement friends how much my "self" was entangled with my by-line, but I recognized it somewhere and admired my friends all the more for their obscurity, for their not-needing that kind of prop. Once, when I visited the Newark SDS project (which I always had vague intentions to join), a woman who was later a friend said: "You mean you'd give all that up and work with us?" Airily, with the proper political spirit, I said, of course, it means nothing (implying: "my work is not for myself; only the cause matters"). But of course that was not true. It was much more difficult than that to give it up.

I felt that the work was beginning to hold me back as a writer, which was perhaps true, and that it was not useful work, which was not true. The political idea that I held then was a translation into my own situation of the general idea that "the people"—masses—would move the nation. I felt it was useless to provide information to the elite readers of *Science*. It was also my variant of the agent-of-change syndrome. I didn't know who it was; but I was pretty sure who it wasn't. The scientists' protest against chemical and biological weapons, growing at that time, came to seem disreputable to me because it was based on knowing-people-in-Washington, petitions of famous prizewinners, and high-level manipulations that had nothing to do with "the people." It was made up of the very stuff of privilege. I disliked it also because it was "about" CBW instead of "about" broader issues. It still repels me that the scientists at one time were afraid to taint their "respectable" protest against CBW with an indictment of the war, let alone the forces behind the war. I was also discouraged with the tactical premise on which the narrow protests were based. My own experience writing about CBW was nearly paralyzing. My articles received a great deal of publicity when they appeared, and they were among the foundations on which the attack on the CBW arsenal a few years later stood. But in working on them I had seen how inseparable the positive spirit and institutions that feed scientific research are from their own debasement, and I felt a growing disgust for people who could have anything to do with science at all, even as reformers. I could not understand how abolishing CBW was going to help. One of the same issues that carried my articles carried an early report on the plan for an electronic barrier in Vietnam. It made my work seem ridiculous. We could make campaigns out of individual evils one after another till we died, and fool ourselves and others about it, and gain money and prestige from the effort. To do so was nonetheless a lie. I joined with my friends in thinking we had to find a way to fight the system.

Now I am not sure whether these political ideas were right or wrong, or perhaps just too shallow to be either. At the least, they were or ought to have been part of a much larger question of strategy and goals. But I know I did not hold them autonomously. They were mixed up with other things: with personal depression, insecurity, and the attractiveness of a new lifestyle. I can see now that there are some fine people in the scientists' movement, men (usually) who use their energies and resources imaginatively, and whose conviction is as genuine as that of any kid who trashed the windows of the Bank of America, and certainly as useful. Not many, but some. But I could not see that then. I am thinking of one physician who has consistently used the authority and reputation gained from association with powerful and prestigious institutions on behalf of radicals at home and revolutionaries abroad, and against the destruction of human life and its environment everywhere. Yet there were several years when seeing this person, or thinking of him, made me uncomfortable. He had not given up his jobs in powerful institutions and was not planning to. He had not "joined the movement." He was working alone or trying to use influence in professional circles. It made no sense to me.

I can see now that the difference between Doctor X and many of my other acquaintances and friends has not only to do with political strategy and revolutionary ideas, but with the location or source of a person's moral impulses, and with their age, economic position, and domestic responsibilities. I felt too sullied at some point by my participation in the "establishment" to be able to continue doing it, on whatever liberal terms. I felt like a bad person. I could not feel moral until my ties were cut and I was working or associating with others who could assure me that what I was doing was clean. The movement was a kind of moral cover. It covered self-distrust with political ideas about which constituencies were worth working for, both in a moral and in a revolutionary sense. Doctor X and other stable adults evidently did not need this disguise. Ideology follows emotions just as trade follows the flag. Their choice of constituency did not, as I once thought, make their work less useful or corrode their souls.

My "career" was in excellent shape. I received frequent invitations to write for other magazines and make speeches. The offers usually came in the form of suggesting that I rewrite material (often on medical care or the drug industry) that I had already written for *Science*. But it never occurred to me not to distrust the motives of the people and the institutions making them. I thought they were asking me to repeat myself, like all the professional and journalistic specialists whose one insight appeared one week in the *New Republic*, the next in the *New York Times Magazine*, and the next month in

Harper's, sanitized and boring. I thought they were vultures, hungry for the carcasses of dead ideas. And I felt they were agents of a partly conscious cultural plot to obstruct the emergence of people capable of general radical inquiry by latching their egos and their pocketbooks to expertise: in my case, health politics. I felt flattered, but I also felt insulted and in danger of being used. I would not let them get me. I was conscious of a choice. I could become a chic journalist—and therefore trivial—or I could refuse. I refused. Again, it all had a political logic, it had a line. Making it in America could be neither worthy nor satisfying. The medium is the message, and the media services the status quo regardless of what its pages or images contain. But it is also true that I did not trust myself or my motives: that I pulled away because the weight of a public identity was too heavy for me: and in part it was important to me as a woman not to succeed in too flashy a fashion. I had the idea that I wanted to be loved for myself alone, whatever that would mean, and I stripped away my external activities in part to see if anyone would be interested in what was left. Thus leaving *Science* to participate more fully in the movement was not a simple thing, not a triumph of revolutionary mortality over careerism, not all a forward or positive motion in my life, though in many ways it was liberating. It was very mixed up, even at the beginning.

It was hard, if not impossible, to find work to do or a way to live that corresponded to this combination of personal need and political fantasy. My inner life would take years to straighten itself out. To find political work that got at the heart of the problem—the "system"—was difficult objectively, at best, and was made more so because my self-respect was so dependent on it. Being in the movement was a state of not-being in straight society. But it was also like being ordained as a preacher and not winning a congregation: a calling but not a job. I wanted to leave Washington, to escape my marriage and the confused affairs that followed it, the censorious intolerance of former friends whose own marriages wobbled more uneasily whenever another young bride or bridegroom flew the coop. My political motives were real. My conclusions about America were based on evidence, based on the stuff of my life since college. They were the same conclusions my friends had reached in the South, or in ghettos, or in the universities. I felt shocked, as they did, by what I had learned about America and bitter and ashamed to be identified with it. I wanted to help bring the machine to a stop. But I also had an enormous private agenda, a warehouseful of emotional baggage so heavy it weighted me down. It was mixed up with my family, with my short-circuited professional life, with being female. When I did find the state of being that corresponded to the greatest proportion of what was really going on inside me, that state turned out to be passivity. There was no burst of revolutionary energy, and no clarity, only a heavy physical torpor that went on for years and was made worse by the fact that it contradicted my principles and therefore had to be disguised.

I moved with a current lover, a fellow radical-outcast from Washington, into a foolishly expensive Greenwich Village apartment, a remnant of some domestic fantasy we could neither meet nor shake. It was late 1967, early 1968. Tom Hayden and Rennie Davis and a few others were already planning a major national action for the Democratic Convention. Sometimes there were meetings about it in my apartment, and I attended huge national meetings elsewhere. People connected with it, and other activities, frequently slept in my apartment. These are the days and nights I remember when I think about the question of "authenticity." I can't remember, or perhaps never knew, how those people began staying there or why they did (except for its location) or what they thought of me. We were not friends. I felt still like the liberal hostess, a role I thought I had left in Washington. I frequently did not understand the conversations and I always felt judged, felt that I-wasn't-doing-anything, had not won my bars or stripes in the ghettos or in combat, and that I was privately despised as obviously "bourgeois." My relationships with some of the women were better, but the women were either as awesome as the men (at least in my eyes, if not in their own, because they were involved in the same brave things) or else they belonged to the men, and were silent. With them, too, I felt scared and inauthentic. My biggest problems were my difficulty working, preoccupation with my personal life, and confusion, now that I was "inside," about what movement politics were and what they meant. I kept this to myself. Mostly, I found that I did not understand what the issues were or how people were conceiving them. I remember clearly that in a pre-Chicago meeting to which I had been urged to go, people were battling over whether a "national action" would disrupt "local organizing" and that was very important to the people who were there. But I had no experience in thinking about these questions and no opinions. I was not familiar with the realities to which they referred. In a sense I felt that from being an "expert" I had become a dunce.

My repertorial spirit vanished down some cloggy drainpipe. Instead of finding out what I did think, I spent my energy trying to find out what I was supposed to think. It seemed the only safe course. This was not particular to me. It was also a general problem. It was as if the only way our vague political feelings about revolution and the system could express themselves was in general rhetorical language, and it was very important to say the right combination of words, have the right view. The decay of speech seemed to follow the decade. When Tom Hayden wrote his book on Newark, for example, he was still describing events clearly and patiently, and his language was powerful. But the tendency to dogma was flowering: perhaps people adopted it in some ratio to their own uncertainty. I don't know. I don't know if other people felt as fraudulent and therefore guilty as I did. But it was like living in the stale joke about stale jokes: someone says "12" and the inmates laugh. We said "liberal" and "co-optation" or "chauvinist" and assumed a posture toward those postures, our posture a knowing look, a glance, a nod of the head that we knew or assumed referred to a common source.

The problem of language is complex. Everyone has a moment or moments, flashes of illumination, when we understand what these words, usually "isms," might mean. We understand that America is *really racist* because we can see it in ourselves or respond to a description in a new book. We understand that women *are really oppressed* because reinterpreting our lives in that way gives logic to previously puzzling experience, makes the facts and feelings of our intimidation cohere. A powerful poem or photograph can crash through our dullness and we can feel that *imperialism* is killing babies. A visit home can convince us that, whatever they think, *capitalism* has sapped our families. Whether these visions we have are precise or comprehensive doesn't matter. I know they correspond *at times* to what people genuinely feel, and that makes them, occasionally, fresh. But most of the time they are dead, and living with them is like transporting the corpse of a not-much-beloved relative and wondering if the grief of the other mourners is more sincere. Conversations about events in parts of the world of which we knew very little, for instance a change of government in an African country, would begin "What's our line on . . .?" It was in part ironic, self-conscious mime; in part genuine hunger; in part self-derogation because we knew that in fact there were many things we could not explain.

Our words were part of our vague moral imperative, badges of belonging, initiation rituals, rites of "brotherhood" as certainly as the Masonic handshake. I do not know who they were designed to arm us against, unless it was ourselves. Perhaps it was too painful to say to one another every day what it was that our struggle was about. Perhaps there wasn't time. Perhaps we didn't always know. But in fact our words armored us against the very people we needed to have fighting on our side. They made us into a secret society, a reasonable posture, perhaps, for a revolutionary movement in, say, a Tsarist or a fascist country, but absurd for us, both because of our actual position in this media-dominated society, and because it contradicted the openness and intelligibility we claimed to be espousing. In "Politics and the English Language," George Orwell points out that most of the political words of the left of his time (lackey, running dog, etc.) were translations, usually from Russia. Most of our words and lines were also borrowed or translated and, by the time they reached us, two or three times defrosted: from Russia, from the thirties, from China. Used language is dangerous, like twice-defrosted food. This is a complicated circle. To be in the movement you had to master the tongue, for no other language could be understood or was respected. But the fact is that this language could rarely be understood either, because its referents were not concrete. It only rarely corresponded to what we saw or felt or needed to express. Thus though we talked a great deal our words did not reach deep or far. I remember an odd moment in Chicago. Rennie Davis had been beaten by the police and was in the hospital temporarily, and Tom Hayden was mobilizing the crowd. As we were about to charge off in some direction or other he waved his arms around and shouted "Remember Rennie Davis," as if Rennie were some great beloved martyr of a peasants' rebellion. It was certainly not just Tom. It was somehow that even in the moments of our greatest excitement and passion, other people's phrases slid from our lips.

Status was acquired not only by manipulating the vocabulary (which was thought to be thinking) but also by some sort of association with the greats. Association did not necessarily involve sex. A cup of coffee with Rennie, a phone call from Paul Potter, a visit from Tom—even if their requests were refused—were a kind of stamp of admission, detectable to the initiated like the light-sensitive tattoos pressed on the wrists of couples at the senior prom. But status could not be secure because it had no basis in work. If I took my identity from readers' mail at *Science* that was ambiguous enough, but at least they were responding to something I had actually done. If my identity rested on Tom's coming to supper it was far riskier. What if I were out of milk or the pork chops were underdone? What was the source of my identity anyway? I had never before been so uncertain.

I avoided most opportunities to work in movement offices, mainly, I think, because I felt physically dizzy when I was in them. Trying to "relate" to the Chicago action in a way I understood, I conceived a research project called something like "Who Rules the Democratic Party?" It was to be power structure research: who contributes and how much and what people and policies they buy with their money. It was meant to be proof to the intellectuals (the "people" already knew) that the Democrats were not democratic. It was meant to support the democratically inspired challenges to party structure. It was meant to uncover specific propaganda material for the left. I got some money and set about furiously ordering books and digging up articles on the Democrats. My office was littered with file cards with two-sentence notations. New books arrived every day. It was a sort of insane frenzy. But every time I sat down on my old green couch with one of the books, I feel asleep.

I have found over the years that when I can't write it is usually for one of two reasons. Either I have nothing to say or I am afraid to say what I think. In the case of the project on the Democrats, it was both those things and more: a too grandiose conception of the work and its importance (the classic cause of "writer's blocks") and the fact that too much of my identity was invested in it. I *had* to do the work, to seal my movement reputation, to prove my radical credentials. It was difficult for me in part because I had reservations about its theoretical or intellectual premises: in this case that the trade-off between money and power, or between the economic interests of party contributions and the policies of the party (particularly when it held office), was a simple one. In a less desperate year a different kind of analysis might have made sense. But as it was, propaganda was the weight-bearing wall of our design. I was signing on to something for external purposes I didn't quite believe. Though I tried to persuade myself that radical action based on simple concepts might be necessary and effective, my own sense of the issues stayed more convoluted, and I didn't quite succeed. I felt terrible and heavy and slept on my green couch a lot. Most of the time I didn't go out at all. And the work never got done.

I took a job as New York editor of *Ramparts*. Frequently I have been asked "what it was like" to work there, and I usually reply that it was difficult to do the job well from New York because power was concentrated in San Francisco. That is true enough, but there is more to the story. It was the reign of Warren Hinckle and Bob Scheer: chaotic and unpredictable. The magazine was always being ripped apart at the last moment according to some whim of Hinckle's, causing delays and confusion and abuse of subordinates that would not have been necessary if he and others in San Francisco had ever agreed to an orderly way of working. My job was impossible because it involved soliciting manuscripts and cultivating writers in the East when I knew the articles would never get printed (they came in fashionable spurts: get Powledge on Bed-Stuy) or the authors paid.

The staff had a self-conscious—or perhaps semi-conscious—fixation on the 1920s. They presented themselves as: debonair, debauched, spendthrift, alcoholic, bedraggled, and inspired by their Terrible-Wonderful times. They celebrated the eccentric, the Runyonesque, the stylized; the hard-bitten reporter, the petty thief, the spectacular swindler. If they believed in honeymoons they would have held them at the Plaza, but there were not enough Zeldas for the Scotts. As it was, they hung out at the Algonquin: looking for future Ho Chi Minhs among the busboys, holding cocktail parties for New York's radical and not-so-radical media elite, and sobering up the morning after with Eggs Benedict and Bloody Marys. The Eggs Benedict were splendid but there were too many mornings-after. At one point the magazine owed the hotel something like $58,000.

Their idea-excuse was that radicalism-doesn't-have-to-be-dull. Revolution is a commodity to be packaged and sold like any other. It was possible to beat *Time* and *Esquire* at their own capitalist game. It was very difficult for me to make sense of. It was OK somehow in the movement's morality (or what I took to be the movement's morality) to work for *Ramparts* because it was "in the movement," "radical," and had in fact published many significant stories. At least it was better than working for *Science* because *Science* was in the Establishment. I knew that *Ramparts* was corrupt in a way that *Science* was not; and I knew that the whole time I worked there I never did a piece of work I was proud of. I was so frightened of saying the wrong thing about subjects that were new to me, and confused by my lack of authority over my own work, that I scarcely wrote. Nonetheless even though *Ramparts* was criticized by people in the movement, it was still part of it, still kept the blessing of our invisible college of cardinals. I refused to draw my own conclusions. Every day I struggled out of my couch and took the E train to our fancy offices on the upper East Side. I saw lights flashing in the subways and thought I imagined them. I heard phones ringing in my head and tried to answer them. I told my doctor I thought I had a brain tumor. He said if I had I might hear telephones but I probably wouldn't try to answer them. He thought something else was going on.

One of the few exceptions I remember to the unhappiness and ineffectiveness of those years is, in fact, the Democratic Convention in Chicago. I was working with many others on a daily *Ramparts*-funded paper, a wall poster called *WallPoster*. *WallPoster*'s purpose was to provide information about the location of demonstrations, to analyze what was happening inside the convention, and to report the news from the streets. We had many sources inside and outside the convention. Though the paper was actually to be put together every night by a small group, it had the feeling of belonging to a huge and justified and free and spontaneous mass. It was destroyed after four issues by the arrival of the official *Ramparts* delegation from San Francisco, who wanted to cut costs, produce the paper from their headquarters in the Ambassador Hotel, and rely on social tidbits gathered by their VIP buddies at the bars.

WallPoster was good work because it was reasonably well organized and clearly useful. But I think the days in Chicago made sense for another reason. Whatever its flaws, the demonstration at the 1968 convention was the most sensible and significant movement action of the 1960s. Of course everyone's "Chicago" is different. Of course it has been both romanticized and distorted. And of course the left had no control over any of the results, from the nomination of Humphrey to the election of Nixon, the subsequent reform of the party under McGovern, or its collapse in his 1972 defeat. Nonetheless I think that most people took away snatches of experience and snatches of understanding of political issues that helped develop a more accurate picture of what America is about. At the very least in Chicago there was still some interplay between the real world of American politics and the movement. Many people understood facts of life we usually did not bother to grasp: the working rules of the party; the complexity surrounding the movement's relation to McCarthy; what the McCarthy people stood for, and didn't; Daley's rule of Chicago, and his style, and his role in the party; internal party conflict, as between Daley and Ribicoff. There were relatively few times during the life of the movement when I had a sense of the external world that clear. I tend to remember private events within the public ones. I remember a shout of joy from open windows in the West Village the night LBJ gave his April Fool's speech. I remember the plainclothesmen dressed as hippies with "Love" on their helmets slipping onto the Columbia campus from the lower staircase, with clubs concealed. I remember how Washington looked when it burned, and later what it felt like to live in a military zone. But I think the times I felt connected with the world outside the movement were too few. What was important about Chicago was not the brutality or the violence. It was that the movement's actions and the officials' reponse x-rayed the spine of power in that ruling party and pinned its x-rays to the light.

But after that, for me, things became worse. On the trip to Budapest to meet with the Vietnamese I had become involved with another man, though I was still living with the one from Washington, and my personal affairs were getting pretty mixed up. My new lover was scheduled to go on trial in California for an antiwar action. I got an assignment from a national magazine to cover the trial, known as the Oakland Seven trial, and went to California for the winter.

Maybe the trial and the political atmosphere of the left in San Francisco and Berkeley were opaque to me because I was a stranger. The atmosphere was opaque enough to me in New York, where I lived. Or because being both a stranger and a journalist in a place bubbling with paranoia and judgment-of-movement-credentials made people suspicious of me. Or because of my relationship with one of the embattled warriors. I do not know. But the trial was weird and depressing, the centerpiece of a lot of heroics and posturing, the occasion of a lot of hollow orations and off-the-track analyses. I don't think anyone saw the issues clearly. This problem—which is no one's fault—is accentuated by the legal system, which encourages its actors to cast about in all possible directions hoping to find the one legal or technical way off the hook. Thus in a trial, one day it is the county's racist method of selecting juries; the next it is the unconstitutionality of conspiracy laws; the sinister private ambitions of the district attorney; his personal morality; the unconstitutional use of spies; the moral necessity and legal right of free speech; the constitutionality of war. . . . The best left lawyers, and Charles Garry, the Oakland Seven's lawyer, is certainly one of them, understand this eclectic property of legal defense very well, and continually find new possibilities in it. But it deposits huge doses of righteousness and rhetoric as it moves along, particularly because it is around regular human beings that these profound questions are swirling. There is something about a trial that becomes a Trial, the combat of Good and Evil throughout all of Time. Energetic and imaginative young men who in great part relished their assault on the Oakland induction station become every martyred rebel in history from Spartacus to Parnell. The county jail becomes the Tower of an English castle. It was difficult to find a human truth on this stage or even to accept the political truth that the outcome was dictated by the decent, liberal judge whose politics we all vilified and whose manner we mimicked. Except for the fact that the defendants would not have to go to jail—which was nice—the acquittal was hollow because it was not tied to a particular set of principles, either liberal or radical, no matter how much we tried to pretend otherwise, and no one could really understand why it had occurred.

The demands of the revolution cut quite heavily into the romantic affair I had pictured in Europe. On the rare weekend days that winter when the sun shone I wanted to climb boulders and visit vineyards. My friend had always to go to meetings, help form committees, make speeches. But the revolution did not get in my way nearly as much as did the fact that in San Francisco he was living with another woman, a fact which I did not exactly know when the affair began, and which I had a hard time dealing with. So did she, and I like to think that she is as sorry as I am now that we couldn't face one another and allowed our suffering prisoner-to-be to keep us both dancing on strings. But my friends in California were almost all men, almost all movement heavies whom I knew from national gatherings or travels. Their women, I understood later, had no reason to trust these relationships, or trust me, or trust them, and at the time I felt we had little in common. I attributed my troubles to a failure of revolutionary nerve. I did not realize until later how much my exhaustion and depression came from trying to keep up with the male Joneses. I finally took refuge in Palo Alto with a friend who was not in the movement, wrote a confused article on the trial, and went home to New York.

I was determined to be a better revolutionary. I abandoned my expensive apartment and ended, at last, my tangled relationship. About that time a new movement project was starting, called the Media Project. It was a product of the film collective, Newsreel, and the research collective, NACLA: the result, at least in part, of a need of some men and women in Newsreel to exercise its authority in a fresh organization that the founders of Newsreel exercised in it. Newsreel functioned as a kind of Mother Church. It gave its priests (and an occasional priestess) exacting training, then dispatched them to establish other missions among the heathen. The Media Project was designed to bring the Word to journalists. In the beginning I was glad to be part of it. Since it was an "organizing" project it meant I could at last be an "organizer." The insecurity that I thought came from my professionalism would dissolve.

The Media Project had much in common with other organizing projects of the New Left, although it started late. We had a few ideas: the media is important because it influences people; all avenues of communication are controlled by powerful corporations and individuals in their own or a "national interest" of interest mainly to themselves. These ideas are true enough. It was the personal corollary—that the writings of journalists are therefore somehow the yappings of His Master's Voice, and they themselves vicious or downtrodden curs—that was a mistake.

This is a complicated thing and I'm not sure I understand it accurately. There *was* a great deal of restlessness and dissatisfaction among New York journalists that summer, 1969. Many felt uncomfortable and somehow strung out by their inability to do anything in their professional capacities to oppose the war. In many cases their papers or news agencies had squelched particular stories they wanted to report or pieces of social criticism they wanted to develop. Many felt themselves to be, or knew they were, tools of arbitrary bosses, though they usually felt this more in terms of a specific editor or department manager than in terms of "the system." They were mostly liberal people, I think, and had liberal complaints, but they did feel compromised by their situations and they did want to do something. What they did not want to do, I think, was quit their jobs. Many people, in a changing flow, came to our meetings. But we had very little to offer.

As usual in those circumstances, I felt confused. I got to know a number of the professional journalists from various committees, meetings, and so forth. I could see that they were opposed to the ideas and rhetoric of the movement organizers in the project. My loyalties were with the movement group, since I was supposed to be one of them, but my sympathies were with the journalists. They wanted the paper we were going to put out to be "good"—i.e., to have professional standards. They felt the movement people were incompetent and vague and didn't know anything about journalism. On the whole they had a taste for the concrete and specific; the movement people for the general and abstract. It was as if the movement people thought the others would be "organized"—"radicalized"—by grand theories about imperialism or the "role of the media." To them "professional" equalled "elitist" equalled "bad." The journalists could see the role of the media pretty clearly, but tended to see it in a more dialectical fashion: it's bad but since it's the only instrument we have, it is also the only realistic source of possible change. The movement people thought you couldn't change it except by being revolutionaries. Being revolutionaries meant quitting your job and being like them. The professionals didn't even like them, let alone want to be like them. Their jobs usually represented

113

some real achievement to them. This was particularly true of some black reporters in the project, some women, and some poor boys and down-and-outs, especially in the wire services, who felt they were getting along with their lives at last. It was also, unfortunately, true in some proportion to the prestige of a reporter's job. If a reporter was on the *Times*, for example, he was on the top of some ladder he had damned well meant to climb. It was impossible and absurd to try to convince him he could do more by dropping out. It contradicted everything he had learned about power in America. And it was hard to give advice about what actions he might begin on the job because he knew his real situation, the possible risks and chances of gain, and we didn't. In my organizing capacity I had many conversations about these subjects and I think my end of them was always pretty feeble. Our combination of lurking moral imperative—Drop Out! and Save Your Soul—and revolutionary rhetoric doomed the project to a short life.

In a small way I think the project fed a positive stream in the press. At least it was a branch of that stream. The magazine *[more]* now published in New York owes something of its inspiration, if not its precise politics, to the project, or perhaps to the ideas the movement and the project tried to clarify. The best pre-Watergate article on Nixon and the press, which appeared in *Rolling Stone*, was by a New York reporter, Tim Ferris, who stayed with the project a long time. Perhaps the most significant movement in the press, however, that centering around the *Chicago Journalism Review*, had an autonomous and professional origin. It was created by journalists in Chicago who were affected by what they saw and heard at the Democratic Convention. That group seems gradually to be evolving toward a conception and a set of demands that would lead to structural changes in the newspaper business. They have proposed, for instance, that reporters get one-third representation on editorial boards with the right to publish dissenting editorials; veto power over the appointment of department heads; and an option to buy their papers if they come up for sale, as well as a veto over prospective buyers. The papers have not exactly rolled over and played dead in response to these demands, but the fact is that the issues—issues of workers' control and of the character of life on the job—are being bargained for the first time, and Guild members are becoming prepared to strike for them. I don't know how our little band in New York could have encouraged the development of comparably significant experimentation there. The only basis on which movement people were able to approach professionals was on the basis of "moral superiority" and "revolutionary consciousness." There was little respect on either side. The movement people thought the journalists were corrupt simply because they were journalists. The journalists thought the movement people were ridiculous. Meetings were either boring or angry, full of mistrust, and always tense. We judged them good or bad by the number of apparent adherents to our position, as if we were in a rope-pulling contest at a country fair. I am surprised now that the journalists listened as patiently as they did, but I think the climate was different then and that the movement still carried enough prestige to make other people—especially white, privileged, and guilt-ridden people—at least try to listen. The project eventually published some useful newsletters. But in the end it consisted of a few people—already movement people in some sense, and more in the publishing business than in the press—talking to themselves. Everyone else had moved on.

Working in the project was a nightmare. The Newsreel people hated me and loaded their hate with political language so specialized that I couldn't even understand what in my behavior it was referring to. I understood it so little that at first I didn't know it was happening. It came to a head in a furious frenzied shouting scene at the Newsreel loft when the project's male heavy screamed at me for about 20 minutes that I was a "liberal" and an "opportunist." I felt very meek and listened carefully and tried to find myself in his charges. I don't want to play dumb. I understood the theory of opportunism and the theory of liberalism. But there was a nexus between theory and practice that evidently had embodied itself in me, and the practice side of it I couldn't quite get. I know now that in many ways I was different from the Newsreel faction, but we had never argued our respective positions. My sense of things was inchoate. As far as I consciously knew I had always tried to do, and thought I was doing, what we all agreed had to be done. And so I listened. "Opportunism" meant doing what was easiest instead of what was purest. It meant going along with some of the journalists' ideas instead of challenging them at every point. "Liberal" was the same thing. What is "purest" might be absurd: it ignored the fact that the great media empires were not going to lie down and crumble at the toot from our radical conch shell. "Pure" was unanalyzed romanticism. I was also an "individualist," which meant, I think, that I had independent relationships with a few of the journalists apart from Newsreel's collective, and meant also that I didn't do what he wanted me to do. But it is hard to think all that through when you are emotionally dependent on sharing the ideas of others—when you are in fact trying to tow the line—and it is impossible

115

when a furious man is denouncing you in a public place. I knew he was wrong in some large important way. But to fight back I would have needed a set of clear, different ideas, and a violent spirit, neither of which I had. He ended his rage: "My god, haven't you even read Mao?" at a high pitch. I walked home through dingy streets fashioning replies like, "Don't you know what country you're in?" But we might have been in China, or some American pre-revolutionary China, for all I knew after being around the movement for so long. I never went back.

Shortly afterward I became involved in the women's movement for the first time. The women's movement has come to mean a great deal to me. I take it for granted. I forgive it its trespasses. I go beyond it when I can and come back to it often. I do not apologize for it. At its best it is a vision of what it might mean to be human in a decent society. Nonetheless, my first experience in it was terrible. I landed by accident in a small group consisting in part of some of the movement's most militant and well-known spokeswomen, and it was the women's movement's most virulent period. It was an extension of my life in the mixed movement, not distinct from it. It was, in fact, the moralistic ideas of the movement as a whole brought forcibly and painfully into my own and my friends' living rooms. And it was made harder to bear because our intimate, autobiographical technique left no room for evasions, and our new rhetoric of sisterhood, collectivity, and struggle unreasonably raised our expectations about what we could hope to become and how fast. In my group—and I think in others—we tyrannized ourselves with ideas that could only destroy us. We fancied ourselves divided into "working-class women" and "middle-class women" though only one woman was, really, working class, and she was then married to a rock critic. The impulse was still, as in the mixed movement, the search for a revolutionary vanguard. The "class question" was used as a club, as lesbianism was later—to be working class or gay was to be in the most revolutionary, therefore correct, position—to attack everything about the others the working-class faction did not like. What is surprising is not that they did it, but that at that point in our political history the rest of us allowed it to happen. Anything we "privileged" women might somehow have needed or felt good about (a piece of work, a job, admission to graduate school) we came to despise and distrust. The radical women's movement in New York was like a permanent purge in which we always identified with those who confessed.

What we were trying to do was difficult, and we were serious about it. We understood class in a microscopic, and I believe accurate, way. It was the shapes of our bodies and the inflections of our speech and the different opportunities we each had in life and the different ways we had each chosen or been forced to turn on men. We recognized that our achievements did rest on other people's backs even if it was not our fault, and that we were not so much smart or skilled as merely lucky. We wanted to destroy the category "intellectual," to root our privilege out, to let the sun shine equally on all the human creatures in the garden. But we had to find some way to "smash elitism" without smashing our psyches, and my group at least did not find it. Another position was possible. We could have admitted our advantage and attempted self-reform and sharing without the pressure of denial that we were who in fact we were. Instead we adopted what gradually came to be known as the lowest-common-denominator theory, by which we attempted to put an egalitarian future into the present by fiat. No one could be smarter than anyone else, or prettier, or more talented, or make more money, or do anything significant on her own. Our responsibility was always to our collective sisterhood, always to work in a group, always to bring others along. It was not a bad ideal, which was one of the sources of its strength. But the vision became a weapon. It was held by powerful individuals with complex private motives they refused to acknowledge, and it was difficult to divorce the social pressure from the ideals. In our group, psychology was believed to be the enemy of revolution and psychologizing a middle-class cop-out. Those of us who were in therapy could not even explain ourselves because the very language of vision was the language of private experience. The others believed that class alone was our real determinant and mediated or controlled all individual experience and family history. To speculate otherwise, even to have the capacity to speculate otherwise, was itself evidence of the great scarlet stain: Privilege.

The pressures accompanying these ideas were so intense, I think, because of our cell-like structure and because we wanted to believe. For most of us our feminist insights were new and powerful. Since some parts of them were so plainly, painfully true it seemed impossible that others should be false. We had a class interest in our unity as women. We needed one another. Our compulsion to arrive at a unified line was enormous. But even though the governing idea of the women's movement at that time was that our-politics-grows-out-of-our-experience, it really couldn't. Our politics made it difficult to be honest about our experience, and sometimes the two were contradictory. We kept notes on ourselves and our thought, and every week attempted to draw up a list of questions we would try to resolve, though we rarely did. The impulse behind this practice was to combat the idea held by male enemies that women couldn't be organized or systematic thinkers, that our talk was unserious gossip. We tried to consider, for instance, "Can women ever oppress men?" or "What is the responsibility of the single woman toward married women?" meaning "Are affairs with married men ever justified?" We seemed to think we could decide these great questions out of the small-sad details of our private lives and arrive at theoretically valid and universal rulings. But the discussions were much affected by the fact that some women were married and some were not. I believe our consensus was that the married woman had to be "right" (i.e., affairs are not justified) because they were the more vulnerable. They were the more vulnerable because it was economic bondage (inability to get a good job, have equal earning power, etc.) which had led them to marriage in the first place. They would not have been in bondage had they not been working class. Now they had children and were all the more restrained. Anyone who would play around with their men or their marriages in these conditions obviously sinned. These arguments were not ridiculous, though they omitted opposite arguments, and the truth of each fragment varied with individual people. But they also carried with them the moral imperative—Don't!—disguised as the responsibilities of a sisterhood which, if fully realized, would promote feminist revolution. Sisterhood is powerful but it is not omnipotent. It doesn't prevent the loneliness and desperation of single women or the romantic antics and suddenly flowering sexuality of married men. In practice if a single woman was sleeping with a married man, whatever her reasons, whatever her problems, it was difficult to bring up and discuss honestly. Fear of censure was stronger than our ability to share the facts of our lives.

I think it is important to say that my group in New York was the worst women's group I have ever heard about. The deformations of the movement there created by life in the city itself and by the relentlessness of the media added a great deal to its difficulties. Relations in the women's movement other places were often painful, I know, but in most places these pressures seemed to be balanced by a slower pace, or by constructive common work projects, or by cooperative living arrangements. In addition, although women are still entering the movement through consciousness-raising groups like mine, the forms of the movement have become more varied. The possible activities within it are so much greater than the destructive intensity that afflicted the New Left and carried over into feminism has largely corrected itself. But my first group met only to struggle over ideas, and that was not enough. I don't remember, or perhaps have repressed, the details of how that group came to dissolve. What I do remember is that one of the last times we met, when we realized we were failing in our agreed goals, we got to talking about what we really wanted in life. Three of us (our middle-class, privileged, psychology-ridden faction) said we thought we might like to be happy some day; we weren't then. The other women were shocked. Disgusted. They had never thought of that before and didn't like the idea. They had no hopes for it. They wanted to make the revolution. Happiness was another bourgeois delusion, just what they had suspected us of harboring all the time we had been together. It was impossible to be happy in an unjust country.

At that point I began to take seriously the work of self-repair. I knew the revolution could not rest on timid neurotics like myself and powerful lunatics like the men and women I feared. I was taken on by a fine psychotherapist who was helping many radicals find some ground to put their feet on. The movement's charges against shrinks did not apply. She had the clearest vision of human freedom I have ever encountered. Slowly, with her help, a picture of the world that did not confuse inner realities with outer ones began to come into focus. That was also about the time of Weathermen. One of my close friends, a long-time activist from the Cleveland SDS project who had been casting around New York for a while went off to Michigan to play some tennis with her lover, stopped at the SDS National Office, and became part of the Weather Bureau. When she finally came back she was in a Weather mood: polemical, cynical, and cruel. Our relationship was sealed in ice. I was hurt and surprised. I knew my political sins but they were the same old sins, nothing new. It was the first time I lost a friend because of political lines, though it was not the last. I believed we were on the same side, and I believe that now. But Weathermen did not represent a political temptation. For me, and for most people I knew, it was not a compelling alternative. Its actions were too spectacularly irrelevant, its lifestyle was too spectacularly intolerable, and it produced its coherent theory too late in the life of the movement to have the commanding impact it might have had before the movement splintered. I had two nightmares. One was that some strong-armed stoned-on-karate women's delegation was going to beat me up because I didn't believe in sexism-is-the-primary-contradiction and was insufficiently feminist. The other was that a different set of men and women

119

was going to trash my apartment because I didn't think racism-is-the-primary-contradiction and was insufficiently militant. Since I was not altogether enfeebled I noticed that the nightmares clashed. Most people did not turn away from the dead end of movement politics that Weathermen symbolizes after they saw its results: they had not been prepared to walk that road in the first place.

In my last year in New York I took two jobs in the non-movement world: one with the telephone company, and one with the hospital workers union, Local 1199. In the first I learned that the consciousness and conditions of workers had little to do with what the movement thought, and gained some appreciation of the subtlety and power of the institutions working to hold them in their place. In the second I learned that an organization attempting to meet the daily needs of workers was too compromised by the methods the system forced it to use to promise much that I could define to myself as freedom. I was able to write about these things—the first serious writing I had done since 1967, and the only serious writing between then and the present—because somewhere in me I was still a reporter, and I loved evidence. But my accounts, if clear, were critical and pessimistic and jarring to my hopes. When I had stayed through that year I had a deeper sense of some of the things that are wrong with the country, and how difficult they would be to change, and a sense of how badly the movement had mistaken and underestimated the system. I had no idea of where we should go, and would have had no vision of how to get there if I had. I visited Vermont often that summer, and one morning, driving back to the city at dawn, I watched the blue sky turn black and the mountains turn to high-rises and the quiet country roads become the beltways of megalopolis and I decided to quit my job and move there. When I packed my bags and left the city I felt like a refugee from war trudging along a debris-ridden highway to a place I hoped only would be quiet and safe.

Movement III: Endings, Beginnings

For more than a year I have wondered how to bring this essay to a conclusion. I feel a ceaseless political ache, a longing, like Simone Weil's, for "the most radical possible transformation of the present regime." The movement is over and by the rules of political autobiography I should be in despair. If my peace of mind and my political destiny were simply linked, the ending would have to be a suicide note. But the fact is that I am not in despair. I am far happier than I was.

I am not certain I can explain this. It reminds me of a session I had with my therapist in New York. I was recalling, I don't know by what association, a childhood event my conscious mind had catalogued "trauma": the day I sent my parents' brand-new postwar Oldsmobile rolling down the hill in front of our house. Or the day, as I then claimed, and as I still remember it, the car happened to roll down the hill when I happened to be in it. As far as I knew I was regretful about the incident, especially about the punishment. I remembered waiting fearfully for my father to come home and hear the news. But my conscious and my unconscious minds had evidently reached different verdicts, for as I told the story I began to laugh, a deep satisfied laugh at odds with external memory. My shrink asked me what was so funny, and I couldn't say. That was all right, she said. Sometimes we don't get the joke for years.

The problem of interpreting the movement is the same. Things that contradict each other at the surface are not necessarily contradictory at their heart. Friends find my account of the movement "bitter," and though I see what they must be seeing in it, bitterness is not my verdict. The opposite. I have a great sense of pride in having been a part of it. The movement produced a major and essentially correct reinterpretation of America. Our understanding of it is constantly vindicated. It was painful and sometimes terrible to be involved. But it was where I wanted to be. I do not regret not having married my high school boyfriend and settling near by family and raising another. I do not regret my divorce. I would not like to have spent that time as a straight reporter, beeping out transmissions from the authorities whose lives are news, or to have remained a Washington hostess, now supporting the Panthers, now SDS, now the Vietnam Vets Against the War. I do not wish that I had merely observed the movement's snake dance without joining the line. If I regret anything it is that I was not clearheaded enough for most of my time in the movement to have helped make it

121

stronger or to prolong or reinforce its impact. I do not see how anyone who scorned or ignored its truths could be "happier" about the 1960s.

My relative sense of well-being, I think, is in part a freedom from ideology. The movement was like a big Russian overcoat, and storing it away makes me feel more agile, independent, alive: like a carved doll escaping the dollmaker and dancing free. I lived on a communal farm for more than a year, and hoped that the vegetables I learned and loved to grow might bear the seeds of a more original and peaceful opposition. I saw for the first time the rings of energy around the rocks and the trees and in the soil and understood, as others have, that the universe is holy and one. Now ideological and religious armies are assembling on all sides again, and though I share the intuitions that give them power, I hope I will have the curiosity to live awhile longer without a prefabricated map of my own boundaries. I am teaching, and writing again. Perhaps these are ideologies of their own. Vermont is a promising and healthy community to belong to.

Yet these are all statements about myself. Where is the "we?" What is the social and political truth? The radical movement of the 1960s has vanished at the time of the most massive, lawless, and ruthless consolidation of state power in United States history. To ask the unavoidable question: What is to be done? The answer cannot be "nothing." Too much is at stake. We are, in 1973, in a new ring. In one corner great numbers of decent people with a clearer understanding of the degeneration of American politics and a host of new energies and techniques with which they hope to escape degeneration or oppose it: diffuse and not always self-conscious personal liberation movements, communes, workers' resistance, consumer boycotts, cooperatives, alternative schools, religion. In the other an implacable social system which will swallow them if it can and smash them if it must. But I do not believe the fight is fixed. I think our best chance for a decent society is to hawk more tickets for our side: to spread out and imbed ourselves with all our demands and visions, incomplete as these may be, in every institution in the country: in schools, colleges, unions, hospitals, churches, community organizations, political parties, radio stations, newspapers, libraries. Whatever stands in the way of the multiple despotisms already upon us is right. Whatever pockets of independence we create are good. To people who will complain that this is not a "strategy," that it does not distinguish useful from deceptive ideas, reform from co-optation, I can only say that I think making these distinctions is part of the work. There will be no simple tests. Whatever we can do, singly or together, to refine our comprehension and prepare a new opposition is important. Let us bury the New Left with the praise and dignity it deserves. To obstruct or curb the monstrous bundle of powers America has become we need something much broader than the movement, less vulnerable to repression, and more livable and long-lasting. This is a strange and confusing period. But there is at least as much chance that the sun is rising as that it has set.

Note

1. The most comprehensive treatment is Kirkpatrick Sale, *SDS: Ten Years Toward a Revolution* (New York: Random House, 1973).

Making History vs. Making Life: Dilemmas of an American Left

RICHARD FLACKS

For most people, the demands of everyday life are all-encompassing. An effective left must integrate its politics with the routines of daily life.

There is little doubt that some kind of "crisis of legitimacy" is occurring in American society. Measures and expressions of public opinion indicate that people are widely disillusioned and cynical. The cynicism extends not only to the Nixon administration but also to many of the major institutions of American life. Yet, despite this crisis, there is no coherent political left capable of offering a credible alternative. In comparison with a few years ago, radical protest is less evident; national organizations of left opposition have disintegrated; symbols and rituals of revolt are gone.

The idea of a left, I believe, makes sense only when it can potentially appeal to a popular majority. The irony of the present is that, just when the possibilities of open communication to a majority seem greatest, no left exists to take advantage of the situation. Even if there were an organized left at the moment, however, it would be a distinct minority, and it would face the problem of bringing its message to "the people." This article tries to understand what's involved in that process of communication. My purpose is to find a basis for language and action that can make a majoritarian left possible.

Specifically, I make the following working assumptions:

1. For the average man and woman, "making history" is radically separated from everyday life.

2. The left is a tradition of thought and action that seeks a world where "making history" and "making life" are intertwined.

3. Political apathy (making life) and "mass movements" (making history) are different means people use to find, protect, and fulfill meaning in their everyday lives.

4. The left can take root in relatively affluent societies provided that the making of history can stand in a meaningful relation to everyday living.

What follows is intended as a "working paper"—a tentative effort designed to provoke response. Comments, however damning, are therefore welcome. In his book *The Power Elite*, C. Wright Mills begins:

> The powers of ordinary men are circumscribed by the everyday worlds in which they live, yet even in these rounds of job, family, and neighborhood they often seem driven by forces they can neither understand nor govern. . . The very framework of modern society confines them to projects not their own . . . But not all men are in this sense ordinary. As the means of information and power are centralized, some men occupy positions in American society from which they can look down upon . . . and by their decisions mightily affect the everyday worlds of ordinary men and women . . . They need not merely "meet the demands of day and hour"; in some part they create these demands, and cause others to meet them.[1]

For Mills, the dominant fact of postwar America is the separation between two modes of human activity: "making history" and "everyday living." "Making history" means taking actions that affect the shape of society or the direction of social change. It is activity that significantly affects the everyday lives of society's members. In contemporary society, Mills argues, the making of history is increasingly deliberate and conscious, since it is increasingly concentrated in the decisions and acts of a small group of men. To be a member of this "power elite" is thus to have two kinds of privileges. First, the constraints that shape most people's lives are not so narrow for the power elite. Second, history making in the sense of control over social institutions is a feature of the elite's everyday roles and routines.

For most people, however, "everyday living" involves neither this kind of freedom nor this kind of power. It is, instead, simply a collection of private activities that are largely taken for granted. Some of these activities are necessary for survival. Others are obligatory and fulfill commitments made to specific people. Still others are needed to maintain a person's sense of self. Everyday life is *real*; it occurs in relation to definite other people whom we know and with whom we feel interdependent. It is *required*, in that our lives seem to depend on carrying through the daily round. And it is *right*, in the sense that these activities constitute our basic obligations to those (including ourselves) that we care most about.

Much of everyday life is highly routinized, involving little chance for self-expression. And a great deal of everyday activity involves meeting other people's needs and expectations, and postponing or denying our own. But daily life provides ways to experience freedom and to obtain direct satisfactions as well. These activities are not mundane. We experience them as separate from daily routine, as "special," or "extraordinary," or even "ecstatic." They may include forms of religious and mystical expression, festivals, athletics, vacations, hobbies, spectacles, the creation or consumption of works of art. Compared to the daily round of constraints, these activities represent an area of comparatively wide choice, of freedom and self-determination. In this sense, people are simultaneously subordinated and free, conforming and resisting, role-playing and being individuals as they move through the day.

People are powerless, first, to the *degree* that the "projects" they do every day are set by external demands and are not freely chosen. Second, they are powerless to the degree that they cannot make history—change those demands and the institutions that make them—without abandoning, disrupting, or threatening the patterns of their daily life.

From this perspective, we can define the political left as a tradition based on the idea that ordinary men and women can and should "make history." This phrase had two meanings. First, society should be organized so that power and everyday life can be intertwined. Second, building such a society depends on the conscious activity of ordinary people to that end.

At first glance, this way of defining the left may seem to be a restatement of what is ordinarily referred to as democracy. Nevertheless, the liberal democratic tradition in America has usually expressed a strikingly different idea about the relationship between power and everyday life. Most liberals have believed that the two domains should be radically separate. Everyday life ought to be inviolately private, immune from the intrusions and controls of unwanted others. Power in turn is supposed to protect the pursuit of private

127

happiness. For liberalism, any other political project is highly suspect, and indeed the good society contains a minimum of power and therefore of collective history.

This liberal vision may have seemed a practical possibility for Jefferson and his contemporaries. Most people now realize, I think, that it is an inappropriate political principle for a highly urbanized, industrialized society controlled by giant corporate and governmental organizations. Americans generally recognize the existence of a "public" world beyond their personal control that profoundly shapes the terms of everyday existence. Despite this recognition, however, most of us continue to believe in the possibility of having a materially secure, physically safe private space within which we can freely be ourselves. As long as power does not grossly intrude on these private spaces, we are relatively passive before it.

Commitment to everyday life at the expense of political participation is not, by itself, either irrational or dishonorable. Everyday life necessarily uses up most of our time, energy, and resources. For most people, an attempt to restructure the terms of everyday life, even if it seemed necessary, would mean abandoning morally binding ties or fundamentally disrupting the very basis of their physical existence. To make history, one must either be in a position to do so as part of the daily routine—that is, as a way of making a living, hence be one of the powerful few—or be somehow free of everyday ties and commitments. Some people find themselves in these situations. But most adults are not, almost by definition, in a position to devote themselves to changing the terms of their existence. They are not in a position to make history. This is the left's fundamental problem.

Rights and Expectations

Everyday life, of course, does not exist in a vacuum. It is built upon a structure of expectations and meanings that give a kind of coherence to daily activities. The elements of this structure are complex. But one key to the political side of it, at least, is that people take for granted certain "rights" that they expect the state to protect. The only condition is that the obligations associated with those rights be fulfilled.

I am referring here not only to the formal rights defined in the Constitution, nor just to the formal obligations of citizenship. Beyond the Constitution and the law is an unwritten cultural charter of rights and obligations that operates in everyday relations. I do not think we know much about the makeup of this charter of rights and duties. But I do think that what people think they have a right to and what they think they owe in return vary markedly according to social class.[2]

The most basic element of a coherent daily life is economic security. For Americans, this means some kind of steady job with a "living wage." After years of political conflict and economic struggle, most Americans now expect the political system to foster "full employment" so that everyone who wants to work can do so. There is a similar broad consensus favoring social security, to provide some measure of economic security to those unable to work.

Alongside economic security, I think, is the expectation of private, "free" space for activity of one's own choosing. Most Americans believe they have some right to individuality, to choice, to self-expression, to projects of their own. But the notion of when and where that space should be available varies significantly with social class. The blue-collar worker, for the most part, assumes little right to individuality or autonomy on the job. Instead, he trades subordination and role conformity at work for choice and self-determination at home, in leisure. Or, as with millions of workers, he sacrifices much of his free time to work so that his children can be "free." For "educated labor" and professionals, however, the situation is usually defined differently. A college education is supposed to entitle one to some degree of freedom and individuality on the job as well as off.

For blue-collar workers, the rights to job security and private freedom seem to entail an obligation to conform, at least minimally, to social roles. To the degree that the private sphere can be maintained, the worker is supposed to be willing to meet the demands of his job, however oppressive or boring it may be. (Workers do, of course, utilize whatever "space" they can, both for doing what they want to do while at work and for protecting themselves from the demands of the job.[3]) The "educated" worker expects the opportunity to do "meaningful," "responsible," "challenging" work. This kind of work brings with it an obligation to "take responsibility" for an institutional or organizational area rather than simply to conform. The obligation is to do well in the job and to accept opportunities for advancement that come as one moves "upward" through a career.

Political stability and legitimacy in contemporary America depends a good deal on the system's capacity in these two areas. It has to deliver and protect "rights" to job security and free space for the traditional working class. And it has simultaneously to deliver and protect "rights" to meaningful work and career advancement for those with higher education and training.

Steady economic growth and technological development are the two principal means by which these requirements have been met. Growth provides jobs for an expanding labor force. Technological development brings increased opportunity for those with advanced education. Economic and technological expansion also allow more choice and freedom in the everyday private sphere. Much of the "consumer package" associated with postwar prosperity—house, car, washer-dryer, TV, stereo, recreation vehicles, and boats—serve to increase people's feeling of personal freedom and private space. People do not seek possessions as such; rather, certain possessions provide the basis for the experience that freedom is still possible.

Insofar as the post-Depression, postwar economy has "delivered" on these terms, then the majority of "traditional" and "educated" working and middle-class adults have supported the established social structure. In this sense, the overall legitimacy of the system rests on the emotional commitment of the majority to their everyday lives. It rests too on the same people's perception that everyday possibilities and meanings are supported and not infringed upon by "the system." Political unrest, in turn, can be traced to groups and situations where, for one reason or another, the system does not "deliver."

One source of unrest is the minorities who find themselves unable to establish the coherent everyday lives that the majority take for granted. Blacks and other disadvantaged groups are often uprooted by economic conditions. They are often unable to establish the stability and security achieved by the white working class. Moreover, this pattern of uprooting and frustration exists side by side with cultural and political promises of full equality.

Another source of unrest is the fact that conventional patterns of everyday life don't offer equal benefits to all. In particular, the structure of work, households and family life fails to provide free private space for most women. Again, this failure has occurred in the context of egalitarian promise. Women, instead of being equal, are assigned the task of making everyday life fulfilling for men.

A third source of unrest is the system's inability to deliver the "meaningful" work it promises to the college-educated. In the last several years, students and educated young adults seem to have experienced this failure particularly keenly. Career opportunities that offer meaningful work seem scarce. Careers themselves are integrated into authoritarian bureaucratic settings. Yet, for children of the middle and upper classes, autonomy and self-expression are supposed to be essential to a satisfying life.

A final source of discontent is the fact that everyday patterns of life embody a variety of social constraints and psychic repressions. These are experienced even by those who cherish the security and freedom daily life provides. Anxiety, boredom, anger, and guilt are feelings intimately related to work pressures, household cares, personal relations within and without the family. These feelings intensify in the present climate of "anomie," in which political conflict, change, and disorder seem to fill city streets, televised news, and other public spaces.

Postwar America thus never witnessed the total consolidation of Mill's "mass society," in which most people find gratification in private experience and cheerfully acquiesce in the historic projects of a "power elite." Nevertheless, the security, meaning, and moral coherence of everyday life are real and powerful. Their appeal, I believe, is essential to an understanding of political life in America.

Movements for Change

Everyday activity tends to cut people off from what I have called "historical activity," or the attempt to change the shape of a society. And yet, powerless people *do* try to intervene in history. We use the term "social movements" or "mass movements" to refer to such activity. Under what kinds of circumstances are such movements most likely to occur?

Most commonly, popular movements arise as efforts to *resist* threats to established patterns of everyday life. Movements are particularly apt to occur when these threats are seen as the fault of those in authority. To a great extent, the goal of such movements is simply to re-establish the rights and terms of stable existence. The disruption of everyday life creates discontent. It also frees time and energy so that those involved may be more available for historical action. One can find examples of this process in the last 75 years of American working-class history—as recounted, for instance, in Jeremy Brecher's recent book *Strike!* The spontaneous strikes and insurrections that Brecher describes were invariably touched off by immediate threats from employers or other authorities (wage cuts, price rises, layoffs, firings, interference with established work rules or practices, and so on).

131

In some cases, a specific event symbolizes not just an immediate threat but a larger process of the erosion of everyday life. Insurrectionary activity—general rebellion against representatives of symbols of authority—may follow. Many of the ghetto uprisings of the sixties can be understood in this light. They were acts of resistance against conditions of rising unemployment, police harassment, and other threats to everyday security and personal freedom. Another illustration is the Free Speech Movement in Berkeley in 1964. It began as a movement resisting incursion by the university administration on political rights that had been taken for granted.

Indeed, most popular struggles in the United States began as efforts to resist various forms of colonization and dependence. One thinks, for instance, of farmers' revolts, native American resistance, Southern secessionism, ethnic urban riots, anti-draft and antiwar protests.[4] Deprivation and oppression alone do not breed revolt. Popular resistance occurs only when triggered by acts or defaults of the authorities that threaten patterns of adaptation or symbolize the disruption of everyday life.

Furthermore, though disruption and threat are fundamental sources of political discontent, they are not sufficient to generate a movement. At least two other conditions appear to be necessary. First, people whose lives are disrupted must see that their fate is shared with others. This requires the possibility of interaction. Accordingly, popular movements most typically occur when people who share a common fate are in close proximity to each other and in some degree insulated from the social control of established agencies.

Second, a movement seems to require the invention of specific tactics that appear effective as means of making history. The history of popular movements is replete with examples of previously passive groups of people being ignited by small, typically spontaneous actions taken by a small number of individuals. All such triggering acts seem to have one characteristic in common: they make it plausible that joining or emulating the initiators might literally enable people to do something—to "make history."

Only when all these conditions are met can popular movements occur. The risks involved in action are taken when they are shared, and when the action seems worth the risk. The outcome, people believe, is likely to involve better guarantees of the security and rights they need to live every day. The rhetoric of resistance involves not so much the notion that action will lead to a brighter day, but that action is necessary to stave off greater darkness.

In short, popular movements are usually defensive, at least in the beginning. They aim at new or more explicit guarantees by authority that the rights in question will in future be recognized. If the movement is successful, its effect may be to strengthen the legitimacy of authority. Or, if the costs of settlement have been high compared to the gain, a legacy of bitterness may remain. Whichever the outcome may be, however, it shouldn't be surprising that even very militant participants eventually leave the stage of history to return to mundane private life once they are able to do so.

Political movements may, of course, go beyond resistance. Previously legitimate patterns of everyday life may come to seem morally wrong or illegitimate. The old routines are no longer real, required, or right. Movements may then be based on aspirations toward *liberation* rather than simply the need to resist. Liberation movements go well beyond resistance: they involve, in effect, a redefinition of self as well as demands for new rights and entitlements.

Liberation movements may involve strikes, direct action, insurrection, and other dramatic political activities. Their unique feature is that historical action can occur within the framework of everyday routines and relationships. A resistance movement seeks to make history by stopping and going outside everyday life to block an external threat. Liberative activity may as likely occur *within* everyday life—for example, doing something that is taboo, unconventional, or unauthorized. What makes this activity historic (rather than merely "deviant") is that it is done consciously, in parallel or together with others who share the same fate. Its intent is specifically to claim new rights, more autonomous "space," or more equality. The contemporary women's movement is, of course, prototypic of a liberation movement; so, too, are many aspects of minority liberation movements. All these movements seek to establish new rights in everyday relations, and all make use of everyday assertiveness as a principal means to achieve social change.

Liberation movements may have significant effects, but they do not necessarily threaten fundamental patterns of power and class rule. If people in everyday life can claim and obtain more rights and more freedom, then everyday life becomes, for them, more attractive. Like resistance movements, liberation movements may culminate in a return to private life, with a resultant strengthening of social stability and legitimacy.

The most far-reaching kind of movement is one that embodies *revolutionary* aspirations. A revolutionary movement seeks to establish a social framework in which the separation between history making and everyday life is broken down, not for a moment but permanently. The movement tries to create institutions and living patterns that will enable full self-government, direct participation, a permanent end to domination. Revolutionary aspirations are most widely felt when re-establishing coherent everyday life appears impossible. The reason may be foreign invasion, prolonged war, the collapse of traditional authority, or endemic deprivation and insecurity—as, for instance, in prerevolutionary China or contemporary Indochina.

Majoritarian revolutionary movements have existed in the past, and do exist in our own time. We know therefore that popular majorities *can* act historically, not just sporadically but continuously, and can be guided by a vision of social transformation. But such movements are poor guides to our own circumstances. They seem to depend fundamentally on total social breakdown—on the impossibility of everyday life—for their emergence and continuation. The problem for the left in post-industrial societies is that it seeks a revolution when everyday life is not only possible but indeed compelling. Who and what then is left?

Activists and Vanguards

Before turning to this, one more general point. Social movements usually include small groups of highly visible people whose everyday lives are defined by the movement rather than by the roles and routines of the established culture. These are the movement's full-time leaders, ideologues, organizers, mobilizers, bureaucrats. They may often draw their livelihood from the movement; in any case, their commitment is to the movement (or to a specific movement organization) rather than to the maintenance of a conventional everyday world. Their world, then, differs quite radically from that of the average citizen. The latter, I have tried to argue, is committed primarily to making and carrying through a private life. He or she leaves off such activity only when the need to do so is compelling, and then returns to primary private commitments when the extraordinary or emergency moment has passed.

There is a good deal of evidence to suggest that movement activists are drawn overwhelmingly from the ranks of those who are separated or estranged from the ties and constraints of everyday life. Activists tend to be people who find it materially or psychologically possible to avoid these ties and constraints; or, less commonly, people who find it materially or psychologically difficult to establish them. Many of the conditions that create such "exemptions" and "maladjustments" are specific to particular social and cultural conditions. Generalizations are thus difficult. But it seems clear that certain features of many societies do generate significant numbers of people who are neither tied to everyday existence nor are members of a ruling class. I would offer one big generalization about who such people are: namely, that movement activists tend to be recruited from the ranks of those who have been socialized for elite roles but denied access to them. A pattern of simultaneously *fostering and frustrating history-making ambitions* can be a systematic feature of a given social order. It can also be a symptom of profound underlying contradictions.

The most obvious and widespread social category that is simultaneously free of everyday commitments and blocked from power is "youth." By youth I mean physically mature people who have not taken on stable work and household roles, and who are exempted from everyday responsibility. The reason for this exemption may be to prepare for elite roles or to perform some special mission requiring a maximum of physical vigor. Or, it may be that they cannot be put to regular work because of economic conditions.

Student and youth revolts historically have often resulted from an overproduction of university-trained young people in economically and technologically underdeveloped societies. Often such overproduction goes hand in hand with official repression of advanced ideas and free discussion. Out of such conditions have come many of the revolutionary vanguards of the last century in many parts of the world.

What roles do full-time activists play in popular movements? Resistance movements apparently can arise quite spontaneously—that is, without the calculated intervention of "vanguard" organizations or "outside agitators." The particular contribution of those who seek to be a vanguard rests on their ability to make sporadic popular actions take on more permanent historical meaning. For example, activists may try to create permanent organizations for the defense of group interests and rights (e.g., trade unions). Left-wing intellectuals articulate criticisms of the established structure and help create new definitions of legitimate rights. Revolutionary ideologists formulate visions of self-determination. Full-time activists can sometimes invent tactics that persuade groups of people they can be historically effective (although I have the strong impression that movement vanguards are most often as surprised—and dismayed—by such tactics, developed spontaneously from below, as any bystander). Finally, movement activists seek to establish

135

an organizational format to sustain full-time agitational activity, to spread the news and the gospel, to maintain continuity when the movement's supporters return to everyday activity, and to contend for power through elections or insurrection.

The separation of activists from the constraints of everyday life frees time and energy for the tasks of influencing history. It enables movements to count on a band of highly dedicated and disciplined workers. But this same separation makes the relation between movement activists and their constituents highly problematic. The activist's experience is radically different from that of the people for whom and to whom he is attempting to speak. Under conditions of profound social crisis, when patterns of daily life have been systematically destroyed, this difference may vanish. Tens of thousands may throw themselves into full-time struggle, and entire communities may organize their lives for resistance. But such moments are rare. At certain times, popular apathy seems to prevail, and the activists strive with perplexity and frustration to "reach," "activate," and "mobilize."

At other moments, insurgency seems to prevail. In such times, activists are typically caught off guard and find themselves racing to catch up with their putative followers.

The history of American social movements reflects this dilemma. On the one hand, this country has witnessed extraordinary popular upheavals and collective action. Indeed, the militance of these upheavals rivals that of any other industrial nation. For as much as ten years at a time, America has seen outbreaks of strikes, community and institutional uprisings, protest demonstrations, acts of civil disobedience, and even insurrection. Although most of these actions were primarily forms of resistance (as I have defined them), aspirations toward liberation and even revolution frequently developed in the midst of the struggles.

On the other hand, despite this history, a self-conscious left has never been able to create a continuously evolving, legitimate revolutionary ideology and organizational format. Indeed, one gets the sense in examining the history of the Socialist party, the Industrial Workers of the World, the Communist party, the Student Non-violent Coordinating Committee, and Students for a Democratic Society (to name the most important left organizations at various periods of popular protest), that a pattern of self-limitation is at work. All seemed unable to make use of opportunities for leadership and growth that were available.

The New Left

To recapitulate: the heart of the left's tradition is the idea that ordinary people can "make history." Not only can they intervene in the process of history, they can also create a social order in which people exercise power in their everyday lives. Leftists agree that such an order requires the abolition of private control over economic decisions. They disagree on many other elements of the vision. But the whole left, particularly in the United States, has in common the following agonizing problem: its vision is alien to most citizens' daily experience and cultural framework. For most, the vision is unintelligible, irrelevant, unrealistic, or illegitimate.

Historically, attempts to solve this problem have taken two major forms. Activists have sought to overcome their isolation by participating in movements of protest, reforms, and resistance. This participation has typically led to a serious dilution of their ideology; often they have come to abandon their opposition to capitalism as such. Or, radicals may try to maintain the purity of the leftist vision. This attempt has typically meant splendid isolation from their fellow citizens.

This inability to construct a nationally sponsored left that is both relevant to the majority and ideologically distinctive is expressed in a series of questions that have recurred on the left for at least the past half century: How can socialism become a live issue for the American people? How can we build an organization that will be both principled and effective? How can we express our long-run political goals while we participate in more limited struggles and movements? There may have been a period in the mid-thirties when most radicals believed that a solution was at hand: the idea of a popular front, the center-left coalition. In the United States, however, the front soon collapsed. It was unable to bear the weight of pro-Soviet apologetics, centrist duplicity, and anti-communist hysteria.

In the late fifties and early sixties, a series of events began to make the idea of a new left plausible, particularly to activist students and intellectuals. Soviet hegemony within the world Communist movement broke down, and left-wing orthodoxies seemed exhausted. A new breed of independent intellectuals emerged, personified in the United States by C. Wright Mills. Domestic and international anti-communist programs declined. And new youth and student movements began to appear in many parts of the world, including the American South. These movements again made credible, after

137

a long hiatus, the idea that powerless people could affect history through collective action.

The new leftists of the early sixties sought to create a movement that would be free of what they saw as the mistakes and failures of the "Old Left." They were skeptical of all established ideological perspectives (including the then-current "end of ideology" ideology). Their new ideological framework for the left would freely synthesize the best insights of the Marxist, anarchist, pacifist, libertarian, and radical democratic traditions. The new leftists would create a vocabulary, a rhetoric capable of capturing the complexity of contemporary experience and appealing to politically uncommitted Americans. They would formulate action in terms of experience rather than ideological categories. They would strive for theory rooted in and tested by practical ability. The fundamental basis of both theory and action would be a kind of pure leftism: people making history and striving to take control of their lives.

This notion of controlling "the decisions that affect our lives" was the principle by which the movement itself was to be organized as well. Hence, new leftists were to be fundamentally anti-dogmatic, anti-authoritarian, anti-bureaucratic. (Dogmatism, authoritarianism, and bureaucracy were identified as fundamental flaws of all Old Left groupings as well as features of the society the new leftists were rebelling against.) Further, since the New Left was democratic and open to experience, it could avoid the destructive factionalism and sectarian infighting that plagued the Old. And since the New Left sought to establish a truly radical movement in the United States, it had to break with the politics of welfare-state liberalism, the cold war, and the anti-communist crusade. Thus the New Left assumed the task of creating a political alternative both to the traditional left and to the dominant forces in the Democratic party.

The final novel element of early New Left thinking was to locate the sources of social insurgency outside the traditional working class. New leftists saw blacks and other politically voiceless minorities, as well as students and young intellectuals, as the main agents of historical action. They thus focused from the outset on issues of self-determination and autonomy rather than material security.

There is always something impertinent about a small group believing that it can make history in opposition to the established centers of power. But the initial expectations and claims of the New Left seem particularly remarkable for their chutzpah. A collection of kids in their late teens and early twenties was claiming the ability to overcome 50 years of left-wing error, failure, and exhaustion. More: they would also initiate a direct challenge to the most powerful ruling elite in world history. Of course, the 50 or so people who met at Port Huron, Michigan, to found SDS did not literally believe that singlehandedly they would recreate the left and establish a new politics. But they did have enormous confidence that a new left was possible, and that their political efforts would have great historical meaning.

As I have suggested, one source of this chutzpah is the fact that many of the new leftists had been socialized for elite roles. Most people are taught to have only limited confidence in their ability or right to engage in significant political action. A narrow stratum of America, however, is taught to think that they can and should affect the shape of society. This stratum is the offspring of the white upper middle class. Most political leadership in this country is in fact recruited from this group, as were most members of the early New Left. Indeed, research on the social origins of the early New Left established a typical pattern of upbringing. Like other children of the middle class, new leftists were encouraged by their parents toward high academic achievement. But parents of new leftists also stressed a moral obligation to work for some kind of social service rather than simply for material gain. The new leftists were taught to feel that they could and should be outstanding, but they felt profound guilt if they saw themselves as self-serving.

It is not hard to see that political activism can be an effective way of realizing and resolving these demands. In the leftist vision, ambition and social conscience came together. The young radicals' relative freedom from status anxiety, and the fact that they were students, provided them the freedom to act historically because they were not constrained by the ties and routines of everyday life. Ambition linked to guilt provided the motivational energy. The moral collapse of both established liberalism and the traditional left made a new left seem possible. From these conditions emerged "the movement."

In times of general apathy, leftist vanguards must have some ideas about what will generate a revival of popular insurgency. One solution to this problem is provided by Marxist orthodoxy: the inevitable contradictions of capitalism will generate the inevitable revival of proletarian consciousness and revolt. Vanguards imbued with this faith are likely to engage in routine organizational politics. Activity revolves around meetings, political education, putting out the party publications. Political activity can thus be fully integrated into an everyday routine. The ideological framework permits members to believe that the routines will eventually prove to have historical meaning—although day-to-day practice seems to indicate the opposite, at least to an outside observer. It is just this style of leftism, of course, that the new leftists were rebelling against—both the ideology of historical inevitability and the routinized, bureaucratic activity that seemed to lead nowhere.

The alternative to ideological encapsulation is to link up with popular struggles for reform and to formulate ideas about potential social movements that are testable through direct action. This is essentially what the new leftists did. They first identified with the Southern civil rights movement. Its development, they hoped, would lead to a revival of the liberal-labor-left coalition. Inspired and goaded by the black movement, dormant reformers would be forced to revive themselves and to lead some kind of movement for a new politics. This movement, in turn, would provide a political niche for the new leftists. Indeed, much of the optimism and joyful energy expressed by young activists in those years can, I think, be attributed to their belief that they were the catalysts of a new reform politics. Out of this ferment, they thought, would come new structures of grassroots action which it would be their vocation to held build and sustain.

This strategy and these hopes were systematically obliterated by a series of events during the mid-sixties. Organized labor and other reformist bureaucracies had little interest in sponsoring social movements. Integrationist strategies for dealing with racism and inequality collapsed. Labor and liberal reform groups continued their commitment to the cold war and interventionist foreign policies. The Vietnam war, ghetto rebellions, and the emergence of Black Power led to deep divisions among the very social groups that might have created a new reformist coalition. The traditional leadership of reformist politics began to be indistinguishable from the rest of the power elite.

What rescued the New Left at this point was the emergence of something that few members had really anticipated: a large on-campus student movement. Most new leftists had previously believed that radical politics and social action could interest no more than a small fraction of college students. The Free Speech Movement at Berkeley shook this view. The outpouring of student participation in the rapidly expanding antiwar movement collapsed it. It didn't take long for most new leftists to come to believe that students and youth could be a potent agency of change. In turn, the New Left was redefined. No longer an effort to create a broadly based left alternative, it now became the vanguard of a movement of revolt based in the younger generation.

I do not want to rehash the factors that gave rise to a student movement in the sixties. What I do want to point out is that in many respects this movement arose spontaneously, without the deliberate, planful nurturance of vanguard groups like SDS. Youth in general, and students in particular, are explicitly exempted from many of the constraints of everyday life; and they are aggregated into segregated enclaves. They are thus the most likely kinds of people to engage in movement activity. The student movement of the sixties was in part a resistance movement. It resisted the draft and the war, and it resisted a variety of threats to the everyday life of the "youth culture." The movement also was a liberation movement. It sought to redefine authority relations within the university. And it maintained a vision of a less constrained, more open everyday life both within the university and beyond.

The particular contribution of new leftists to the youth revolt included, first, the development of tactics that reinforced the idea that students could make history. Many such tactics, such as draft-card burning, seemed to have been spontaneously invented by a handful of people at a particular place and time. Others, such as sit-ins, were also often unplanned—but they were employed by students who had learned them from civil rights or pacifist activity. Finally, some tactics of protest were planned and organized in advance, such as peace marches or rallies. These were either deliberate initiatives by nationally organized groups or more spontaneously organized events on the local level.

Thus, like any movement vanguard, groups like SDS kept the momentum going. Second, they sought to provide a coherent ideological framework for the activities that were occurring. As "vanguardists," SDS and other new leftists tried to make students see their actions as part of a larger historical process. The students had a mission to carry out beyond defending their own social space, the activists argued. Without political transformation, everyday freedom and security wouldn't be possible. A crucial part of this argument was SDS's successful linkage of the Vietnam war and the military-industrial complex to the university. Students thus did get a sense that their particular institutional environment was integrated with a larger structure.

To a considerable extent, new leftists were successful in their efforts. They generated a climate of radical disaffection with authority on the campuses. They also gained support for the idea that students had an historical mission. The ranks of the New Left grew enormously in the middle and late sixties.

SDS itself became a mass organization, claiming upwards of 50,000 members by its peak in 1968. Independent estimates, such as that provided by the Yankelovich surveys, suggested that at least 11 percent of students by the end of the sixties identified themselves as adherents of the New Left. In other words, there were possibly half a million or more students who defined themselves as left political activists. Beyond this, there was a still broader consensus among students that they had a responsibility, and a credible chance, to affect the course of history. The mood reached its culmination in the national student strike of May 1970, but it had been growing for several years before.

Failings and Failures

Four years later, all of this seems totally deflated: history that requires an effort to recall. I want to sketch some of the reasons for the disintegration of the New Left as an organized vanguard. I am not here offering an account of the decline of student protest itself, although such an account would overlap with the one I will offer.[5] For one thing, a general withdrawal from history making into everyday activity is relatively unsurprising. For another, any assertion that student political activity is "over" is quite likely to be falsified by events. It is clear, however, that the specific vanguard group that adopted the label "New Left" and that was concentrated in SDS did disintegrate. It does not now exist as an identifiable group at the national level. Indeed, the disintegration of the New Left occurred well before the decline in overall student and youth protest. SDS, for instance, fell apart in the summer of 1969; in the year that followed, student action spread out and intensified despite the lack of national coordination.

We need to know more than we do about how a vanguard group can maintain itself and develop its capacities for leadership. Maintenance is, in part, a problem of providing material sustenance: if people are going to be professional activists, there must be some means to support such a vocation. Maintenance also requires an organizational format. There must be means of communication, role allocation, planning, and so on. Maintenance also seems to require an ideological framework to justify the impertinence of assuming leadership. The framework needs to reinforce the idea that one's attempts at history making have some meaning, and it has to provide the intellectual resources to defend against attacks from outside. Finally, vanguard groups must realize that members are being continuously tempted to return to private everyday activity that will merge everyday life with political participation. Or, they must create a new, totalistic reality more compelling and self-fulfilling than life outside the group.

In the early days of the vanguard's existence, such problems are less pressing, especially if its members are young and well-off. Youthful activists have some independent means of support or the energy to find them. Few have dependents. There will be some financial resources to provide subsistence to the full-timers. In the early days too, the cognitive and moral framework of the group has yet to be tested by competition, repression, or failure. In short, if a vanguard group has been highly successful initially, it is likely to avoid serious concern with problems of survival and maintenance. These come up only later.

For three or four years, new leftists experienced these heady "first days." Their ideas and activities were receiving steadily growing support and respect. They were in control of a viable organization, SDS, that was gaining adherents and developing resources. But note that the central tenets of New Left thinking militated against seriously considering the problems of group survival and maintenance. The new leftists were dedicated to overcoming the Old Left tendencies of ideological dogmatism, sectarianism, bureaucratism, and authoritarian discipline. They were thus specifically opposed to the very measures that might have led them to form a cohesive leadership group. I make this point not in criticism but to highlight a fundamental dilemma. The only possible left for America was one that was ideologically open, free-wheeling, relatively undisciplined, decentralized. Yet his created enormous problems for sustaining what little cohesion and leadership there was.

In addition, new leftists' commitment to participatory democracy created strong resistance to self-perpetuating leadership groups. Official leaders of the organization were annually replaced. Informal leaders felt, and were made to feel, that they should limit their attempts to influence the organization's development. Finally, it began to seem inappropriate that aging ex-students were still participating in what was supposed to be a student organization.

By 1966, virtually all of the founders of SDS were no longer exercising formal or informal leadership within it. A new group had taken over with no personal ties to the founders; indeed the new leadership was hardly acquainted with the old. The influx of newcomers into both the leadership and the rank and file also brought with it a striking political change. The "New Left" ideas and sentiments originally envisaged by the founders no longer prevailed. Instead the organization became a kind of umbrella group for a multiplicity of outlooks. It had some agreement on organizational strategies but very little on basic philosophical or moral approaches. Not only had the original new leftists given up their personal influence within the organization; they had also failed to communicate their vision so that it would be carried forward by any self-conscious group of successors.

In part, this failure was beyond the new leftists' control. Although they knew what kind of left they did not want, they never concluded what the alternative was to be. The hoped-for revival of the liberal-labor-left coalition had failed to materialize. There was no time, by the middle sixties, to have developed anything else.[6]

But I think a part of the failure of the New Left during this period was self-imposed. For example, once the early new leftists had "graduated" from SDS, they could have created a new organization for leftist "non-students." Indeed, many expressed the intention to do so, and several full-dress conferences were convened for the purpose. Yet little or nothing came of it. James Forman, in his book *The Making of Black Revolutionaries*, describes in detail a similar failure of SNCC leadership during this period to help the organization reach beyond its student activists. In a chapter on "internal disorder" in SNCC, he analyzes what he calls the "negation of power" within the organization. What he is referring to is a persistent refusal to assert leadership, an almost willful abandonment of opportunities.[7]

Consider too: charismatic leaders within the New Left often abandoned their positions just when they could have generated a real following. Bob Parris Moses of SNCC is a dramatic example: at the height of his capacity for personal influence, he abandoned public arenas and sought total anonymity. Mario Savio of the Berkeley Free Speech Movement did much the same, and so did most New Left "personalities." What was true for individuals, moreover, was also true of the group as a whole. Beyond a certain point, the New Left drew back from opportunities to solidify its organizations and to further its long-run aim of building a left alternative.

What accounts for this self-limitation? Fundamentally, it was a growing feeling that a group of white middle-class intellectuals did not have the *right* to lead in the creation of a left. A true vanguard, it was argued, would be led by representatives of those most oppressed, those most capable of revolutionary commitment. An organization initiated by the new leftists would be insufficiently militant: unable to articulate the real needs of the oppressed. This theme reappeared whenever the possibility of an adult New

Left was raised. It was an argument put forward both by those who were antagonistic and by new leftists themselves.

Beyond such ideological reasoning, we may conjecture less publicly admitted sources of self-limitation. Essentially, the linkage between ambition and guilt that was the initial motivating force for the history-making chutzpah of new leftists had snapped. The ambition to lead was now itself a source of guilt. To fulfill their vanguard role, the new leftists had to assert themselves. But without a coherent ideological justification for self-assertion, guilt prevailed. This guilt resulted not only from the fact of being white and middle class, but also and perhaps most deeply from the fact of having power, gaining recognition, and exercising influence. The situation was exacerbated by the increasingly seductive efforts of the media to make new leftists into celebrities. Severe psychological conflict resulted from this situation, and rancor and envy from below began to appear.

The result, in brief, was that leadership was largely abandoned by new leftists to those less troubled by self-doubt and those more self-justified by fixed ideological commitment. Accordingly, in the late sixties, the public definition of the left was being provided by those who found legitimation in traditional revolutionary doctrines. It was not that new leftists retreated from activism, for most remained highly committed to movement activities. It was that they failed to seize, and then lost, the opportunity to develop their own capacity to exercise leadership. An important reason for this, I am suggesting, is their inability to suppress guilt in the interest of self-assertion.

Such a "flaw," if it is a flaw, did not have to be fatal to the New Left project. But the project would then have required an organization that did not depend on centralized, assertive leadership. In fact, many movement organizations did contain the seeds of such an alternative form. Organizationally, SDS, the Resistance, and other national student-based movements of the middle sixties were loose networks. Their real life occurred in hundreds of autonomous local groups and chapters. Few coherent policies were adopted nationally. Few manifestos were issued from above. The national organization gave a kind of historical dimension to local activity, but it did not direct it. Had this experience been taken seriously, it could have helped create the basis for a sustainable New Left organizational format. But by the late sixties many of the most politicized student activists, including many early new leftists, had virtually abandoned the goal of creating a broadly appealing left in favor of the goal of Revolution.

Revolution, as it was expressed in the years after 1968, was not perceived as the outcome of prolonged organization and struggle. It was an immediately necessary apocalyptic insurrection. I do not want to detail the conditions that made Revolution Now seem plausible. It may seem incredible that such a perspective had such a grip on many politicized youth only a few years ago. To understand its hold we would need to reconstruct the historical circumstances of that time, especially the apocalyptic character of 1968, and recapture the feeling that prevails in the midst of popular uprisings—the feeling that anything is possible. No doubt, too, the rhetoric and style of apocalyptic revolutionism were a way of meeting some deep psychic needs having to do with guilt and self-doubt. Finally, a reconstruction of this period would have to attend to the influence of the mass media. History making, by the late sixties, had come to be defined as appearing on the six o'clock news. The only way to ensure such an "historic" appearance was to resort to visually exciting acts of insurrection.

The acts of confrontation and insurrection that occurred during the 1968-71 period were typically not the result of deliberate planning by movement vanguards. They were either spontaneous expressions of unrest, or the result of official provocation and suppression, or some combination of the two. The contribution of the various vanguards, again, was to create a rhetoric to justify the activities. One possible rhetorical framework would have emphasized that confrontation constituted a form of resistance to the war and police suppression. But the rhetoric of resistance and civil disobedience was typically overwhelmed, both in the media and within the movement, by the rhetoric of Revolution.

In this climate of totalism, SDS turned into the very opposite of what its founders had envisioned. SDS had begun with the intention of avoiding dogma, doctrine, top-down discipline, factional warfare, and sectarian style and language. Its purpose was to create the basis for a left that could appeal broadly to the American people. By its final convention in 1969, SDS had not only fallen prey to all of these supposed failures of the Old Left, it had become an incredible caricature of its worse excesses. Monolithic, slogan-chanting factions met in open combat over obscure points of dogma, beyond any hope of intelligibility to the uninitiated. As these factions mutually destroyed the organization, they also destroyed whatever framework existed for a nationally organized student left or a general New Left.

In the aftermath, the great bulk of student activists were left to their own resources. One group of leaders encapsulated itself in the psychological comfort of ideological orthodoxy. The "Weather" faction, closest in social origin and personal history to the original new leftist group, transformed itself into a pure history-making elite. It self-consciously sought to break all ties to everyday life, and thus to test the limits of total commitment to historical action. It found those limits in death.

Revolutionist rhetoric and activism thus undermined new leftism by drowning it out. It also undercut it morally. By demanding total commitment to historic action, such rhetoric blocked those on the left who favored patient organizing, ideological tentativeness, and majoritarian politics. Yet because of the critical importance of guilt over privilege in the character structure of those drawn to the New Left, activists found it hard to avoid submitting to demands for total commitment.

The disintegration of SDS, followed by the collapse of the late-sixties' vision of apocalypse, signaled the death of the New Left. In the upsurge of popular historical action, one could merge oneself with the movement and forget longer-run projects. Most new leftists did this. Or one could prepare for an ultimate historical act. Those with most guilt and fewest ties to everyday life took this route. The nature of the New Left's vision, and the qualities of its adherents, proved unequal to the task of historical self-assertion.

Reassembling a Left

The tragedy of the late sixties is not so much that the New Left project was abandoned. It is that the aftermath of this period has witnessed an unprecedented fragmentation of the left. The centers of power are in disarray, and disillusionment is widespread. Why, then, has it seemed so difficult to pick up the pieces?

One key to the present situation is this notion: once large numbers of people engage in historical action, they discover the limits of their ability to affect history. Political action, in a word, contains the possibility of disillusionment. The degree of disillusionment is of course related to the movement's extent of success. If a movement has limited goals and wins them, members will return to everyday life. But they will not have been disillusioned. If goals are limited and gains are partial, then momentum for action may continue, especially if the authorities seem vulnerable to further pressure. But if political action is thought to have failed, then cynicism and disillusionment may set in. The more that members have developed far-reaching liberative and revolutionary aspirations, the more disillusionment there is likely to be. In this situation, partial gains are seen cynically: they are cheap and morally irrelevant buy-offs.

Whatever gains there are, moreover, are likely to relax some of the threats to tolerable everyday existence. The return to private life may therefore be easier. It will be easier still if previous actions have been intense, disruptive breaks with everyday existence. Most participants in movement activity may feel a certain relief at its end. They can now go on living, having been saved from falling over the brink into total apocalypse. Relief and newly perceived powerlessness lock people back into everyday life. The struggle is renewed only with difficulty.

This pattern of withdrawal may be even more likely if the movement has won over only a minority of the population. The more disruptive and militant the movement, the more likely it is to have been seen by others as a threat to their everyday lives. This of course is the famous "backlash." A minority movement in particular is likely to create a backlash; and in the aftermath, those who supported the movement and many who opposed it may try to reduce polarization. An agreement to respect each other's everyday existence replaces the drift toward civil strife.

Revolutionary totalism is the complete antithesis of everyday life. For the young people who see the coming constraints of adulthood as something akin to death, it is a compelling image. In the late sixties, for many, apocalypse was a way to avoid everyday adulthood, or at least a way to avoid thinking about it. Once it was clear that the apocalypse was not coming, the problem of how to live every day had to be confronted. Radical activists then discovered that the movement had only helped crystallize a set of moral commitments. It had not helped them understand how to live every day in terms of these commitments.

In fact, the activists' estrangement from everyday life created an enormous barrier between themselves and the non-young majority—*and between themselves as youth and their own futures as adults*. Those who remained committed to the original New Left project came to see that the project could only be fulfilled by somehow transcending this barrier. Furthermore, most activists began to confront the problem of everyday life on a personal level—how were they personally going to resolve the tension between making history and making a life? There were no clear answers.

There would be no basis for a left if every citizen had the opportunity for a safe, secure, and autonomous private life. When private security and freedom are systematically disrupted or invaded, conversely, the left's appeal is greatest. Advanced capitalist societies, particularly the United States, stand somewhere in the middle. Gross inequalities and everyday discontents persist. Massive structural contradictions give rise to periodic crises in the economy. Misallocations of power and resources generate chronic threats to security and safety: crime, pollution, deteriorating public services, rising tax burdens. These structural contradictions create a continuing basis for movements aimed at resisting threats to everyday life. There is, too, a rich diversity of cultural contradictions, stemming from values emphasizing equality, freedom, and dignity, and from the ceaseless clash of ideas about the good life. The culture legitimates a variety of personal needs, and the social order fails to implement them. The resultant restlessness generates impulses toward liberation.

These structural and cultural contradictions, impinging as they do on everyone's everyday life, create the conditions for a popular movement and hence for a left. But there is a problem. People intervene in history to make it possible for them to live every day. The leftist, however, dreams of a situation in which people will take permanent control of the historical process. To the extent this vision implies the abandonment of everyday life, it makes no sense unless there is no everyday life to return to. In fact, everyday life persists, and it still continues the overriding practical and moral reality for most people. Thus, insofar as movement vanguards do not share everyday commitments with "the masses," their ability to exercise leadership is limited. At one point they are engulfed in the tide of popular revolt. At a later point they are stranded on the beach.

For the idea of a left to be more than just the property of vanguards, there must be theoretical and practical links between the making of history and the making of everyday life. So long as the separation between "vanguards" and "masses" is perpetuated, and so long as history making is defined as the antithesis of everyday living, the left's vision remains pure utopia. This will be true unless our society undergoes a thorough, rending social crisis.

Many new leftists have continued to work on their project. Their activity is an attempt to find ways to make history through everyday activity. Such activity includes countless experiments to reconstitute patterns of everyday life: communal living, cooperative child rearing, economic independence,

149

grassroots psychotherapy, aesthetic expression, and so on. These experiments try to free participants for historical action while maintaining the possibility for satisfying everyday needs. They also intend to make history directly. Their effect is to create real change in the culture, the social structure, and personal character from the bottom up.

A second, related type of activity involves efforts to reconstitute work activities. So far we have seen the development of alternative institutions, the organization of dissident members of various professions, and attempts to press for change in established work institutions. Although much of this activity has been devoted to professional work, ex-student leftists are increasingly involved in blue-collar and white-collar work situations. Their activities focus, often, on issues of alienation and union democracy.

Another important post-sixties initiative is the effort to develop grassroots political coalitions. These coalitions aim at winning majority support for programs of community self-determination. In some locales, the efforts involve a return to electoral politics. In others, grassroots organizations have used direct action to win reforms. These struggles seem to seek a majoritarian politics of the left based on local resistance to corporate colonization of communities.

Finally, the New Left of the sixties brought with it a new generation of left-wing intellectuals. The intellectuals' work is to develop an ideological framework, social analysis, and vision that are theoretically rich, empirically informed, and rooted in American reality. The political importance of this work is enormous. A left has to persuade people that society *can* be organized so that power and everyday life are intertwined. Left intellectuals must, of course, clarify and illuminate the structural sources of private troubles. But once such connections have begun to be made spontaneously, the most important task becomes envisioning concrete alternatives. Despite the death of the organized New Left, this work of intellectual reconstruction is accelerating.

The post-sixties turn of leftists toward local politics, personal development, intellectual work, and a majoritarian outlook contains the elements of a possible breakthrough in left politics in the United States. Yet, ironically, we remain in a situation where local, personal, and intellectual projects appear to have little or no historical effect. Indeed the separation between the power to take historical action and everyday activity seems to grow. This dilemma occurs at a time when popular contemplation of radical alternatives seems increasingly possible.

There is no single strategy that can solve the dilemma of the left. But at least three frameworks of action seem to offer some immediate means of resolution. These I would call: (1) building an authentic popular front; (2) decolonizing communities; and (3) liberating the workplace. I will attempt to develop these themes in a later essay.

NOTES

1. C. Wright Mills, *The Power Elite* (New York: Oxford, 1957), p. 3. The influence of several others in addition to Mills permeates the argument to follow. Most especially, Jeremy Brecher, *Strike!* (San Francisco: Straight Arrow Books, 1972); and David Sallach, "Marx and Schuetz," (Indiana University, mimeo, 1972).
2. The following discussion is indebted to Richard Sennett and Jonathan Cobb, *The Hidden Injuries of Class* (New York: Alfred A. Knopf, 1972).
3. For a beautiful illustration of this, see Barbara Garson, "Women's Work," *Working Papers* vol. 1, no. 3 (Fall 1973).
4. Richard Rubenstein has written an interpretive history of these movements based on this supposition. See his *Rebels in Eden* (Boston: Little, Brown, 1970).
5. I have discussed this rather fully elsewhere. See Richard Flacks, *Youth and Social Change* (Chicago: Markham, 1971).
6. Cf. Kirkpatrick Sale, *SDS* (New York: Random House, 1973), for a detailed account of the fortunes and internal tensions of the organization.
7. James Forman, *The Making of Black Revolutionaries* (New York: Macmillan, 1972). See especially pp. 411-33.

Primary Groups in Social Movements: A Memoir and Interpretation

ROBERT J. ROSS

INTRODUCTION

"In unity there is strength."
"An injury to one is an injury to all."
"Solidarity forever."
"We shall overcome."

The slogans of protest and radical groups arch out over their programmatic demands, evoking an aura of human aspiration for renewal and community. This aspiration both transcends and forms the basis of the "politics"—the cognitive elements of belief—of movements which nevertheless are considered instrumental as distinct from expressive (cf. Blumer, 1951). Expressive social movements may withdraw from public struggles, attempting to create humanly satisfying microcosms of a new order. But ostensibly political groups ask their members to come "All Out for Mayday!" They link arms and sing "We shall overcome." They, too, in ritual and ceremony, in movement folkways and in comradely embraces, plumb the depths of profound emotion and a longing to be linked with others in ways not typical of the social structure they seek to change.

The role of face-to-face, more or less intimate personal relations within larger impersonal structures has been a persistent theme in the social science analysis of public and business bureaucracies. The purpose of this article is to reflect on the role of such primary groups in the organizations within the protest movements which began in the sixties.

"Fellowship" (Blumer, 1951) and solidarity (Gamson, 1975) have, of course, been discussed by observers of social movements and social movement organization (S.M.O.). By bringing together my observations with other documentary and analytical work, it is my hope that the scattered nature of the existing literature may be made somewhat more coherent.

I should note that my interest in these matters did not originate in an academic context. As part of the founding cadre of an activist left-wing student organization (Students for a Democratic Society, S.D.S.), I was perplexed by changes occurring within it in 1965-66. This was a time of rapid growth in S.D.S., in which new groups gained prominence. And it also brought the first stirrings of the counter-culture to left politics in the form of a search, even a demand, for "community." Around that time I formulated notes about some of the determinants of internal tone, emotional atmosphere and strategic direction of social movement organizations. My life within the tempestuous sixties left that paper behind. But then, at the turn of the decade I was once again part of a leadership cadre of a new organization of leftist academics (The New University Conference—NUC).

In the factional atmosphere of the early seventies I found my old notes were helpful in understanding—though not, alas, ameliorating—organizational changes. Recently, while teaching and writing about some of this material at a small university, I have found that students and others engaged in leftist groups continue to face many of the same issues I did, and that upon occasion the material in this paper is useful to them. Thus, while sharing my thoughts in a research journal, I believe they can be useful to organizers and activists. This dual concern is reflected in the organization of the paper. It divides the role of primary relations in movement organizations into two general areas. The first is organizational growth and maintenance. This leads to the second area: policy formation, democracy, and response to crisis. Each of these segments draws on both my own experience and the observations of others. At the end of the paper I suggest the implications of the role of communal aspiration for enduring concerns in the theory of modern society. Finally, in an appendix, the previous observations are listed as formal, testable hypotheses.

I. PRIMARY GROUPS IN THE GROWTH AND MAINTENANCE OF PROTEST GROUPS

A. General Considerations

Some of the rewards of social movement participation, even in political or economic movements, are always expressive. Blumer referred to the function of movement participation as in part, overcoming loneliness and isolation; Zald and Ash (1966) use the felicitous phrase "the joys of participation." Staughton Lynd, an historian and New Left participant, had this experience in mind when he referred to the movement as a "band of brothers in a circle of love" (Lynd, 1966:8-9). This rewarding experience has one of its key "points of production" in the primary groups which develop within organizations among participants.

Describing a 1969 occupation of a Harvard building, a student participant expressed the euphoria involved in humbling awesome Harvard (cited in Hampden-Turner, 1970:381).

> What was most euphoric, however, was us and what we were to each other. For those few hours we were brothers and sisters. We did reach out and hold onto each other. You couldn't be flip about it. 'I haven't seen so many friends together in two years,' one girl said. But you had to realize—whatever your politics and tactics—that we were very beautiful in University Hall, we were very human, and we were very together. . . .

Confrontation is not the only source of such feelings. Kopkind (1973:30) describes his first visit to an S.D.S. organizing project in Newark:

> Their commitment to a common cause cut into the loneliness of work, which I had always assumed was inevitable. . . . In that intense mood, I fantasized an end to alienation, despair, emptiness.

Turner and Killian (1972:366) refer in general to the "ecstatic experience of membership in a cohesive, committed, like-minded group" becoming "an independent source of satisfaction."

Primary ties to a social movement, and within an s.m.o., are important in other ways as well. Killian suggested one of the consequences of joining the informal fellowship within social movements when he wrote "Admission to the intimacy of the inner circle, where one may associate on an informal basis with the leaders of the movement, is an important step in transforming the

155

adherent into the convert" (1964:445). Analysis of trade union militancy has repeatedly shown the importance of class "community" in tying members of locals together (Cumbler, 1974; Lipset, Trow and Coleman, 1956; Kerr and Siegel, 1954).[1] Turner and Killian (1972:199-205) have used the studies of information diffusion to describe the role played by primary groups in collective movements of public opinion, and Gerlach and Hine (1970:111, 113, 158) report the importance of face-to-face contact in the recruitment to both pentecostal and Black Power groups they studied; "Initial contacts develop by means of pre-existing significant social relationships" (p. 111). Freeman (1975) makes the same observation about "networks" of feminists who became mobilized in the Women's Liberation Movement.

In passing, we may note that some of these generalizations focus on the rewards of solidary membership; others, on the usefulness to group formation of pre-existing trust and sympathy among potential participants. Charles Horton Cooley would have been pleased: Cooley early on recognized the importance of primary groups to learning empathic skills and thereby communicating moral sensibility (See Cooley, 1918:249-50; Swanson, 1968).

Since most protest or radical organizations are materially poor, incentives for membership or participation are not, generally, services or material rewards. Indeed, leftist movements ask much from their members materially and only rarely reciprocate in kind. Moreover, the benefits sought by such groups are, as Olson (1956) pointed out, "public goods." Movement participants will not necessarily or usually get more or less of the benefits which the movement demands for the much larger beneficiary group. There remain but two alternatives: the internalization of ideology (persuasion) and "the joys of participation" (expressive gratification).[2] And these are apt to be different sides of the same coin. The general point is that primary groups are among the most important source of both kinds of incentives for individuals.

The reader will note that no reference is made to particular types of personalities or "needs" or character types. The wholistic and spontaneous nature of primary group interaction makes personality important, to be sure, in determining which persons play which roles in any given group. But the basis of the observations I make is the generic nature of group process, not any given type of individual personality. In greater or lesser degree, that is, expressive rewards and successful group pressure to learn its ways will be present for any movement participant.

B. Recruitment

When we speak of recruitment to social movements we are talking about the diffusion of participation in a movement's activities and the degree of its intensity. In any given locality the process can be conceptualized as one radiating from a core—we may call it a clique—of highly involved individuals ("militants") who interact with one another with great frequency. This core is made up of active individuals with a strategic place in a lattice of primary relations. In this network they carry their particular style, set of substantive concerns, and propose their current projects. In any given locality such people are, from a national association's point of view, a "cadre," sometimes middle-level leadership, and more infrequently, national leadership.

Frequently, one finds groups of friends, who are not formal members of any given organization, but including among them constituents of many. So, within a circle of college friends from 1960-64 there may have been a number of people who received mailings from SNCC (the Student Non-Violent Coordinating Committee), another from the W.E.B. Du Bois Clubs, another from S.D.S., etc.

Besides being a local chapter leader and a member of national executive bodies, I had at various times regional organizing responsibilities. As I travelled I noted in the early sixties, and later, when I travelled nationally for NUC, that even while one of these organizations was growing nationally, in a given area, or on a given campus, it might be failing. My observation was that local chapter growth was heavily influenced by the social location and status attributes of their initial cadre.

The higher prestige and more attractive the individual members of an activist clique or friendship group, and/or the higher the prestige of the group as a whole, the more likely they were to have channels to successfully communicate their concerns, the latest news, etc., to a broader group of people. And by their own attractiveness as individuals or leaders, they attracted people to participation.

Where such groups and individuals were lower in status and prestige, they found a smaller scope for recruitment, and may even have found their group negatively valued, and an obstacle to gaining movement adherents. This, of course, is the meaning of "personal" factors in the local success of a movement; it is the generalized restatement of the reaction expressed by potential "supporters" of a movement that "the association here is no good, I wouldn't join it."

157

Prestige and status are, of course, relative terms. The pristine sense of them—honor, and life-style groups exhibiting behavior to which varying degrees of such respect is attributed—must be seen in terms of a given target group for recruitment. For example, the New University Conference attempted to organize leftist graduate students and faculty members. It was my experience as an organizer that chapters established by graduate students—the most frequent type—were relatively unsuccessful in recruiting faculty members, regardless of questions of ideology. In part, the reason had to do with life-cycle impact on styles of life. Faculty members with families, for example, found the typical graduate student disregard for family life (late meetings, weekend projects, etc.) an obstacle to their participation. And graduate students in the late sixties were apt, once they had been involved in leftist activity, to put the problem of the morality or political propriety of their vocational choice at the top of their moral agendas. Among faculty members, for better or worse, these were issues long since settled.

Another set of examples of personal, status and cultural styles in relation to different target groups may be found in dress and appearance. Clean-shaven and short-haired in the late sixties, I found that I could no longer walk into an S.D.S. or a leftist meeting and assume I had legitimacy. Things improved in 1969 when I grew a beard.

Movement organizations vary in the extent to which they recognize these status phenomena, or approve of them. The highly visible use of "notables" may alienate rank and file leftists; it is less problematic to groups without highly developed egalitarian ideology. Another factor which will determine variation in the extent to which organizations make use of personal status of central members is the degree of outreach it seeks. If it is appealing to groups socially different from it—in base or style—then it will tend to put forward its most "attractive" members. Since the farther the social distance from the activist group, the more likely a widely recognized criterion of attractiveness will be used, ambitious outreach tends to make more visible members who are more conventionally prestigeful, or at least acceptable to conventional constituencies. This is part of the social economy of a social movement organization—a dismal science for leftists, for it helps create some of the oligarchic tendencies, noted by Michels and his commentators (e.g., Zald and Ash, 1966), and of such concern to leftist movement participants.

Primary groups also influence recruitment to social movements by legitimating action in face-to-face and salient terms—by making it conventional. In conventional milieus and in periods of stability relatively noninstitutionalized forms of political action are dissensual—at least in Western societies. One might say that, to support a decision to act for a collective goal in irregular ways, a person will generally be meeting some positive expectation of significant others. In this perspective, movement-related primary groups are the carriers of norms which encourage "commitment." They act as channels of communication biased in favor of action on the basis of political or moral judgment, especially when these channels are prestigeful. As an observer of political demonstrations, for example, one notes the characteristic clustering of individuals who join a march or rally, or congregate at a demonstration or before a speech. The clusterings at such events groups friends with one another, and quite importantly, turns some acquaintances into friends. There are higher densities around notable personalities of the movement. These groupings, starting with twos and threes, tend to arrive at the event together, collect other group members, and can be seen clustering again when it is over.

The provision of legitimation is a factor when an individual is indecisive about participating in an event or more long-term program. This may be due to ambivalence on the issue, or a reluctance to give the time involved for personal reasons. One may then observe the interchange:

"Are you going to the march?"
"I dunno . . . you?"
"Yeah, I think so."
"I guess I'll go."

The embodiment of the principle or the commitment in a concrete person, a trusted, valued friend, is almost always more effective than a written appeal. In my experience, movement participants tacitly recognize this in another way, when, for example, they are collecting names for petitions: organizers try to contact "outsiders" through activists with whom "the outsider" has some positive relationship.

C. Socialization and Ideological Maintenance

The recruitment of members may disrupt or change the associations of a social movement. When social unrest and/or movement activity is high, any association will have to choose either to limit membership, or to recruit rapidly. This corresponds to the distinction between inclusive and exclusive membership criteria, as used, for example, by Duverger (1963) and Zald and Ash (1966). If the more rapid course is chosen, the association risks "dilution" or change in its political or social outlook as the "uninitiated" pour in. S.D.S. experienced this after it sponsored the April 17, 1965, March on Washington to end the war in Vietnam.

Having organized the first national demonstration against the Vietnam War, in April 1965, S.D.S. grew spectacularly. One estimate (Sale, 1973) is that the number of chapters doubled between December 1964, when the March was first decided upon, and June 1965, the first convention after it was held. In most chapters individual participation increased even more. But who was a member? S.D.S. had never been very tightly administered, nor overly concerned about formal membership: now it was a shambles. At the University of Chicago, where I was, meeting attendance went from a couple of dozen to a couple of hundred while the March was being organized. And the new participants had little or no sense of the outlook of the organization or its recent history. Those of us in the "old guard" realized that the group was growing away from us. By 1966, a new "generation" (cohort is more accurate: see Ross, 1976) of leadership had taken control of S.D.S. For S.D.S. growth meant change.

Whether or not an association chooses an "open door" policy, it still has the task of socializing new members to the culture of the group. And as well, the association tries to make its ideological view comprehensible for those recruits with less highly developed outlooks than those already active. Associations vary in the degree to which they manage such socialization and maintenance. In periods of rapid recruitment and low socialization an association may be qualitatively transformed—and this often happens. Another example is the transformation of CORE. In the fifties CORE was an obscure band of pacifist-oriented middle-class individuals with many white members; it was committed to racial integration through direct nonviolent action, and passive resistance to nonviolence. Under the impact of the direct action phase of the civil rights movement CORE grew enormously, its membership changed to include more Blacks, and it became less middle class and more militant: nonviolence was transformed from a philosophy to an organizational tactic. Its strategy was transformed from action on the symbolic level (e.g., bus and lunch counter) to the concrete (rent strikes and employment); later its nationalism led it to adopt "Black capitalism" as its strategic perspective.

Primary groups within the social movements and organizations in which I worked influenced the absorption by new members of the style and beliefs of the group more than any other single factor. The variability in their ability to do so determined whether waves of new recruits produced the smoother or more discontinuous appearance of movement "generations." S.D.S.'s period of growth is a good example.

As with the New Left in general (see Unger, 1974; Teadori, 1969; Lynd, 1969), there is broad agreement about the timing of a 1965-66 shift in the tone and style of S.D.S. Though there is little doubt that spring '65 through June '66 was the period of transition, this author's experience and observation is that the winter of 1964-65 was the seed-time of the change.

In the fall of 1964, the Free Speech Movement at Berkeley mobilized thousands of students in protest and direct actions against restrictions on campus-based political activity. The response in S.D.S. was immediate (see crisis response, below). The network of chapter contacts and officers, with National Office encouragement, set up a nationwide tour of a number of Free Speech Movement leaders, and it was clear as they travelled that a sympathetic response from S.D.S. chapters and toward S.D.S. chapters had been found. Throughout 1965-66, the militant on-campus confrontation of the Free Speech Movement acted as a kind of model for on-campus protests, but now they were focused on the war and the draft.

The reader will recall that in August 1964 the Tonkin Gulf incident revealed that the Johnson Administration was willing to use direct American armed intervention in Vietnam. By December 1964, before the February '65 bombing of Hanoi and the escalation of troop landings which followed it, there was widespread perception in S.D.S. circles that a full-scale war was imminent. With much controversy, the National Council of S.D.S., meeting between Christmas 1964 and New Year's 1965, called for an April 1965 March on Washington to End the War in Vietnam.

Despite opposition from the anti-communist Left, the March was a success and S.D.S. became, as its sponsor, the recipient of a large influx of new recruits.

The scholarly and other writers about this period have failed to observe that the vote to hold the April 1965 March prefigured the later generational split in S.D.S. The decision was very close; indeed, the March was defeated in a first vote, and then only narrowly passed on reconsideration. The most influential bloc opposed to holding the March was that part of the founding group—the most prestigeful part—which had left college and was engaged in off-campus community organizing. They argued that the nationally focused activity of the March would take energy and resources from local grass-roots organizing. When the March took place, bringing with it a new wave of student members, the group which included most of the central old guard figures tended to withdraw from commitment to S.D.S. inner organizational matters.

Turner and Killian (1972:284) have a nice formulation which, by analogy, was similar to the situation in which S.D.S. subsequently found itself:

> Publics typically ascribe unannounced broader goals to any movement that attracts attention, and the public definition affects the adherent's conceptions of their purpose in the movement.

Although S.D.S. had always (since its manifesto of 1962, the Port Huron Statement) been *inclusive* in recruiting policy, it had remained a slowly growing, relatively small group. Face-to-face contacts and the use of intellectually oriented working papers were its media of diffusion. Now, in 1965, the mass media did S.D.S's recruiting for it. One consequence of this was the transformation of the meaning of the phrase "participatory democracy." Coined in the Port Huron Statement, the phrase was interpreted by some mass media and even friendly observers, to imply "consensus in group decision-making." To this author's knowledge, that meaning was not used at all at the Port Huron meeting in 1962, and rarely until 1965-66. Its original usage more nearly intended to extend the socialist idea of industrial democracy to all forms of public life. But the new recruits (and later, scholars; cf. Turner and Killian, 1972) came to S.D.S. with this impression, and they made it into a partial reality.

Beyond such specific transformations, the observers agree on change in the tenor of the group.

Sale's research is congruent with my impressions at the time: "The new spirit in S.D.S. was the genie that April 17 [1965: The March] let out of the bottle." At 1965's June Convention the President elected was the first from outside the founding group.

Sale (1973:204) summarizes it this way:

> . . . Now S.D.S. was starting to become the home for a new breed of activist, a younger (sic) more alienated, more committed (sic) student. . . . They were new to national politics, had never before attended an S.D.S. convention, knew the organization essentially as the caller of the April March. . . . Much to the bewilderment of the older S.D.S.ers now irrevocably christened 'the old guard.'

For the first time at a convention most of the people were unknown to each other, the proceedings were out of the hands of a group of old friends, the Port Huronites no longer dominated.

Participants shared Sale's sense of the change over that year. Haber (1969), the first President (1960-1962) and most important single founder, noted the new recruits have "no time for educational work . . . because the urgency of direct moral expression outweighs for them all other considerations." On the other side of the developing generation gap, Shero, elected Vice-President, proclaimed, "We were by instinct much more radical, much more willing to take risks . . ." (Sale, 1973:206). Shero in fact attributed his election to his *disaffiliation* with the most prominent of the old guard, Tom Hayden: "I thought he was a great dude, but I wasn't in awe of him at all. . . . I got a certain amount of respect . . . for taking him on" (Sale, 1973:209).

As 1966 wore on, the old guard realized S.D.S. was changing. In December an "educational" conference was held. Sale comments (1973:252):

> The December meetings were a touching symbol. Called by the old guard to re-establish the kind of S.D.S. they had known and loved, it actually served to indicate that, inevitably, the organization was headed in new directions, the clock could not be turned back. The S.D.S. that was family, that was shared assumptions and shared lives, was fading now, and something new and uncertain was growing in its place.

The breakdown of a former, perhaps intuitive consensus was indicated by an "ideological" workshop of about fifteen persons, attended by the present author. The span of participants' views covered free market anarchism to technocratic planning. Not a single participant, except for the author, had read S.D.S's strategic 1963 document, *America and the New Era*, and none had read C. Wright Mills' "Letter to the New Young Left," a piece with wide currency among the old guard.

By 1966 the change in leadership and style was complete. "A new group had taken over with no personal ties to the founders, indeed the new leadership was hardly acquainted with the old" (Flacks, 1974:36).

The small group of persons among the old guard who advocated coalitions with labor and liberals were now out altogether (Unger, 1974:95). The new guard, tremendously diverse, with views ranging from counter-culture utopianism to a budding Marxism "had joined S.D.S. after the inception of its anti-Vietnam program, and . . . came from schools without much tradition of student activism" (Skolnick, 1969:96-97).

163

Participant journalist Kopkind (1973:30), in fact, delimits the usage New Left to "a rather small group of white and black students and post-students committed to a Radical socialist reformism, who were working from about 1961-1966."

II. PRIMARY GROUPS AND CHANGE IN SOCIAL MOVEMENT ORGANIZATIONS

A. Leadership Change

In the presentation of the "old guard-new guard" shift in S.D.S. the observers and participants we cited above were struck by the absence of friendship and even acquaintance between the two leadership groups. Recall that Flacks (1974:36) referred to "no personal ties to the founders"; Skolnick (1969:96-97) makes the same point.[3] Sale pointed out the "group of old friends" displaced in '65 by conferees who were new to meetings (1973:204). He describes the antipathy to the old guard

. . . based in part on nervousness, awe, and unfamiliarity, in part on the remoteness and inaccessibility of the old guard" (1973:206).

By 1966, Sale says, "the S.D.S. that was family" was gone (1973:252).

These observations can be supported by some more objective evidence about organizational activity (Sale, 1973:272). In the spring of 1966, before the vital 1966 convention, five new regional structures were formed in S.D.S. One of these (The Midwest: Ohio, Indiana and Michigan) was in an "old" area of S.D.S. work, but new institutions were brought in; another, the Niagara (upper New York State) was heavily infiltrated by the FBI, but also included a new set of institutions (Rosenbaum, 1971, as cited in Marx, 1974).

The other three regions were the Plains States (Iowa, Kansas, Missouri and Nebraska), the Mid-South (Texas, Oklahoma, Arkansas and Louisiana) and the Northwest (Oregon and Washington). At the 1966 convention, the acrimonious defeat of the "old guard" was, by the new guard, referred to as the victory of Prairie Power, a consciously populist reference. And indeed, the elected officers reflected this. The three most prominent figures at the convention were respectively from Texas, organizing in Nebraska and attending Iowa State. Texas, Iowa, Los Angeles, Iowa again, Texas again, were the homes or residences of members of the new National Council. Every member of the N.C., except for one, and the First Alternate (myself) were identified with Prairie Power (Sale, 1973:272, 283-85).

The leadership of the new guard, then, was largely drawn from regions without face-to-face contact with the old guard. Even within campus chapters, where founders were present, new recruits and old hands could be socially segregated. But important figures in the old guard had already *left* campuses (Sale, 1973:214-15) and so were hardly available to the bulk of new recruits. The new guard then, complete with its diversity and ultimate internal contradiction, nevertheless felt itself arrayed against the most unifying of adversaries: the strangers.

Sophisticated observers of S.D.S. may take exception to interpreting primary group ties as the key to office turnover in particular: they will be right. The founding leaders of S.D.S. almost unanimously believed in rotation of office and in making way for new leadership. But *office turnover* is not what is under consideration here; rather, we seek to explain discontinuous waves of movement generations (or cohorts) in their impact on movement change. Flacks puts it well (1974:36):

> In short, not only had the original new leftists given up their personal influence within the organization, but they failed to communicate their particular vision in such a way that it would be carried forward by any self-conscious group of successors.

Flacks' analysis correctly implies that the socialization process in S.D.S. broke down when the organization expanded rapidly. This is supported by the personal memoirs of older recruits which have recently appeared (Kopkind, 1973; Langer, 1973; Potter, 1971). For each, the original New Left vision became a "thematic heritage" (Kopkind, 1973:33), no longer attached to S.D.S. as an organization.

Thus, my hypothesis is that if integration to preexisting primary groups within an organization is low, but new members remain in the organization nevertheless, these new members are apt to be a change element in the organization. Of course, the qualifier here is that this change will be heavily dependent on the existence of usable democratic procedures.

A recurrent symptom of inadequate socialization is the formation of new member cliques which feel disaffected from the "old" leadership in vague, but deeply felt ways. In S.D.S., we saw that disaffected new-member cliques arose most frequently in areas which had either been without former chapters before, or where new members were much younger or for other reasons were personally segregated from older members. It is here, in the relative ability of groups to absorb new members to primary group association, that the genesis of movement "generations" takes place.

The more complex and subtle an organization's ideology and/or intellectual content, or the greater the commitment membership implies, the more necessary highly integrated primary group life is for its maintenance. When primary ties break down or are highly discontinuous within the organization, change in political content is more probable.

In movement organizations there is always a tendency to view new issues in simple terms, or, in the absence of obvious salience, to ignore them. Moreover, there is a tendency to act on the known and predictable consensus rather than upon an unborn one which may be occasioned by new events. Strong group ties which consistently involve the participant in discussion of the movement's perspective and its problems, will bring new issues and problems into the group's and the participant's frame of reference, and adjust the individual's reactions, as well as the group's formulations, to new events.

A social movement must constantly define and redefine the social situation if its substantive ideas are to remain important to its membership. As elsewhere in social life, the redefinition of the situation is crucially dependent on one's primary group ties.

Useem (1972) has demonstrated, for example, that those engaged in organized resistance to conscription during the Vietnam War entered the movement with various liberal to radical views. But after entry the proportions of those with radical views increased dramatically. In exploring this, Useem shows that friendship choices shifted, after entry, toward other movement participants. Since the resistance was organized by old hands from the New Left, Useem attributes what, for the organizers, represented successful socialization to radicalism as a result of the successful integration of old hands and new ones. As the resistance grew in the area Useem studied (Boston), the changes influenced by new recruits did not create discontinuous changes in policy or in clique leadership.

Interestingly enough, however, the resistance's success in smoothing the flow of movement generations was obtained at the almost direct expense of S.D.S. Many of the radical anti-draft organizers Useem studied were faction or clique members who were growing discontented with S.D.S.—as an inner social experience and also because of its inconsistency on the issue of the draft. Their exit, which was variable in completeness, was part of the

166

regionalized and generationally divided ferment within the organization in the 1966 period—which was when the "prairie power" group became prominent. Note should be made here that we have spoken of social movements from the point of view of its associational core. In the looser, less clearly defined lattice of constituency primary groups—i.e., among "adherents" and "supporters"—the same problems are confronted and functions observed, except that in these more loosely organized sectors one would expect the latitude of socialization and maintenance to be much broader. And the pressures to conform, since the objects of conformity would be much less clear, quite a bit milder. It is just because such groups are less demanding that they proliferate so easily. Both S.D.S. and the anti-draft resistance, in the mid-sixties, were characterized by extraordinarily inclusive membership: they had only the most diffuse criteria for social membership. Discontinuous movement generations were therefore made more probable as new member primary groups were less likely to reach very far into the old-hand cliques.

B. *Internal Processes and Social Control*

Union Democracy provides evidence for the proposition that organizational democracy rests on the possibility for small group interaction with others concerned about organizational direction. (Of course, the existence of such groups does not mean they are, as Faris [1957] points out, primary groups.) Other internal processes discussed here include the ability of an organizational core to effect its decisions, the degree of tolerance of internal dissensus, and the role of cliques in decision-making.

A movement organization's ability to carry out its programs, aside from the adequacy of material resources, depends upon the mobilization of sympathy and support for these programs. Pressures generated in friendship and clique groups within the organization mobilize commitment to program through a process by which the general commitment (loyalty) to the organization becomes embodied in specific individuals with which an individual interacts in diffuse primary relations. Obligations to the collective are thereby transformed to obligations to specific persons.

Once an association has taken a decision, it then attempts to mobilize resources to carry it out. This is no small problem when a movement's "personnel" are (a) volunteers, (b) rather amorphous both in terms of their identification with the association and in their politics, and (c) perhaps untrained or unskilled in terms of a particular program (e.g., S.D.S. proposals in the fall of 1965, and 1966, for a nationwide network of draft—or anti-draft—counselors. These required a large number of persons familiar with the intricacies of the selective service system and the regulations for conscientious objectors). Members must be convinced that the program is worthwhile, good, or right, possible, etc.; and their own participation must be cast as critical for its success. The symptom of failure is typical and clear: groups pass "paper" resolutions on the national level, but cannot implement local programs. This reflects both their origins and their reception. Because the typical non-Leninist movement organization partakes in the atmosphere of movements themselves, they have little inner discipline: people act preponderantly on their own locally generated initiatives. Most programmatic proposals brought to national bodies are generated within such local groups and reflect a particular group's perceptions and strategic outlooks. Although they may succeed in convincing representatives of a national meeting of the general desirability of a given project, it will not be implemented unless they, or others, can impress local groups with their outlook. Programs are generated then, among small groups, more or less intimate, more or less homogenous. They are received by other such groups. If a program "fits" the current style and profile of concern of a local group, and more decisively, if it has a strong local advocate who "embodies" it to his colleagues, it has a greater chance of successfully involving constituents and participants.

In a locality there may be groups composed of persons whose commitments and identities are "referenced" to the organization as a national entity. This is not necessarily or even usually abstract; rather, the organization symbolizes a series of long-standing and warm relationships with concrete individuals. For those individuals and groups with such a reference, a national decision may be taken as a major personal and collective responsibility. An example of this occurred in the S.D.S. March on Washington against the Vietnam War, in 1965. Many clusters of older S.D.S. hands, including those in Chicago, were indifferent to or opposed the idea of a March. However, once the December 1964 decision was made, they considered its success as their personal *cum* collective responsibility. In Chicago, the two S.D.S. activists (myself included) with responsibility in this area shared the organizational tasks of launching local committees to charter buses and so forth, despite their personal feelings. It is interesting to note that neither would have done the job if left alone; only the fact that the work was seen as their collective responsibility enabled them to prompt each other to action. Similar instances occurred in other cities at this time—e.g., Cleveland and Newark.

In the draft resistance, only an occasional and widespread sharing of organizational literature knit the local groups together. They displayed wide variation in projects undertaken and methods used. But the overlap of friendship ties and common commitment produced very similar themes in these projects: coffeeshops for youth and GIs, community newspapers and pamphlet publishing, counselling work (Ferber and Lynd, 1971).

In organizations in which formal rules demand discipline, that is, in Leninist organizations, it is still the identification with the organization, and the creation of personal *cum* collective responsibility, that operate in motivating volunteer functionaries. Studying a religious group, Lofland and Stark (1965) suggest the generalization that the more intensive the affectively positive interaction is between movement participants, the more likely personal sacrifice (material or ideal) will be made.

Related to the problem of acquiescence is the fundamental problem of the toleration of dissensus. Obviously, organizations and movements are, in historical terms, distinguishable by the broadness or narrowness of their political and social ideas, and to the extent to which they demand adherence to a "line" or consensus. This paper conceives of movements—and most any voluntary association—as lattices of fairly homogenous groups of persons interacting as social wholes. The extent to which heterodox individuals will be permitted, or will choose, to stay within these groups is a complex variable. Not a small part of it is determined by forces generated outside of the primary group. It would be a mistake, however, to conceive of movements as static, located once for all time on this dimension. For example, local groups should find that high attraction to newly arrived members, or older members who are out of sympathy with part of the movement's perspective, will widen the legitimacy afforded to dissensual views. And we can envision, in similar fashion, this new legitimacy spreading in ripples through the lattice of groups within the organization or movement.

In the late sixties, the influence of Marxism spread through the S.D.S., in part, because leading members who shared in the shift toward Marxism were part of, or able to organize, "collectives" of high solidarity to advance their budding perspective.

C. Cliques and Democracy

We have proposed that the way in which founding groups relate to new recruits is an important factor in what may appear to be the arrival of a new movement "generation." The most obvious kind of organizational relationship is dominance—organizationally and ideologically. In this relationship the older group has a monopoly on legitimate leadership. Gusfield (1957) analyzed this sort of generational dominance for the Women's Christian Temperance Union. In this kind of inner organizational life, which gives rise to the Weber-Michels tradition of analysis of oligarchy, relations to constituencies may be strained or, indeed, nonexistent. The W.C.T.U. found itself *without* a constituency.

The experience of the student movement of the sixties was that loosely tied constituencies were held or lost to the extent to which their members felt they had direct accessibility to organizational decisions. This eventually led movement groups to adopt procedures to allow anyone who attended a meeting to vote on questions before it. Organizations may avoid this problem with constituencies, through maintaining clique control, by concealing this control (as was the case in the role of the CIA in the U.S. National Student Association) or legitimating it through principles of strategy—e.g., "democratic centralism."

Thus, "old hand" cliques may dominate organizations by (a) co-opting new members to their primary groups, (b) concealing their dominance, or (c) using an ideological justification of principle. Each strategy has its limits and problems. Co-optation is limited by size; concealment by the ability to suppress historical information; and ideology by the absolute cohesion of the dominants, and the effective indoctrination of new members.

More common than a single clique dominance, however, is clique evolution. This was the process within S.D.S. In the early sixties a small founding group co-opted "leadership types" to itself, unintentionally but effectively socializing new members to new ideas, new friends, new styles... for a while. As the organization grew too large for any given small group to know everyone in the organization, in 1965, this tactic created significant strain. Socialization could not be carried out in a single, even though geographically dispersed, primary group. More formal programs, institutes, readings would have been required, and some were attempted. Strategically, the early dependence of clique—primary group—socialization meant that when the period of mass infusion occurred, S.D.S. was unprepared to assimilate great numbers of new members. The result was a period of great confusion over organizational goals, strategy, and structure; in turn, this caused a withdrawal from action at the time when the organization was larger than ever before, in 1965-1966.

Geschwender (n.d.) has provided indirect evidence for seeing formal institutes as functional equivalents to informal socialization in his analysis of factions in the League of Revolutionary Black Workers. The League began at one Dodge (Hamtramck) plant and the spread among Blacks in the Detroit automobile industry. At that juncture League internal education programs were attempted; they failed because competing cliques among the intellectuals disagreed over their content. The League did not survive this clash.

The maintenance of organizational democracy has a peculiar relationship to clique formations which is not necessarily solely negative, and not anticipated by the Weber-Michels school. A social movement organization, because of turnover, (sometimes) expansion, and loosely tied constituencies, and of course events in the world outside itself, is, as we have seen, constantly redefining its strategy and outlook. Its new members or loosely identified constituencies are likely to lack either organizational experience of specifically relevant experience with which to formulate issues in a malleable manner.

Despite the New Left's notable distrust of leadership, two illustrations of this process are among the many I had within S.D.S.

At the Port Huron Convention of 1962 the business at hand was consideration of a draft "manifesto," submitted by Tom Hayden. There were a variety of major and minor points of contention about the document, and these were raised in the first day of the meeting. The document was lengthy—more than ten thousand words. Hayden, and Al Haber, the dominant personalities at the meeting, proposed that work groups, dividing the document into sections, should formulate their revisions as "bones": simple statements of shift in analysis or strategy. For example, one "bone" was: "the last section should point out that students cannot make change without allies, especially working class and trade union allies." These bones, rather than detailed, line-by-line rewording, were what came before the plenary for voting. Those passed were given over to a "drafting committee." The idea worked—even though it made more convenient the transformation of Hayden's own document.

Much later, at the University of Chicago, in 1969, the S.D.S. chapter had decided to hold a sit-in in support of a fired female leftist professor. Needing mass support, the chapter called for a campus-wide meeting to consider various proposed actions. It became evident that a couple thousand people would attend—with a significant number hostile to S.D.S., the issue, and the idea of a sit-in. At the time I was not active in the local chapter. I was working as national organizer for the New University Conference. And I was far from being on the best of terms with the local or national S.D.S. leadership. However, I had had considerable experience of chairing large parliamentary-type meetings, and none of the chapter leadership had. They asked, and I agreed, that I lead the meeting. It went as they hoped—a sit-in was legitimated in a tumultuous late-night session.

There is irony in the incident, but no iron law of oligarchy. I was personally skeptical, and mildly *opposed* to the sit-in tactic.

If old hands cannot use their experience for the common good, either because of inadequate information, skills, motivation, or (even) insoluble conflict, the old hands find themselves discredited and the organization in a period of confusion, and/or in the hands of a new group with new definitions of reality. This succession need not necessarily be democratic in the sense of a positive political choice; it may be succession by default. And maintenance of the status of the old group may reflect their ability not necessarily to dominate but to facilitate democratic processes. All of these variations occurred within S.D.S., some within SNCC. In SNCC, where the organizational decisions were made by and for full-time staff (Zinn, 1964), strategic problems were more nearly zero-sum games determining the activity of an individual over a period of (often highly dangerous) months. Under these conditions clique succession was more complete.

It is, therefore, my hypothesis that one requirement for organizational democracy is the existence of a more or less influential group with skill in facilitating decision-making. Cliques of old members may maintain status and influence on the basis of this ability, without necessarily being oligarchic in their control of the decision-making process. The more rapid the recruitment (the higher the proportion of new members eligible to participate in decision-making), the more important such groups become to the maintenance of orderly decision-making processes.

This proposition, and the one before it, have direct bearing on studies such as Michels', which focuses on turnover of leadership. In fact, a stable leadership *may* perform a democratic function by leading an organization to issue resolution. Of course, stable leadership cliques may, and probably do, frequently use their agenda control to maintain their positions. The point here is some of the counter-intuitive possibilities in clique analysis.

D. *Primary Groups and Response to Crises*

When a major political or social event occurs in modern society, individuals are apt to learn about it directly from the mass media, before organizational channels can be mobilized. Sometimes initial organizational response is solicited from a central office, with telephone calls, telegrams, etc., to relevant leadership groups. Or, response may be from constituent elements to national centers. In either case, individuals may not spontaneously respond in the same political terms, or intensity of feeling. In a given locality, however, some participants will call, visit, discuss with one another. Only then, when the various relevant (or irrelevant) aspects of the event have been brought to collective attention and balanced one way or another, does the perception of crisis occur and become communicated up or down, and across the organization.

An example of this process will illustrate it. In fall 1964 S.D.S. was growing, but still small. It had been highly influenced by the direct action techniques and spirit of the civil rights movement. Its own programmatic agenda at the time called for student volunteers to leave campus and help organize "an interracial movement of the poor." Then, as mentioned earlier, the Berkeley Free Speech Movement began. In Chicago we heard of the large sit-ins through the various media. My sense of each of our individual reception of the news was quite warm and positive. But it was only as and when we met together, and were in contact with the National Office to arrange speaking tours for FSM leaders (some of whom had had personal contact with the founding cadre at Michigan), that we collectively realized something momentous had happened for our own organization. Only then did we all, locally and elsewhere, go into "high gear" in terms of the university as an arena of direct action.

Thus, my conclusion is that speed of organizational response in a potential crisis depends upon the effective coverage in primary group lattices throughout the organization and its constituency. Intensity of response, following Lofland and Stark (1965), should be positively related to the intimacy of group relations. Furthermore, to the extent that the lattice of interpersonal relations extends far into nonmember constituencies both locally and nationally, the crisis perception within an organization will be more effectively promulgated as a public event.

The influence of primary groups in crisis response flows naturally from the characteristics of such groups: the medium of primary group communication is as much affective as cognitive; its distinctive characteristic is the legitimacy within it of the exchange of "wholistic" human behavior, not merely the instrumental exchange of more impersonal environments. (This characteristic of primary group communicative modes is, of course, decisive for many of the other relationships discussed in this paper; whereas it is implicit throughout, it is mentioned here because of the clarity of the relationship in this particular context.) Crises are defined not only by whether or not they are seen as "bad," but by the *degree* of threat, promise, or moral extremity which they may signify. It is in the primary group, then, that the communication of intense feelings is most legitimate, and the variety of legitimate modes of communication most diverse. Sympathy with another's feelings, a central aspect of primary relations, allows what is often called "contagion" to move rapidly and intensely. In this context one is reminded of the sentences by Blumer alluded to previously, to the effect that fellowship in a social movement promotes the taking of roles and sharing of experience.

Overview

Through personal ties which legitimately carry affective expression, primary groups, to summarize broadly, offer a series of secondary gains which support movement participants emotionally and help to mold them intellectually. Primary groups become the locus of an individual's collective orientation. In movements like the late New Left these processes may provide a base for a decentralist ideology. But primary groups may also be components of organizational or movement control in quite different ways. They may be instruments which mediate discipline and unity.

If a movement meets serious opposition within the larger society, if its members do not easily procure status gratifications from other stable societal roles (as doctors who fought Medicare did and as students or Blacks do not), if the movement's beliefs are far enough from current perceived reality for it to be seen as "disloyal" or otherwise subjected to calumny—if these conditions prevail then there must be some source of personally meaningful social support and legitimacy available to participants if they are to stay on. This may come from individual moral and religious beliefs. More frequently it is as part of the secondary, often expressive gratifications of group membership that participants gain social support and normative legitimacy for their views. In this sense, all movements which meet opposition are counter-communities which sustain the personal and moral needs of their members. And to a greater or lesser extent, by creating new and counter-sources of legitimacy, their participants begin to *live* in the new order they seek to create, even as they work for its construction. The extent to which this experience is made an explicit part of the prescribed new order, however, is the extent to which utopian and/or communalistic withdrawal is the eventual solution to the movement's problems—but it is all a matter of degree.

To some extent, even the "broadest" political movement has, therefore, its own new society within which members experience a new life.

III. THE NEW SOCIETY OF SOCIAL MOVEMENTS

With the material we have compiled and interpreted so far, the basis for the theoretical interpretation of primary group life in modern social movements has been sketched. That interpretation begins with the idea that participation in social movements *is*, by and large, participation in a more or less intimate primary group life which may be characterized, as did the French Revolutionaries, as *fraternite*. The comments which follow, though somewhat speculative, rest on the kinds of observations described in the foregoing sections of the paper.

Students of social movements have always been sensitive to the "new order" of society implicit in the subjective experience of participants. It remains for us, however, to examine the affective (as more or less distinctive from the cognitive) content of this new order.

In primary groups related to social movements, a person's experience of fraternity generates a significant portion of his or her image of the good society. In some senses, and in most movements, primary groups come to embody the ultimate, though perhaps not consciously realized, aspirations of the movement. In other words, the immediate circle of friends, "a band of brothers (and/or sisters) in a circle of love" *is* the hoped-for new society. Cooley asserted no less, by the way, in his view of primary group life and the social order in general. We suggested earlier that the sources of legitimacy—or more aptly, counter-legitimacy—generated in movement-related primary groups laid the basis for a person's taking on a new series of roles, beliefs, and valued symbols. The general contention here is that the new order implicit in social movements is a "project" of the comradely ties within the movement. The ways in which this applies to social theory can now be restated.

This new order is and has been a difficult and hazy conception—general enough so that its different bases allow their proponents to war against each other. That is so because the yearnings satisfied by movements of both left and right are only ultimately, and not obviously, related to formal or procedural definitions of institutions. This is inherent in the kind of "project" the fraternal order represents. Specific procedural or formal goals—democracy, planning, universal suffrage—are composed of cognitive elements of belief about cause and effect: e.g., free elections lead to the greatest good, etc. But the fraternal order has as its goal concrete and wholistic relations between persons. Its models are in people's affective experience with one another. These aspirations for affective states are highly refractory to institutional definition. The relationship between a hoped-for fraternal commonwealth and the abolition of poverty or exploitation is not "incorrect": according to the analysis presented here, it is just that the abolition of poverty is but indirectly, and distant in time, a condition of meeting fully the affective projection of comradeship.

Consider events which sociologists have chosen to characterize as "expressive." These may be formal or ceremonial ritual, but may also be observed in the informal, incidental aspects of movement life. An instance in the student left and civil rights movements was, for a time, the singing of *We Shall Overcome* at almost all important mass meetings, rallies, etc. Linking arms in large, rhythmically swaying circles, participants from those days of the movement now reflect on them with touching nostalgia. The spontaneous song during free time at conventions or meetings, or the excited and joyful greetings exchanged by friends in the movement when they met at national meetings after periods of separation, still lives in their memories.

The affective tone which is left over after these occasions is as significant as the experience itself. People remember them as exceptionally happy. They are apt to explicitly recall the exaltation they experienced. Crisis situations, in similar manner, are recalled, in retrospect, as expressive experiences. They are described in emotive tones and in terms of the solidary content of feelings.

They are almost always defined in group-relevant ways—hardly ever as happening to or acted upon merely by individuals. It is at the height of such states of feeling that movement participants most clearly experience what is called fraternity.

For me, this means that modern mass movements, to some degree, all share an implicit image of a new order of fraternal relations. The affective experience of comradely relations in primary groups is the most relevant and clear basis for the projection of this order which is not defined so much cognitively (and therefore institutionally) but more as a world of experience in which loving and spontaneous personal relations are predominant.

If this proposition has merit, then the period of disillusionment which seems to follow revolutions can be conceptually ordered in its terms. When a movement is victorious it has emerged from a period of intense conflict; its participants have experienced the exhilaration of comradely union in struggle and sacrifice. But people cannot and do not sustain such emotional heights indefinitely. At some point the revolution consolidates and defines itself institutionally. Because its institutional creations answer aspirations which are cognitively operationalized—e.g., redistribution of land will boost our level of living or security—it does not always address itself, directly, to the creation of a new affective order of brotherhood. So emotional attachments to it become more matter of fact. Everyday daily rounds replace the experience of charisma—of "grace"—embodied in the movement.

Implied here is the larger proposition that there is a limit to the influence of organizationally rational factors, to the amount of impersonality in the development of modern society which will be accepted without social unrest. In sociological work, structural differentiation (alternatively, rationalization of social structure) needs to specify a maximum, not infinite, ability to adequately motivate its own acceptance. At various points in the development of Western capitalism, groups participate in large-scale movements which include an implicit demand to be treated as social wholes, and to organize society around that demand. At the level of macro-sociological theory, then, our excursion in the analysis of primary groups has led to an overarching proposition: the "rise of rational efficiency" will be challenged by the "revolutionary" (sisterhood) or brotherhood." This may be left or right; the class factors and institutional crises which determine that are properly the foci of macro-level theory, as the genesis of crisis is properly the focus of political economy. But in moving from primary groups to rationalization, we have dealt with dimensions of theory which are rooted in interpersonal relations.

That these are structured for their participants by larger systems is undoubtedly the case. That they are directly and humanly experienced as personal relations is also true. City planners may see maps; construction workers see scaffolds.

NOTES

1. In fact, the Hawthorne studies of the Bank Wiring Room, where work groups restricted output through informal norms, were begun, in part, because Western Electric was anxious to prevent unionization—i.e., the emergence of an opposing solidarity. See Loren Baritz (1960).
2. In a recent critique of utilitarianism (Olson, 1965), Fireman & Gamson (1977) employ the equally good usage "consciousness and solidarity."
3. It should be noted, however, that Flacks helped prepare Skolnick's chapter, so that this is not independent verification (cf. Skolnick, 1969:xvii).

REFERENCES

Allen, Robert
   Black Awakening in Capitalist America. New York: Doubleday, 1969.
Baritz, Loren
   Servants of Power. Middletown, Ct.: Wesleyan University Press, 1960.
Blumer, Herbert
   "Social Movements," in M.A. Lee (ed.), *Principles of Sociology*. New York: Barnes and Noble, 1951.
Cooley, Charles H.
   Life and the Student. New York: Knopf, 1918.
Cumbler, John Taylor, Jr.
   "Continuity and Disruption: Working Class Community in Lynn and Fall River, Massachusetts, 1890-1950." Ph.D dissertation, Department of History, University of Michigan, 1974.
Duverger, Maurice
   Political Parties. New York: John Wiley, 1963.
Faris, Elsworth
   "The Primary Group: Essence and Accident," in Lewis Coser and Bernard Rosenberg (eds.), *Sociological Theory*. New York: Macmillan, 1957.
Ferber, Michael and Staughton Lynd
   The Resistance. Boston: Beacon Press, 1971.

Fireman, Bruce and William A. Gamson
"Utilitarian Logic in the Resource Mobilization Perspective." Paper prepared for Vanderbilt Symposium on "The Dynamics of Social Movements: Resource Mobilization, Tactics and Social Control," March, 1977.

Flacks, Richard
"Making History vs. Making Life: Dilemmas of an American Left," *Working Papers*, 11 (Summer, 1974), 56-71.

Freeman, Jo
The Politics of Women's Liberation. New York: David McKay Co., 1975.

Gamson, William A.
The Strategy of Social Protest. Homewood, Ill.: Dorsey Press, 1975.

Gerlach, Luther P. and Virginia H. Hine
People, Power, Change: Movements of Social Transformation. New York: Bobbs-Merrill, 1970.

Geschwender, James A.
"Internal Ideological Conflict and the Development of Splits Within Social Movements: The Case of the League of Revolutionary Black Workers." Mimeo. State University of New York at Binghamton, n.d.

Gusfield, Joseph
"The Problem of Generations in an Organizational Structure," *American Sociological Review*, 35, (1957):323-30.

Hampden-Turner, Charles
Radical Man. Cambridge, Mass.: Schenkman Press, 1970.

Kerr, Clark and Abraham Siegel
"The Interindustry Propensity to Strike—An International Comparison," in Arthur Kornhauser, Robert Subin and Arthur Ross (eds.), *Industrial Conflict*. New York: McGraw-Hill, 1954.

Killian, Lewis
"Social Movements," pp. 426-55 in R.E.L. Faris (ed.), *Handbook of Modern Sociology*. Chicago: Rand McNally, 1964.

Kopkind, Andrew
"Looking Backward: The Sixties and the Movement," *Ramparts*, 11, (1973): 29-34.

Langer, Elinor
"Notes for Next Time: A Memoir of the 1960s," *Working Papers*, 1, (1973): 48-83.

Lipset, S.M., M. Trow and J.S. Coleman
Union Democracy. Glencoe: The Free Press, 1956.

Lofland, John and Rodney Stark
"Conversion to a Deviant Perspective," *American Sociological Review*, 30, No. 6 (1965), 862-74.

Lynd, Staughton
"Towards a History of the New Left," pp. 10-13 in Priscilla Long (ed.), *The New Left: A Collection of Essays*. Boston: Porter-Sargent, 1969.

Marx, Gary T.
"Thoughts on a Neglected Category of Social Movement Participant: The Agent Provocateur and the Informant," *American Journal of Sociology*, 80 (1974), 402-42.

Michels, Robert
Political Parties. New York: The Free Press, 1949.

Olson, Mancur, Jr.
The Logic of Collective Action. Cambridge, Mass.: Harvard University Press, 1965.

Potter, Paul
A Name for Ourselves: Feelings about Authentic Identity, Love, Intuitive Politics, U.S. Boston: Little-Brown, 1971.

Rosenbaum, R.
"Run, Tommy, Run!" *Esquire*, 76 (1971), 51-58.

Ross, Robert J.
"Generational Change and Primary Groups in a Social Movement." Paper presented at American Sociological Association Meetings, New York: August, 1976.

Sale, Kirkpatrick
SDS. New York: Random House, 1973.

Skolnick, Jerome H.
The Politics of Protest. A Report Submitted to the National Commission on the Causes and Prevention of Violence. Washington, D.C.: Government Printing Office, 1969.

Swanson, Guy E.
"To Live in Concord with Society: Two Empirical Studies of Primary Relations," in Albert J. Reiss, Jr. (ed.), *Cooley and Sociological Analysis*. Ann Arbor: University of Michigan Press, 1968.

Teodori, Massimo
The New Left: A Documentary History. Indianapolis: Bobbs-Merrill, 1969.

Unger, Irwin
The Movement: A History of the American New Left 1959-1972. New York: Dodd, Mead, 1974.

Zald, Mayer and Roberta Ash.
"Social Movement Organizations: Growth, Decay and Change," *Social Forces*, 44 (1966), 327-40.

Zinn, Howard
SNCC: The New Abolitionists. Boston: Beacon Press, 1964.

APPENDIX

Hypotheses on Primary Groups and Social Movement Organizations

1. Social movement diffusion moves along networks of primary group relationships.
2. The success an initiating group will have recruiting others is dependent, to some extent, on the attractiveness of its style of life and other status attributes for a specific target group.
3. Primary groups within social movement organizations act as sources of counter-legitimacy for action outside the regular political process of the society.
4. Primary groups are the location of socialization of new members to organizations.
4.1 If new members are not integrated into preexisting primary groups, but stay within the organization nevertheless, they are more likely to be a change element in the organization.
4.2 When new members form their own networks of primary group attachments, and are conscious of their new member commonality, they will have the appearance of a new "movement generation."
5. The more complex and/or demanding an organization's outlook, the more important primary group interaction is to its absorption of new members.
6. Programmatic effectiveness, defined as an organization's ability to carry out programs it has legislated, is dependent, in part, on the ability of primary group attachment to become a generalized attachment to the organization's goals and programs.
7. The more rapid recruitment to an organization, the more dependent it is on old-hand cliques to maintain orderly decision-making.
7.1 Old-hand cliques may maintain their positions in an organization on the basis of their ability to *guide* democratic decision-making; this does not necessarily mean they will "guide" it so as to get their way.
8. Speed and intensity of organizational response to crisis will depend on the extensivity and intensity of its lattice of primary group networks.

A brief comment on the applicability of these hypotheses is in order. It may be that the role of primary groups in social movement organizations is accentuated in student and youth movements. Not having formed their own families yet, peer groups are apt to be more important to the young and educated than to others. Feuer (1969), for example, lists as a characteristic of modern student movements the desire to create in them family substitutes. However, as mentioned in the text, the community context of trade union and working class action has been shown to have a formative impact on militancy and effectiveness. So, besides the hypotheses themselves, an overarching one is in order:

9. The general importance of primary group life to social movement organization is probably higher in youth and student groups than for adults.

9.1 Because of the family and community severing impact of higher education and professional work, the hypotheses are apt to be more true for the highly educated than for others.

But please note, these last propositions assume that the original hypotheses continue to have applicability, to greater or lesser degree; the application to youth and students and the highly educated is one of degree, not kind.

The Achievement
of the
Anti-War Movement

TODD GITLIN

As my generation teeters uneasily between late youth and early middle age, and American expeditionary forces are launched toward new wars in the Third World, a good number of my old political buddies are wondering whether the antiwar passions of the 1960s were worth the effort. The Vietnam War dragged on and on, after all, and in the end, didn't Khmer Rouge genocide and Vietnamese authoritarianism discredit our hopes? Prompted by once-over-lightly media treatments of the era, today's campus activists also seem to believe that the '60s demonstrated conclusively that you can't change history to match your ideals. So why go to the trouble of letting tainted politics interfere with the rigors of preparing for the law boards?

Meanwhile, it's the so-called conservatives, neo- and paleo-, who give the antiwar movement credit. They firmly believe that the country was seized during the '60s by a "new class" of overeducated left intellectuals, tantrum-throwing students, media liberals, uppity minorities, feminists, hedonists, homosexuals and assorted bleeding hearts, who not only succeeded in trashing tradition, standards, the family and all natural hierarchy, but also broke the back of national security, leveling America's just position in the world and costing us an achievable and noble victory in Vietnam. They have spent the past ten years trying to figure out how to recapture lost terrain from the barbarians. And they are haunted by the specter of revived antiwar activity—for good reason. For despite their paranoid exaggerations and their self-serving refusal to acknowledge just how much ideological ground they have already reconquered, they know in their bones what many veterans of the '60s don't know or have forgotten: that the movement against the Vietnam War was history's most successful movement against a shooting war.

Not that there's much reason for unqualified self-congratulation. The napalm no longer falls on Vietnam, but the country still lives under dictatorship, on a perpetual war footing. Moreover, while the movement counted heavily in American politics, much of the leadership, eventually, wasn't satisfied simply to be against the war. Feeling either futile or giddy, they finally wanted a revolution, and came to define success accordingly. Those who persisted in that course made themselves irrelevant to the politics of the '70s and '80s. If the movement was effective, a less insular and more sophisticated movement might have been all the more so. To understand both the achievement and the limits, to learn lessons apropos impending wars, we have to look carefully at the movement's effects on the war and, with equal care, at the war's effects on the movement.

Already, the passing of time shrouds the '60s; the end is confounded with the beginning, the consequences with the causes; the all-important sequence of events is obscured. Our collective memory, such as it is, rests on a few disjointed images snatched out of order. For example, I was shocked in 1975 when the most sophisticated student in a class I was teaching at the University of California, Santa Cruz, said to me one day, "You were in SDS, right?" Right, I said. "That was the Weathermen, right?" How could I explain easily that the Weathermen were one of the factions that *ended* Students for a Democratic Society, exploded its ten-year history? (As an early leader of SDS I had fervently opposed them, in fact.)

The media and popular lore have dwelt on the lurid, easily pigeonholed images of 1968-71, as if they encompassed and defined the whole of "The '60s" in living color once and for all: the flags of the National Liberation Front of South Vietnam flying at antiwar demonstrations, singled out by TV cameras however outnumbered they were by American flags; window-trashers and rock-throwers, however outnumbered they were by peaceful marchers; the bombings and torchings of ROTC buildings; and the lethal explosions of the Weather Underground townhouse and the University of Wisconsin Army Mathematics Research Center in 1970.

To fathom the antiwar movement, though, we have to go back to 1964-65, when the Johnson administration committed itself to the war. In September 1964, while Lyndon Johnson was campaigning for peace votes with the slogan "We seek no wider war," American gunboats just offshore North Vietnam provoked an attack by the North Vietnamese, and a gullible Senate gave Johnson a carte blanche resolution that was to supply the questionable legal basis for years of subsequent escalation. The political climate of that moment is measured by the fact that the dissenting votes numbered a grand total of two—Wayne Morse and Ernest Gruening. That Christmas, Students for a Democratic Society, with all of a few hundred active members, presumptuously called for a demonstration against the war, to be held in Washington, D.C., in April. In February, Johnson began the systematic bombing of North Vietnam. In March came the first campus teach-ins against the war, and in April more than 25,000 marched in Washington—the majority dressed in jackets, ties, skirts. During the fall of 1965 there were the first coordinated demonstrations across the country, some of them more militant (a few symbolic attempts to block troop trains); there were a few widely publicized draft card burnings and a national media hysteria about a nonexistent SDS plan to disrupt the draft. Within the next 18 months, some leaders of the civil rights movement began denouncing the war—first the militants of the Student Nonviolent Coordinating Committee, then the Reverend Dr. Martin Luther King, Jr. There were attempts to get antiwar measures onto local ballots and to carry the war issue into professional associations.

With the number of American troops steadily swelling to almost the half-million mark and the bombing continuing mercilessly, antiwar militancy—still nonviolent—grew apace. In October 1967 there were vast mobilizations at the Pentagon and in Oakland, California, where, for the first time, armed troops and riot-control police wreaked havoc on active nonviolence. Only in 1968, after the assassinations of Martin Luther King and Robert F. Kennedy, did significant numbers of antiwar people murmur about the need for violence to raise the political cost of the war at home. There were also the first activities by government *agents provocateurs*.

We don't know nearly enough, and are not collectively curious enough, about government provocation. But one item may suggest how tantalizing this subject should be for a new generation of researchers. In August 1968, a few thousand demonstrators went out into the streets of Chicago. The tear-gas clouds and media spotlights during the Democratic convention polarized public opinion and established a new threshold for militancy while fatally discrediting the Democrats. Who were these protestors? According to army intelligence documents pried loose by CBS News ten years later,

"About one demonstrator in six was an undercover agent." As flag-burning and cop-provoking increased, the movement became open territory for tough-talking infiltrators. With glacial slowness, information seeps into the light; but our famous investigative press—busy now uncovering the startling news that the KGB tries to influence antinuclear politics in Europe—is largely uninterested in this ancient history.

In any event, to gauge the effects of the movement as a whole, we might begin by asking what would have happened if the war had gone on without any material public opposition. Suppose, in other words, that without a movement in the streets there had been only a passive and ambiguous dissent in the polls as the American body-count mounted. Suppose also a numbed and passive Congress. Suppose, that is, a war very much like the Korean War.

What would have kept the war from escalating even more intensely than it actually did, with more ordnance and more troops producing more devastation, more refugees, more death? There were, of course, other forces working against the war: the economic drain; the breakdown of military discipline (inspired in a curious way by the movement); and the political mainstream's sense of the war's futility. But the North Vietnamese and the NLF were prepared to suffer huge casualties indefinitely rather than surrender. And once "Vietnamization" had changed the color of the corpses, the United States could have withdrawn its combat troops and still continued the air war for years without producing massive disgruntlement, for the bomber missions cost relatively few American lives. Support would likely have grown for the military's designs to press the war to the screaming limits of military technology in order to maintain an anti-Communist South Vietnam, indefinitely, at all costs.

Concrete evidence of the movement's influence was hard to come by. So much so, in fact, that, day to day, many movement people felt we were accomplishing next to nothing. After all, although the worse escalations *might* be averted or postponed at any given moment, this was abstract surmise; concretely, the bombs kept falling, and successive administrations weren't handing out public prizes for tying their hands.

Meanwhile, public opinion after the Tet offensive of early 1968 was ambiguous. It registered the growing conviction that the war was a mistake and a futility, coupled with the desire to "get it all over with" by any means possible, including bombing. This was the combination that Nixon brilliantly exploited to win the presidency in 1968, with vague references to a secret plan to end the war. So emerged the movement's desperate cycle of trying to raise the stakes, double or nothing—more fury and more violence—especially when the media dutifully played their part by amplifying the most flamboyant gestures of antiwar theatre.

Nonetheless, evidence is coming to light that the movement had a direct veto power over war escalations at a number of points. David Halberstam tells us in *The Best and the Brightest*, for example, that in late 1966 the military was already urging President Johnson to bomb Hanoi and Haiphong, to block the harbor and, in Halberstam's words, to "[take] apart the industrial capacity of both cities." "How long [will] it take," Johnson lamented, "[for] five hundred thousand angry Americans to climb that White House wall . . . and lynch their president if he does something like that?" "Which ended for a time," Halberstam writes, "the plan to bomb Hanoi and Haiphong."

Despite their denials at the time, Nixon administration officials were no less sensitive to the actual and potential political threat of movement protest. Early in the first Nixon administration, for example, during a lull in demonstrations—so writes Henry Kissinger in *White House Years*—Secretary of Defense Marvin Laird argued against the secret bombing of Cambodia for fear of "[waking] the dormant beast of public protest." At another point, Kissinger refers to "the hammer of antiwar pressure" as a factor that they and Nixon could never ignore.

The denials were, at times, actually a backhanded index of the movement's real influence. Unbeknownst to the movement, its greatest impact was exerted just when it felt most desperate. In the summer of 1969, while withdrawing some ground troops amidst great fanfare, Nixon and Kissinger decided on a "November ultimatum" to Hanoi. Either Hanoi would accommodate to Nixon's bargaining terms by November 1, or Nixon would launch an unprecedented new assault, including, as Seymour Hersh writes in *The Price of Power*, "the massive bombing of Hanoi, Haiphong and other key areas in North Vietnam; the destruction—possibly with nuclear devices—of the main north-south passes along the Ho Chi Minh Trail; and the bombing of North Vietnam's main railroad links with China." For a full month, in utter secrecy, Nixon kept American B-52s on full nuclear alert—the first such alert since the Cuban missile crisis.

Some White House staff members objected to the November ultimatum plans on military grounds, but by Nixon's own account, antiwar demonstrations were central to his decision not to go ahead with this blockbuster escalation. The massive October 15 Moratorium, and the promise of more of the same on November 15, convinced Nixon (as he wrote later) that "after all the protests and the Moratorium, American public opinion would be seriously divided by any military escalation of the war."

For public consumption, Nixon made a show of ignoring the demonstrations and claiming they were of no avail. The movement, for its part, had no way of knowing what catastrophe it was averting, and thus felt helpless. Nixon, meanwhile, moved to split militants from moderates. He combined stepped-up repression, surveillance and press manipulation with a calming strategy that included markedly lower draft calls and, eventually, a draft lottery system that defused opposition by pitting the unlucky few against the lucky. Within the movement, the minority who faulted the Moratorium for its relative moderation began arguing that a new level of militancy was required: first came trashing, then sideline cheerleading for the newly organized splinter group, the Weathermen. The result was a general demoralization on the Left.

At the moment of its maximum veto power, much of the movement's hard core fell victim to all-or-nothing thinking. White House secrecy was one reason the movement misunderstood its own force; the intrinsic difficulty of gauging political results was a second; the third was the movement's own bitter-end mentality. Much of the movement succumbed to a politics of rage. Relatively privileged youth had been raised in child-centered families and conditioned by a consumer culture to expect quick results. An excess of impatience made it easy for them to resort to terrorism. Thus, the movement drove itself toward self-isolating militancy and, by 1971, away from most activity altogether. A desperately revolutionary self-image drove the hard core to disdain alliance with moderates, which, of course, was just what the White House wanted.

When Nixon ordered the invasion of Cambodia in the spring of 1970, hundreds of thousands poured into the streets in protest. But the old movement leadership had burned out or burrowed into underground fantasies, and the new activists lacked leadership. This new round of protest flared and disappeared quickly, especially as shrinking draft calls eliminated the immediate threat to many college students. At the same time the killings at Kent State stripped students of their feeling of safety. With their sense of exemption gone, results invisible and leadership lacking, it wasn't long before they subsided into inactivity. And yet, even then, the demonstrations convinced Nixon to limit the invasion's scope and cut it short. "Nixon's decision to limit the Cambodian offensive," Seymour Hersh concludes, "demonstrated anew the ultimate power of the antiwar movement." Even though the frequency and size of demonstrations declined over the next two years, their threat restrained Nixon's hand.

By this time, the movement's influence on the war was mostly indirect: a nudging of the elites whose children were in revolt, which paved the way for Establishment skepticism. Although radicals didn't want to think of themselves as "mere" reformists, they amounted to a small engine that turned the more potent engines that could, in fact, retard the war.

The movement continued to stimulate moderate antiwar sentiment in Congress, the media and churches even in later years, when demonstrations had become only a ghostly echo. As early as 1968, political, corporate and media elites grew disillusioned with the war. It wasn't "working." Although they accepted little of the antiwar movement's analysis, the elites capitalized on the movement's initiative and sometimes—as in the case of the McCarthy and Kennedy campaigns for the Democratic nomination in 1968—recruited troops as well.

The pivotal moment came just after the Tet offensive, when Johnson's top advisors decided that the war was costing too much in political, economic and military terms. Clark Clifford, Johnson's new secretary of defense, lost faith in the war effort and set out to mobilize influential opposition among the political elite that had represented foreign policy consensus since 1945. At the same time that the Joint Chiefs of Staff were requesting 206,000 new troops for Vietnam, Clifford was persuading Johnson to meet with the informal advisory group later known as the Wise Men: Dean Acheson, McGeorge Bundy, George Ball, C. Douglas Dillon, Cyrus Vance, General Maxwell Taylor and others, men who had occupied top positions in the Truman and Kennedy as well as Johnson administrations. If there was an Establishment, this was it.

Cyrus Vance said later, "We were weighing not only what was happening in Vietnam, but the social and political effects in the United States, the impact on the U.S. economy, the attitudes of other nations. The divisiveness in the country was growing with such acuteness that it was threatening to tear the United States apart." As guardians of America's world position, the Wise Men were sensitive to European doubts and frightened by the war's economic consequences—deficit financing, incipient inflation, a negative balance of payments and gold outflow. Some of them were also aware that American troops were becoming unreliable in the field and that, in an unanticipated echo of the antiwar movement, some soldiers were wearing peace symbols on their helmets.

"The meeting with the Wise Men served the purpose that I hoped it would," Clifford exulted later. "It really shook the president." Three days later, Johnson refused the Joint Chiefs' troop request, announced a partial bombing halt—and took himself out of the presidential race. Major new shipments of American troops became politically taboo for the duration of the war.

Nevertheless, the war went on for years, leaving hundreds of thousands of corpses as testimony to the movement's failure to achieve the peace it longed for. If it had been more astute, had cultivated more allies, it might have been able to cut the war shorter and reduce the general destruction. The largely middle-class antiwar movement could have broadened in several directions. If it had supported the growing GI antiwar faction more concertedly, had gotten over its squeamishness toward soldiers, the combination might have succeeded in frightening Johnson and Nixon earlier. A more serious alliance with antiwar veterans and working-class draftees might have broken the movement out of its middle-class ghetto, might have established before a hostile public and a cynical administration that the movement was more than a rabble of middle-class kids trying to preserve their privilege of avoiding combat. If the largely white movement had paid more attention to broad-based interracial alliances (as with the 1970 Chicano National Moratorium) and less to the glamour of revolutionary showmanship, it might have capitalized on high-level governmental fears of what Air Force Undersecretary Townsend Hoopes in his memoirs called "the fateful merging of antiwar and racial dissension." A we now know, the White House was terrified of black protest even into the Nixon years. A full year after Martin Luther King was assassinated, J. Edgar Hoover was sending memos on King's sex life to Henry Kissinger, who kept them on file, one National Security Council staff member said, "to blunt the black antiwar movement."

If anything, the movement should be faulted for not being effective, ecumenical, persistent enough. It is even conceivable (history affords no certitudes) that a stronger movement might have kept the ferocious U.S. bombing from driving Cambodian peasants into the arms of the increasingly fanatical Khmer Rouge. All civilized people who are revolted by the Khmer Rouge mass atrocities should also remember that it was the Nixon administration, not the movement, that encouraged the overthrow of Prince Sihanouk and weakened opposition to this regime of mass murderers.

Moreover, whatever the movement's willingness to overlook authoritarianism in North Vietnam, a shorter, less destructive war might also have made postwar reconciliation easier in a unified Vietnam. And if the movement had survived to demand that the U.S. keep up its end of the 1973 Paris peace agreement, the promised American postwar aid might have overcome some of the austerity that later served Hanoi as a rationale for repression.

The movement left a mixed legacy. Even with most of its force spent, after the McGovern catastrophe of 1972, the phantom movement, coupled with the belated resolve of congressional doves, succeeded in keeping Nixon from a wholehearted new assault on Vietnam. Watergate was the decisive turn, though, that distracted Nixon from keeping his secret promises to Nguyen Van Thieu and short-circuiting the Paris agreements with a resurgence of American bombing. By the cunning of reason, Nixon's paranoia about the antiwar movement, among other betes noire, led him to such grossly illegal measures that he was ultimately prevented from continuing the war itself. And, of course, the antiwar feeling outlasted Nixon. As late as 1975, Congress was able to stop American intervention in Angola.

Even today, the memory of the movement against the Vietnam War works against maximum direct military intervention in Central America. Again, there's no cause for pure and simple jubilation: the doves failed to anticipate how easy it would be for later administrations to substitute heavy military aid and troop maneuvers for direct combat forces. The movement also failed to persuade enough of the country that democratic revolutionary change is often the superior alternative to hunger and massacre in the Third World, and that American support (what the New Left used to call "critical support") might soften the most repressive features of revolutionary regimes. The result of simplistic Cold War thinking is hardened revolutions and Third World dependency on the Soviet Union—which after the fact seems to confirm the Cold War notion that revolutions are nothing more than props for Soviet expansion. American troops en masse are not at this moment being sacrificed to unwinnable wars, but the same bitter-end purpose is supporting Somocista guerrillas in Nicaragua, genocidal killers in Guatemala, death squads in El Salvador, a seemingly permanent U.S. base in Honduras—at a relatively cut-rate cost to American society.

The movement against the Vietnam War can be counted a real if incomplete success, even despite itself. But what happened to the movement in the process?

The movement sloppily squandered much of its moral authority. Too much of the leadership, and some of the rank and file, slid into a romance with the other side. If napalm was evil, then the other side was endowed with nobility. If the American flag was dirty, the NLF flag was clean. If the deluded make-Vietnam-safe-for-democracy barbarism of the war could be glibly equated with the deliberate slaughter of millions in Nazi gas chambers—if the American Christ turned out to look like the Antichrist—then by this cramped, left-wing logic, the Communist Antichrist must really have been Christ. Ironically, some of the movement anticipated the Great Communicator's jubilant proclamation that Vietnam was a "noble enterprise," but with the sides reversed. This helped discredit the movement in the eyes of moderate potential supporters—who were, in turn, too quick to find reasons to write it off. For too long the movement swallowed North Vietnamese claims that it had no troops in South Vietnam, even though, by the logic of the movement's argument that Vietnam was one country, artificially kept divided by American intervention, it should not have been surprising that northern troops would be in the south.

Romanticism and rage dictated that North Vietnamese and National Liberation Front heroism be transmuted into the image of a good society that *had* to exist out there somewhere. American activists who thought they were making a revolution, not a mere antiwar movement, borrowed their prepackaged imagery—their slogans and mystique—from Vietnamese cadres whose suffering and courage were undeniable but who had little to teach us about how to conduct a modern democratic society. In 1969, when zealots chanting "Ho, Ho, Ho Chi Minh" confronted other zealots chanting "Mao, Mao, Mao Tse Tung" and tore up SDS between them, both sides were surrendering political reason and curling up to father figures.

This kind of moral corrosion has become all too familiar in the 20th century: the know-it-alls explain away revolutionary abominations, try to corner the market in utopian futures and, in the process, become mirror-images of the absolutist authority they detest. In the end, the revolutionists have helped return moral title to conservatives.

Even today, we hear voices on the left conjuring rationalizations for crimes committed by left-wing guerrillas. A curious partial freedom is parceled out to state-sponsored socialism, as if revolutions are responsible for their accomplishments, while their brutality, if acknowledged at all, is credited to American imperialism. Why is it necessary to keep silent about the shutting down of newspapers in Managua in order to oppose American intervention on behalf of death squads?

There is no simple explanation why much of the antiwar movement leadership found it hard to criticize authoritarian socialism. Partly there was the fear of putting ammunition in the hands of the Right—as though if the Right were right about anything, it might be right about everything. Then, too, dressing up for revolution was easier than reckoning with the strangeness of being a radical movement, based on youth, spunk, marginality and educated arrogance, in a society that not only permitted dissent but made it possible to act in history without wholesale bloodshed. The heavily middle-class revolutionists tried to bull past their own isolation: they made themselves Leninists of the will. Others went the Yippie route, with toy machine guns and glib youth-cult gestures. The publicity loop boosted the most flamboyant leaders into celebrity and helped limit the movement's reach.

Caught in a maelstrom of images, the rest of the movement became massively demoralized by 1970. This vast, unorganized, indeed silent majority was appalled to watch SDS decompose into warring sects speaking in Marxist-Leninist tongues. They didn't think revolutionary Vietnam was the promised land. They hated illegitimate authority in all forms. If they were understandably sentimental about peasants shooting at fighter bombers with rifles from alongside their water buffalo, they also knew that by far the greatest bloodbath going on in the world came from American firepower—and that no halfway desirable objective could be worth it. And they were right. From their impulses, on top of the civil rights movement, came a more general refusal of unjust authority, which led, most profoundly, to the movement for the liberation of women. To choose political passivity today on the spurious ground that the antiwar movement of the '60s "failed" is to succumb to all-or-nothing petulance, to insist that history promise to bear out all one's dreams before one tries to stop a slaughter. We'll travel lighter now without the burden of revolutionary myths.

A final legacy of the antiwar movement is that it battered the unreflective anticommunism of the 1950s and made it possible to open new doors. Now it also becomes possible to think past the kneejerk anti-*anti*-communism of the '60s, and to oppose American interventionism on the ground that it violates the elementary rights of human beings, not that it obstructs the Third World's revolutionary emergence into the highest stage of social existence. Anyway, movements are compost for later movements. The Vietnam War bred succeeding wars, and so, in a sense, the meaning of the movement against the war is still up for grabs. That meaning depends on what happens as we try to stop sequels in Central America and elsewhere. After throwing weight against a juggernaut once, and slowing it, the right lesson to learn is: Do it better and smarter next time. I like what William Morris wrote: "Men fight and lose the battle, and the thing that they fought for comes about in spite of their defeat, and when it comes, turns out not to be what they meant, and other men have to fight for what they meant under another name."

Recommended Reading

Carson, Clayborne. *In Struggle: SNCC and the Black Awakening of the 1960s*. (Cambridge, Mass., 1981). A thoroughly researched and carefully written study of the Student Nonviolent Coordinating Committee, which explores its relationships and roles in every facet of the Civil Rights Movement and the New Left.

Evans, Sara. *Personal Politics: The Roots of Women's Liberation in the Civil Rights Movement and the New Left*. (New York, 1979). A critical study of the growth of feminism in the New Left. The author discusses how male attitudes served as an important catalyst in the liberation movement.

Farber, David. *Chicago '68*. (Chicago, 1988). An in-depth study of the National Mobilization Committee and the Youth for International Peace roles in protest against the Democratic National Convention. Farber also relates the protest story from the viewpoint of the city government and the police.

Flacks, Richard. *Making History: The American Left and the American Mind*. (New York, 1988). An evaluation of the left and its history, particularly that of the New Left. The author also details how he believes the left can play a more significant role in the future.

_____. "What Happened to the New Left?", *Socialist Review*, 19:1, (Jan.-Mar., 1989): 91-110. Argues that the New Left never disappeared and that a new generation is becoming active in political and social activities.

Fraser, Ronald (ed.). *1968: A Student Generation in Revolt*. (New York, 1988). A mistitled book. This is an oral history of people who participated in the major movements and events of the entire 1960s in several different countries. The editors skillfully interweave oral history with narrative.

Gitlin, Todd. *The Sixties: Years of Hope, Days of Rage*. (New York, 1987). A part-history, part-memoir, part-analysis by an early SDS leader who was involved in many of the decade's major events.

Gitlin, Todd. *The Whole World is Watching: Mass Media in the Making and Unmaking of the New Left*. (Berkeley, 1980). A fascinating study of the role of newspaper and television reporters in making the New Left an important component of the American political and cultural scene and how their focus on the most violent and spectacular acts pushed the New Left toward a more violent course.

Isserman, Maurice. *If I Had a Hammer... The Death of the Old Left and the Birth of the New Left*. (New York, 1987). An important account which attributes a much greater influence of the Old Left on the New Left than previous writers. Isserman argues that Socialists and Communists of the 1950s were much more active and played a greater role in shaping New Left ideas than others have realized.

_____ and Michael Kazin. "The Failure and Success of the New Radicalism," in Steve Fraser and Gary Gerstle, *The Rise and Fall of the New Deal Order*. (Princeton, 1989). Argues that the influence of the New Left was much greater in the area of culture than politics.

King, Mary. *Freedom Song: A Personal Story of the 1960s Civil Rights Movement*. (New York, 1987). A long memoir of the author's involvement in the Civil Rights Movement. She was active in SNCC for several years and, with Casey Hayden, drafted the famous memorandum on the role of women in the movement.

Miller James. *Democracy is in the Streets: From Port Huron to the Siege of Chicago*. (New York, 1987). The first half of the book details the activities and ideals of the early leaders of SDS at the University of Michigan. The second part focuses on the events of the post-1965 years, including a detailed account of Tom Hayden's activities.

Rorabaugh, W. J. *Berkeley at War, the 1960s*. (Berkeley, 1989). A thorough treatment of the Free Speech Movement, Berkeley area anti-war activities and the battle for People's Park. Rorabaugh views developments from the perspectives of both the students and the administration.

Sitkoff, Harvard. *The Struggle for Black Equality, 1945-1980*. (New York, 1981). A well-written introduction to the modern Civil Rights Movement.

Zaroulis, Nancy and Gerald Sullivan. *Who Spoke Up? American Protest Against the War in Viet Nam, 1963-1975*. (Garden City, N.Y., 1975). A year-by-year account of the anti-war movement, which emphasizes the role of Catholic militants while criticizing the failure of SDS to lead the movement.

Index

AAAS, 101
Abelson, Philip, 100
Acheson, Dean, 189
ACLU, 87
Activists, 134-136, 137, 148
AEC, 68
Affairs, extra-marital, 118
Age of Jackson, The (Schlesinger), 79
AMA, 101
America and the New Era, 163
American Institute of Architects, 42
Antiwar movement, 183, 190
Autobiography, 66, 116
Avakian, Bob, 44

Ball, George, 189
Bartok, 77
Beethoven, 77
Berg, 77
Best and the Brightest, The (Halberstam), 187
Black Panther party: armed, 9; convention, 31, 40-43; as dominant force, 8; and integration, 6; and liberation, 45
Black Power, 22, 156
Black separatism, 6
Booth, Paul, 24, 54
Bourgeoisie, 105
Brecher, Jeremy, 131
Brown v. the Board of Education, 71
Bullock, Alan, 76-77
Bundy, McGeorge, 189

Calvert, Greg, 25, 54
Cambodia, 10, 188
Camus, Albert, 3, 77
Capitalism, 106
Career opportunities, 130
Carnegie Endowment, 79
CBW, 102
Chaney, James, 4

Che, 78
Chicago, 30-31
Chicago Eight, 10
China, 91
Chutzpah, 138-139
CIA, 80, 170
Civil rights movement, 22, 140, 185
Class analysis, 94
Clifford, Clark, 189, 190
Cliques, 170-173
Collectives, 169
Columbia University, 9, 26-28, 31, 110
Commitment, 159
Conservatives, 183
Cooley, Charles Horton, 156
Co-optation, 27, 93
CORE, 160
Cuba, 41, 45, 46, 91-92
Cultural disaffection, 77

Daley, Richard J., 30, 110
Davidson, Carl, 25
Davis, Rennie, 4, 9, 53, 105, 107
Days of Rage, 10
Democracy, and cliques, 170-173
Democratic centralism, 170
Democratic National Convention (Chicago), 9, 97, 105, 111, 114
Democratic Party, 108
Detroit, 25, 45
Dialectics of Sex, The (Firestone), 96
Dillon, C. Douglas, 189
Dylan, Bob, 77

Economic Research and Action Project. *See* ERAP
Economic security, 129-130
Egleson, Nick, 54
Elite roles, 139
ERAP, 4-5, 59-62
Expressive gratification, 156

197